MANOR HOUSE

Life in an Edwardian Country House

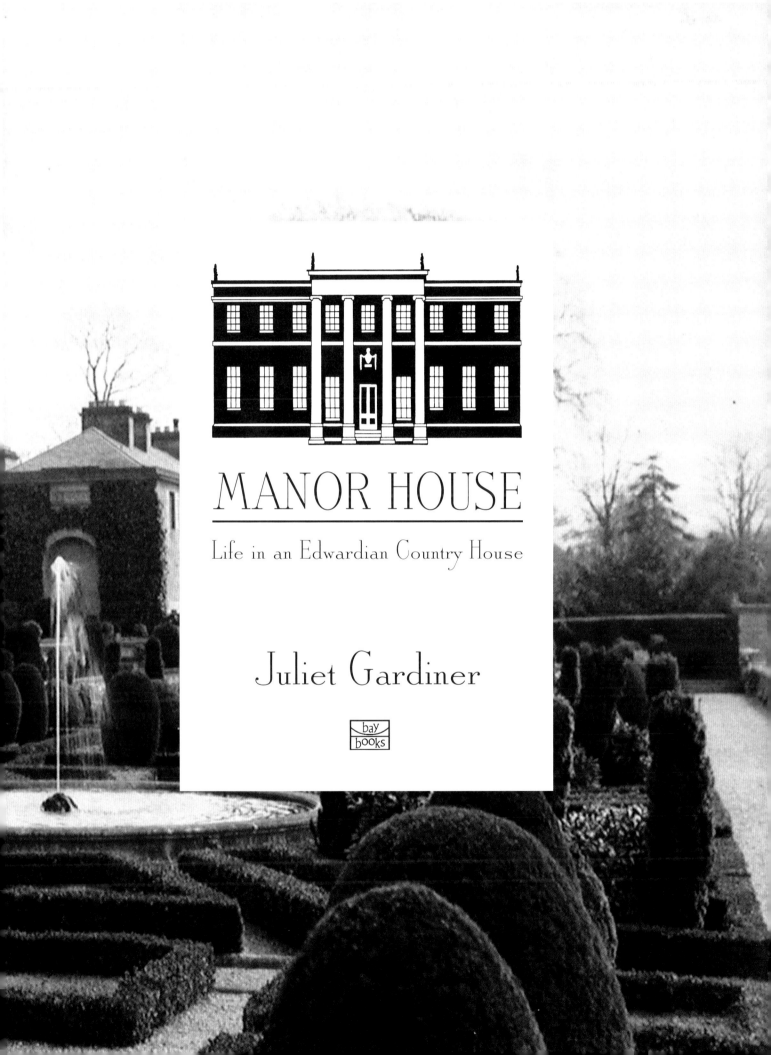

MANOR HOUSE

Life in an Edwardian Country House

Juliet Gardiner

bay books

First American edition published in 2003 as *MANOR HOUSE, Life in an Edwardian Country House* by Bay Books, an imprint of Bay/SOMA Publishing, 444 De Haro Street, No. 130, San Francisco, California 94107.

First published as *The Edwardian Country House* in 2002 by Channel 4 Books, an imprint of Pan Macmillan Ltd, London.

Text © Juliet Gardiner, 2002

Library of Congress Cataloging-in-Publication Data available

For Pan Macmillan:
Design by Isobel Gillan
Illustrations by Amanda Patton
Photography © Simon Roberts/Growbag, © Simon Grossett,
   © Mark Pinder and © Debi Treloar

For Bay Books:
Cover design by Michael Geiger

Colour reproduction by Aylesbury Studios Ltd
Printed by Butler and Tanner, Frome, Somerset

This is the companion book to the Public Television series *MANOR HOUSE*, originally titled and produced as *The Edwardian Country House* by Wall to Wall for Channel 4

For Wall to Wall:
Executive producer: Emma Willis
Series producer: Caroline Ross Pirie

ISBN 1-57959-082-9

Printed in England

10 9 8 7 6 5 4 3 2 1

Distributed by Publishers Group West

CREDITS
While every effort has been made to trace copyright holders the publishers will be glad to make proper acknowledgements in future editions of the book in the event that any regrettable omissions have occurred at the time of going to press.

L B Chappell: 15; Simon Grosset: 8, 10, 55, 68, 75, 76, 77, 78, 79, 83, 87, 117, 125, 140, 142, 144, 147, 149, 150, 151, 154, 156, 157, 162, 163, 169, 174, 175, 182 (right), 187, 203, 225, 248 Hulton Getty: 179, 221, 241, 269; Isobel Gillan: 16; Mary Evans Picture Library: 244, 271, 272, 274; Lord Palmer for permission to reproduce photography from the Manderston family albums: 2, 11, 20, 22, 23, 24, 40, 71, 73, 74, 107, 108, 118, 158, 170, 176, 181, 182 (left), 188, 195 (inset), 196, 215, 218, 222, 224, 226, 227, 230, 233, 237, 238, 256, 264; Mark Pinder: 208, 209, 255, 256, 257, 260, 262, 263; Simon Roberts: 7, 13, 17, 18, 21, 26, 28, 30, 31, 32, 33, 34, 35, 36, 37, 38, 39, 41, 42, 43, 44, 46, 48, 49, 50, 51, 52, 53, 56, 57, 58, 59, 60, 64, 65, 66, 82, 86, 88, 89, 92, 95, 96, 97, 100, 102, 103, 106, 110, 115, 121, 122, 123, 124, 126, 127, 128, 129, 130, 132, 133, 134, 135, 136, 139, 166, 167, 171, 172, 180, 184, 185, 192, 193, 194, 195, 199, 200, 201, 206, 207, 210, 211, 214, 229, 243, 245, 247, 249, 251, 254, 267, 268, 277, 278; Fritz von der Schulenburg: 19 ; Debi Treloar: 62, 85, 90, 98, 104, 152, 161, 164, 252, 259

'Huntin', Shootin' and Fishin' (p. 178) reproduced by permission of A. P. Watt Ltd on behalf of Mrs Teresa Elizabeth Perkins and Jocelyn Hale.

Thanks to Paula Pryke Flowers for recreating the table flowers (p. 90) and the table centrepiece (p. 259), Denis Dubiard for creating the jelly (p. 85), Sugar Mountain, Hawick, Scotland for supplying sweets (p. 152), Caroline Rose at Rose & Co Apothecary for supplying the beauty remedies (p. 104) and floral bath soaks (p. 161).

Contents

Introduction

The stately homes of England
How beautiful they stand!
Amidst their tall ancestral trees
O'er all the pleasant land...

FELICIA HEMANS

John Betjeman wrote, 'The Edwardian was the last age in which a rich man could afford to build himself a new and enormous country-house with a formal landscape garden, a lily pond and clipped hedges.'[1] Such country houses, which became the markers of society's 'Saturday to Monday' house parties (Monday being the significant day since anyone who could regularly be at leisure on a weekday must not *need* to earn a living), have come to epitomize the years between the Boer War and the Great War: the Edwardian era in which the privileges of the rich were made possible by the labour of their servants, an age when the inequalities of wealth and poverty were starkly delineated and the conventions of class were still rigidly, if complexly, defined.

The period from 1905 to 1914 is the subject of this book, involving a unique social experiment in Edwardian living. Manderston, a large, beguiling, classical-style house on the Scottish borders near Berwick-upon-Tweed, rebuilt by an Edwardian plutocrat in 1905, was the container for the experiment. The house, which still functions today as the family home of the descendants of the Edwardian owner was taken over by the television production company Wall to Wall. They chose a family, the Olliff-Coopers, to live 'upstairs', and recruited a dozen or so individuals who were prepared to live 'below stairs' as servants for three months.

However, this was to be no 'upstairs, downstairs' costume drama, but as faithful a re-creation as possible of the way in which such a wealthy household would have functioned in the Edwardian era. Manderston is virtually unchanged in all the essentials from that time, and it was possible to reconstruct the material conditions with authentic Edwardian cooking facilities, food, clothes, toiletries and remedies, the lavish entertainments and the endless, menial work, while the social 'rules of engagement' that framed Edwardian lives were replicated from household manuals, reference works and memoirs of the time.

The intention was to see how a set of twenty-first-century individuals, comprising a range of people from a variety of jobs and modern ways of life, would interrogate the Edwardian way of life, how they would cope with the various demands put upon them – whether cleaning grates or dealing with visiting cards – negotiating a very different set of social mores, and accepting or rejecting the rules and regulations that pertained both upstairs and down a century ago. The Edwardian country household was described by its contemporary admirers as a 'well-oiled machine'. This did not refer just to the organization of the household but to social arrangements too, the acceptance of hierarchies, of place and of class distinctions. How that 'machine' ran, how smooth was its operation and if and how and why grit got into the workings causing it to judder uncomfortably, or even to throw into reverse, is the subject of both this book and of the television series.

CHAPTER ONE

The Golden Years

Over the past century, the Edwardian era has assumed a crystalline fragility. The long decade is caressed with a nostalgia for time stood still, for innocence, and for a world lost; in the words of Samuel Hynes, it is viewed as a 'leisurely time when women wore picture hats and did not vote, when the rich were not ashamed to live conspicuously, and the sun really never set on the British flag'.[1]

The years from 1901 to 1914, which constitute what is now designated the Edwardian period, are of course an infinitely less static and more complex time than that suggested by the clichés of sunlit lawns, games of croquet and tennis, tinkling bone china teacups, twirling lace parasols, fox fur stoles and sprays of Parma violets, frock coats and tweed Norfolk jackets, shooting and boating parties, fabulous wealth and conspicuous display. Indeed, not all the summers were golden – rather the reverse. In 1901 the weather was near perfect, and in 1911 the sun shone almost continuously, but in the years between, summer skies were often grey and lawns were rained on rather more than they were anointed with the sun's rays.

An enthusiastic welcome for the Edwardian era: Sir John Olliff-Cooper (left), Mr Jonathan, Master Guy, Miss Anson and Lady Olliff-Cooper.

The nostalgia for this era is occasioned largely by the contrast between the periods that preceded and succeeded the Edwardian years, and which seem to endow it with a shape and a completeness denied to other epochs. When Victoria died she was the longest-reigning monarch in British history, and the succession to the throne of her overweight, much-pleasured, many-mistressed fifty-nine-year old son, after more than half a lifetime spent in the wings, seemed to suggest a trepanning of the oppression of the Victorian era. 'The queen is dead of an apoplectic stroke and the great Victorian age is at an end,' noted the poet Wilfrid Scawen Blunt in his journal. 'This is notable news…it will mean great changes in the world.'[2]

On 4 August 1914 Britain declared war on Germany. Nothing that had happened before that event had made it possible to predict or imagine the harsh and terrible reality of the Great War that scythed a generation of young men, either in its almost unendurable longevity, or in its unprecedented and unrelenting carnage. As well as all the myriad other things that the First World War was, and represented, it became a distorting optic. It is impossible to focus the Edwardian period other than through this prism. This gives those years a sharp poignancy and an undercurrent of melancholy that is the very substance of nostalgia and regret. It makes their glitter appear tawdry at the same time as rendering it strangely and compellingly innocent.

The ex libris *of Lady Eveline Miller,*
wife of Sir James Miller who rebuilt Manderston,
showing the house and its gardens.

It is facile to envision the Edwardian period as unique, as wholly different from what preceded and succeeded it, and to focus on the detail is to dissolve the picture and reconfigure it in a different, more nuanced pattern, one of contrast and plurality. Much from the Victorian century persisted well into the Edwardian period and beyond: many of the currents of 'modernism' apparent after 1918 were clearly eddying before 1914. The First World War was less of a terminal event or a watershed, than an accelerator of change, or, in some instances, even an inhibiter of progress in the social, political and economic affairs of Britain. As Jose Harris points out in her survey of British social history of the period:

> Many features of pre-war society – changes in the structure of family life, the emergence of the
> labour movement, the challenge of feminism, the investigation of poverty, the rise of aesthetic
> modernism, and the growth of religious and moral uncertainty – seem to anticipate concerns of the
> later twentieth century…[while] other aspects of Edwardian life – the fashionable predominance of
> a leisured aristocracy, the sheer immensity of the poverty of the poor, the omnipresence of infant
> death, the restricted scope of central government, and the ingenuous confidence in the future of the
> British Empire (and indeed of European civilization in general) – seem so utterly remote from a
> later age that it is tempting to see them as part of a wholly vanished society…[3]

The word that echoes down the years from the Edwardian era is 'golden'. Gold glows, it gleams, it glitters, and it glistens. The rays of late summer afternoon sun burnish the landscape with a lingering golden glow that seems reluctant to fade. Gold is the hue of sunlight – and of display.

Gold conjures up secured wealth and fortunes of avarice; it connotes investment and acquisition, nuggets and money markets, the exchange of fungible assets rather than the stability of the settled old money of land. 'The Bank of England gives gold unconditionally and exchanges its notes for gold, therefore international trade can rely that all claims on London will be paid in gold, and as gold is, among all circulating mediums, the least subject to fluctuations, for this reason bills on England are negotiable everywhere…' explained a foreign investment banker to a meeting of the Institute of Bankers in March 1907.[4]

Gold has become a seed-metaphor for the Edwardian age. The historian of the City of London, David Kynaston, writing in the final decade of the twentieth century, calls the volume that covers the near-quarter of a century from 1890 until the outbreak of the First World War, *The Golden Years*. As he points out, one of the most popular books at the time by the author of *Wind in the Willows*, Kenneth Grahame, was *The Golden Age*, 'little though it touched on monetary matters'.[5] The 1911 edition of the *Encyclopaedia Britannica* explains that 'gold [has] been valued from the earliest ages on account of the permanence of its lustre…gold is the universal symbol of purity and value…when pure [it] is the most malleable of all metals. It is also extremely ductile.'

In the popular imagination, the golden image is still potent. The novelist and critic Marghanita Laski, who was born the year after the Edwardian age came to its tragic end, suggests:

> In so far as any single group in a community imposes a popular image of its domestic life on an age, for Edwardian England that group was the very rich…[leaving] a crude impression of an aristocracy and a plutocracy whose gay and often gaudy glitter was maintained by hierarchies of submissive servants, of homes adorned – as George, Duke of York [later to be George V] wrote to his wife in 1901 – 'with all that Art and Science can afford', the background for gargantuan dinner parties and gorgeous balls in the metropolis, and for weekend parties of near-feudal splendour in the country. Because it is the rich who impose this image and because it is the rich who can take fullest advantage of the new range of choices – social, technological, aesthetic – that the age has to offer, any account of Edwardian domestic life must give to the rich more attention than their numbers might seem to warrant.[6]

And it was 'the home adorned' that seemed to exemplify these riches. Property underpinned all other social institutions in Edwardian Britain, and mapping who owned what and how they acquired it and in what manner they held it became a preoccupation of the late Victorians' and Edwardians' curiosity about their nation's prosperity. The value of land, the traditional focus of property ownership, had been in decline, particularly after the agricultural depression of the 1880s. Britain's land had been worth around £2,000 million in the late 1870s; by 1914 it had fallen steadily to a little over £1,000 million, and by then it constituted only around a twelfth of the national wealth compared to a quarter some forty years earlier. In contrast, the value of housing and business premises rose from around £1,000 million in 1865 to nearly £3,300 million in 1909.[7] And in the place of land, other forms of property came to embody the indices of wealth, the bestowal of rights (such as the vote), privileges and citizenship, and connotations of thrift and of moral rectitude that had previously adhered to it.

Despite the increase in taxation as part of the spread of the tentacles of the administrative state, a huge amount of property remained in private hands – and much was concentrated in a few. The age of opulence was an exclusive one. In 1905, the aptly named economist, Sir Leo Chiozza Money, explained that 'more than one third of the entire wealth of the United Kingdom is enjoyed by one thirtieth of its people…the wealth left by a few rich people who die approaches in aggregate property possessed by the whole of the living poor'. Four Edwardian plutocrats who died between 1906 and 1911 left estates valued in excess of £5 million (somewhere around £300 million in today's money) which were fortunes without precedence. Yet of the 343,000 deaths in England and Wales in 1901, only 33,400 (17 per cent of the population) left anything at all other than a few chattels.[8] More recent calculations by historians, far from contradicting these Edwardian figures, have suggested that the situation was if anything more acutely unequal. These suggest that for the years 1911 to 1913, 10 per cent of the adult British population owned 92 per cent of the nation's wealth, making Edwardian Britain one of the most unequal societies in early-twentieth-century Europe in terms of access to property, and possibly (though this is harder to determine) less equal than at any other time in Britain's history.[9]

And the Edwardian rich in many cases were of a different order, as a character in W. H. Mallock's satire *The Old Order Changes* makes clear: 'You, the gentleman of the country, the old landed families…you no longer stand on your own proper foundations. You are reduced financially to mere hangers-on of the

Deliveries for the big house: vegetables await the kitchen maid's attention.

bourgeoisie. Your material splendour, which once had real meaning, is still, no doubt, maintained. But how?…The yellow stucco of ninety years ago has given place to the towers of a Gothic castle…[but only because] his Grace…has five million dollars' worth of railway stock in America…You could no longer live like seigneurs if you were not half tradesmen.'[10] The new plutocrats were outrunning the aristocrats in the gold stakes with money made from finance and investment, fortunes built on trade and manufacture and spent on property not in the form of land from which to draw income, but on building or acquiring or extending houses as showcases for their wealth and the fabulous lifestyle it enabled. 'In King Edward's reign,' wrote John Betjeman, the poet, nostalgist and conserver of things Victorian and Edwardian, 'most British people regarded architecture as an expensive luxury. They liked expensive luxuries.'[11] And there were plenty of luxurious houses, many 'with an Osbert Lancaster touch to them',[12] such as those built for the Rothschilds at Waddesdon, Mentmore and Tring; Château Impney in Worcestershire built for a salt manufacturer 'in the style of a grand hotel'; Overstone Park in Northamptonshire built for a banker (or rather his wife's fancy) which Pevsner cited as an example of 'asymmetricalissime', and of which the owner himself was not proud. 'I am utterly ashamed of it,' he raged. 'I grieve to think I shall hand such an abortion to my successors… [We might as well] have undertaken to whitewash a blackamoor'; and there was Alfred Rothschild's Halton House in Buckinghamshire which was described as 'memorably vulgar…a combination of a French Château and a gambling house…gaudily decorated…hideous…the sense of lavish wealth thrust up your nose',[13] though its owner seemed pleased enough as he trotted round his home in a dog cart pulled by two zebras.

These plutocratic residences may not all have been architectural gems: Lord Leverhulme employed half a dozen different architects to design Thornton Manor in Cheshire, admitting that his taste ran to a preference for 'Georgian dining rooms as the rooms in which to give large dinners. For small dining rooms I prefer Tudor. For drawing rooms I prefer what is called the Adam style; for entrance halls the Georgian.'[14] But however eclectic, even vulgar, the aesthetic of such establishments, leisured lives were congenially spent in them hosting fabulous balls and fancy dress parties, shoots at which game rained down in convoys, more than ample breakfasts, formal lunches and multi-course dinners, with champagne awash 'at moments when a glass of barley-water might have been acceptable' as J. B. Priestley observed.[15] There was an indulgence of (or turning a blind eye to) a degree of sexual licence (and sexual double standards), an enthusiasm for hunting, shooting, fishing, boating and gambling. And to keep this life afloat, a troop of servants labouring below stairs and toiling in the grounds was a necessity.

But, as are most societies at most times, Edwardian society was in a state of flux. The era was to witness the election of a Liberal government that was to mount a gradual assault on 'unproductive wealth' in the interest of the social welfare of the many; the development of the Labour Party, representative of the interest of the working man in Parliament; industrial unrest and the consolidation of trade union rights; the arrival of the 'new woman' with her demand for education, the vote and changed economic and legal status; the stirring of nationalist movements throughout the Empire, and its implacable demands in Ireland; threats to the balance of power which, exacerbated by the ultimately bruising experience of the Boer War, reconfigured British foreign policy in Europe, and would bring about the Great War.

The Edwardian country house, that quintessential icon in the gilded portrait of early-twentieth-century England, did not escape the breezes of change. As the economic historian Martin Daunton has written, 'The tax system is a very effective way of articulating assumptions about the market, consumption and social structures.'[16] In the mid 1850s Gladstone had recognized that 'the operation of income tax is severe on intelligence and skill as compared to property',[17] and had always hoped to be able to abolish income tax and transfer the burden of taxation to death duties which would have hit the landed estates hardest. In 1890, the American economist Henry George's influential work, *Poverty and Progress*, argued that land was failing to pay its proper contribution to the national community. What was required was an increase in taxation on property and on unearned income. 'For many years,' remarked the son of the Chancellor of the Exchequer, Sir William Harcourt, 'the budgets have been more or less rich men's budgets; it is time we had a poor man's budget' – and the 1894 budget consolidated the duties paid on death in ways that penalized large estates. One per cent was levied on estates of £100 to £500, and this rose to a maximum of 8 per cent on estates over £1 million; increases in land value where no improvements had been made were taxed, and graduated income tax rose. It was not as powerful an assault on property as it might have appeared at the time, and it was not until Lloyd George's 1909 'people's budget' or, as he called it, 'war budget...for raising money to wage implacable warfare against poverty and squalidness' that most of the tax increases fell on the wealthy and unearned income, but it was a substantial straw in the wind for the wealthy and the propertied.

A silver stairway to a golden age: the staircase at Manderston which prior to the First World War took three men three days to dismantle, polish and put back.

In addition 'the servant problem' was beginning to make itself manifest. Between the census of 1891 and that of 1911, although the number of domestic servants in England, Wales and Scotland fell only marginally from 1,949,606 to 1,822,169[18] (in a ratio of roughly two-thirds female servants to one-third male), there were far more families seeking servants than there were servants to fill the vacancies, and after 1911, the situation got worse – as far as employers were concerned.[19] It was, in fact, a problem that affected the middle-classes more than the rich, but it was a potent augury of changes in society. In Vita Sackville-West's *roman- à-clef, The Edwardians*, this was portended when Wickenden, the head carpenter at Chevron, comes to see the young master, Sebastian; his 'eyes swimming with tears', he says:

> 'It's my boy, your Grace – Frank, my eldest. Your Grace knows that I was to have taken him into the [carpenter's] shops this year. Well, he won't come. He wants to go – I hardly know how to tell your Grace. He wants to go into the motor trade instead. Says it's the coming thing. Now your Grace knows...that my father and his father before him were in the shops, and I looked to my boy to take my place after I was gone. Same as your Grace's son, if I may make the comparison. I never thought to see a son of mine leave Chevron so long as he was fit to stay there.'[20]

The Edwardian country house, while not sheltering the poorest in the land (indeed, it was frequently pointed out that most domestic servants were better off than their counterparts in industry, retail or commerce since they had room, board and in some cases uniforms provided), can be seen as an exemplar of many of the features and tensions of those years. It serves as an index of the shift in financial and thus political and social power, the shift from old to new money, and the social conventions and aspirations that accompanied these. It exemplifies the change in the perception of aristocratic property as being a local landmark, a part of the national heritage and thus of legitimate interest to the public, to functioning increasingly as a private home, excluding all but the invited.[21] It regularly staged a variety of occasions of ostentatious consumption, it formed a staging post in the social circuit of the wealthy,

The genuine article: Christine Mason, a Scottish Edwardian parlour maid.

it made manifest the evolution of class as a powerful social category with the calcification of social distinction not just between masters, mistresses and servants, but also among gradations of servants. The Edwardian country house thus stands as a micro-society by which to describe and interrogate fundamental aspects of Edwardian life.

The challenge of the Channel 4 series, *The Edwardian Country House* (renamed *Manor House* for Public Television in America) was to have a group of modern-day 'explorers' inhabit as authentic a house as possible, representative of the home and habits of an Edwardian plutocrat. Dressing in the clothes, eating the food, and using only the things that would have been available at the time, guided by the conventions and mores of such a society and regulated by the rules inscribed in contemporary memoirs and manuals, a collection of twenty-first-century individuals would move into an Edwardian country house for three months and live out an experiment in Edwardian living to the best of their ability. There would be a real family upstairs serviced by an appropriate number of 'servants' downstairs, and each would strive to absorb and re-create their understanding of Edwardian society within the parameters provided by the house and its contents, and the recollected experiences of the early years of the 1900s.

After a great deal of searching, considering and rejecting, the house was selected: Manderston, near Duns in Berwickshire close to the Scotland–England border. And after even more advertising, reading, sifting, meeting and interviewing, a family, the Olliff-Coopers, was invited to live upstairs, a 'tutor' was engaged, and twelve (later to rise to thirteen) individuals from different parts of the country and from a variety of walks of life, none of whom had ever met before, were engaged to work downstairs. The experiment began on 21 August 2001.

The house is marvellous, it's wonderful, it is simply better than anyone could possibly have imagined. It's so *huge*,' enthused the elegantly attired Lady Olliff-Cooper, as the gleaming Napier swept her and her family through the heavy wrought-iron gates and drove slowly up the long drive to Manderston, an imposing neo-classical country house set in 56 acres of formal gardens and parkland on the Scottish borders.

As the car scrunched to a halt on the gravel, the front doors opened and a pewter-haired butler emerged, followed by two footmen. Mr Edgar stood at the top of the steps to the porticoed entrance to welcome his new master, Sir John Olliff-Cooper, while the two footmen hurried down the stone steps to open the car door and assist the family to alight. The Napier had been built in 1903, and at the time was in the same league as a Rolls Royce or a Lanchester. A seven-seater with a six-cylinder, 45-horsepower engine, it is capable of a maximum speed of 40 mph; it sold for £495 plus an extra £25 for the hood.

The disembarkation did not go quite as smoothly as it would have done in a period drama since the family were as yet not fully conversant with the niceties of Edwardian etiquette and precedence, and all were anxious to get a closer look at the stately pile that was to be their home for the next three months. But soon Sir John, his wife Anna, their sons Mr Jonathan (known to the family as Jonty) and Master Guy, and Lady Olliff-Cooper's sister, Miss Avril Anson, managed to scramble out, and stood gazing in awe at the façade of Manderston, which has more the dimensions of a terraced street than a family home.

Exploring the territory: the Olliff-Cooper family stroll in the grounds of the Edwardian Country House.

The butler, Mr Edgar, welcomes the Olliff-Cooper family to their new Edwardian domain.

Gathering up their skirts, the ladies followed Sir John up the steps and were led into the house. Mr Edgar introduced them to the waiting staff, who lined up to give a bow or bob, before conducting the family through the marble-floored and -pillared hall, opening doors to offer the family glimpses into a bewildering array of grand rooms all 'filled with wonderful antiques', as Lady Olliff-Cooper gasped. There was the dining room with its ornate ceiling featuring a relief of Mars, the Roman god of war, in the centre and with the largest private collection of 'Blue John' (*bleu-jaune*', a valuable, semi-precious stone mined only in Derbyshire) in Scotland – urns, obelisks and candelabras – arrayed on the mantelpiece and sideboards. A full-sized slate and green baize billiard table dominates the library, the walls of which are lined with leather-bound volumes. The romantic ballroom is decorated with panels depicting Venus, goddess of love, with cherub-filled roundels at the corners and a ceiling showing the sun god, Apollo, with his cupids, from which hangs a pair of magnificent Italian crystal chandeliers. Finally, the Olliff-Coopers trooped into the drawing room with its pastel-tinted Adam ceiling, and fireplace over which hangs a Madonna and child painted by Murillo, where the footmen served them afternoon tea.

The sense of awe that the Olliff-Coopers felt on first seeing the house that was to be their home was similar to the impressions of a young reporter on the local Berwickshire newspaper as, bored with dancing, he had wandered round Manderston on the night of a 'house-warming' ball held at the house in 1905:

> You roam say for an hour, through halls, in and out of rooms. Through vestibules and along corridors, up superb staircases and through more corridors and chambers. Returning, you are startled to find new beauties crowding themselves on you from out-of-the-way corners – places that you have missed – and you get lost, and you want to begin all over again. Presently, it dawns upon you that it is absurd to attempt to do the place in an hour, and that it is necessary to do it in instalments, a little at a time in order to appreciate in any adequate way the exquisite treasures with which the mansion is literally deluged.[22]

In that year, 1905, the Russo-Japanese war was raging, and there were already signs of unrest in the great Russian Empire that would erupt into revolution a little more than a decade later: 22 January 1905 was to go down in history as Russia's 'Bloody Sunday', when troops of Tsar Nicholas II fired on peaceful protesters led by a young priest, Father Gabon, who were making their way to the Winter

Palace in St Petersburg with a petition for the Tsar – 500 strikers were killed. In June that year mutinous sailors aboard the battleship *Potemkin* attacked their officers and, shouting 'Liberty, Liberty', threw them into the Black Sea and ran the Red Flag up the pole.

At home Edward VII was on the throne. His mother, Queen Victoria, had died in January 1901 aged eighty-one, and the next year Edward was crowned, king at last after the longest-ever reign of a British monarch: sixty-three years. The accession of the late-middle-aged playboy King promised a transformation from the 'dullness and decorum' of the Victorian court into the 'glitter and vivacity' of the Edwardian era. There was certainly little sign that the 'smart set' of plutocrats and socialites (sometimes of dubious social origin) that had surrounded Edward when he was Prince of Wales would be likely to moderate their behaviour – an endless round of pleasure, comprising parties, balls, theatre visits, dinners, country house weekends, gambling, cards, horse racing, illicit love affairs – now that he was king. There was political change afoot too. In December 1905 the King invited a lowland Scottish Liberal, Sir Henry Campbell Bannerman, to form a government after the resignation of the Conservative Prime Minister, Arthur Balfour, his party in disarray over tariff reform. The following February the Liberals were to have a landslide victory at the general election, reducing Tory representation in the Commons from 401 to 156 seats, and – a portent of things to come – the Labour Representation Committee, the forerunner of the Labour Party, led by Keir Hardie, won 30 seats and trebled its share of the vote.

The year 1905 saw the completion of the rebuilding of Manderston – hence the celebratory ball. It had taken two years, and when it was finished the house was a masterpiece, a near-flawless example of the finest Edwardian craftsmanship, and a monument to the riches and excess of those gilded years

An Edwardian vista: the Robert Adam-inspired hall at Manderston.

between the death of Victoria, who symbolized the bourgeois propriety and sober industry of the nineteenth century, and the Armageddon of the Great War. The first house on the site, near Berwick-upon-Tweed, just over the English–Scottish border in fine fishing country, was built in the late 1780s for a Mr Dalhousie Watherstone. Watherstone had bought the land from an East India Company surgeon, John Swinton (Swinton village is a few miles from Manderston). The architect was either Alexander Gilkie or John White (drawings by both of a proposed house exist).[23] In 1853 the square, stone house was sold to Richard Miller, and on his death his younger brother, William, bought the estate from Richard's widow for £78,050. Descendants of William have lived in Manderston ever since, and his great-great-grandson, Lord Palmer, is the present owner.

William Miller was a rich man. He had made his money in the Baltic trade in hemp and herrings, and after spending sixteen years in St Petersburg as the British Consul, he returned to Manderston and was elected as Liberal Member of Parliament, first for Leith and later for his home county of Berwickshire. More of a constituency politician than one active in the House, Miller was created a baronet by the then Prime Minister, William Gladstone, in 1874 in gratitude for the political dinners he hosted in the Liberal interest.

The rebuilding of Manderston, the Edwardian Country House, took two years from 1903 to 1905.

Sir John and Lady Olliff-Cooper

John Olliff-Cooper (or John Cooper as he is more usually known), a former Lloyd's 'name', has run his own successful flooring company for the past thirty years. Aged fifty-six, he has a love of the Edwardian period stretching back many years, and is a connoisseur of Edwardian fishing – restoring antique fishing rods is one of his hobbies. 'I am completely 1905 between the ears,' he admits. But in his twenty-first-century mode, John writes on fishing and travel for an Internet magazine. He has two adult sons from a previous marriage, who did not take part in the project, though one of them managed to pay a couple of visits to his temporarily ennobled father and stepmother.

Anna Olliff-Cooper, who is fifty-two, works part-time as a doctor in the casualty department of Southampton General Hospital. She also runs the family home (in the New Forest in Hampshire), looks after her two sons and in her 'spare' time is studying for a philosophy degree with the Open University. She was quite clear why she had wanted to take part in the experiment: she was at something of a crossroads in her life and had begun to feel that she was on a treadmill of relentless hard work. She felt exhausted most of the time and yet somehow unfulfilled: she desperately wanted a change. When she saw the advertisement for people to live in the Edwardian Country House for three months, it seemed like the answer. She thought she would apply to be a servant – after all, she thought ruefully, she was pretty used to looking after other people. But a moment's further thought made her realize that that just wouldn't be possible. Guy was only nine; he still needed her. But if they *all* went as the family upstairs…

Sir William had already started to enlarge the modest Georgian house, adding a Doric *porte-cochère* to the existing Ionic pillared entrance porch, a French Renaissance-style mansard roof and additional bedrooms for the servants.[24] Tragically, his heir, William, choked to death on a cherry stone while still a schoolboy at Eton in 1874, so on Sir William's demise, the baronetcy, the estate and the fortune all passed to his second son, James, who was twenty-four at the time.

Sir James was the perfect country landowner of the 'new money' variety: a career soldier (though he had failed the 'examination' for the Blues which probably indicated that he was not out of the top drawer socially), he was also an excellent shot, good at sport, a fine horseman and generally popular – 'Lucky Jim' was the nickname his friends gave him. He was also, as the magazine *Vanity Fair* pointed out in 1890, 'one of the most wealthy commoners in the country [his horse racing activities added a total of £118,000 – over £7 million in today's money if one uses a rather crude and not entirely accurate

Sir William Miller Bt. M.P., the wealthy merchant who
bought Manderston from his brother, and left it to his son…

multiplier of 60 – to James's inheritance] and a bachelor' – a very eligible young man indeed. Predictably, he married well. The bride he took in 1893 was the Hon. Eveline Curzon, the fourth (and supposedly the prettiest) daughter of Lord Scarsdale (who could trace his family lineage back to the Norman Conquest). Her older brother was George Nathaniel Curzon, who was Viceroy of India from 1899 to 1905.

Lady Miller's father's seat was Kedleston Hall in Derbyshire, a magnificent eighteenth-century house designed by the architect Robert Adam. Sir James was determined that his new wife would have a home to match her father's. Indeed, when he had ventured to Kedleston to ask for Eveline's hand in marriage, he had replied to the traditional paternal inquiry: 'Can you keep my daughter in the manner to which she has become accustomed?' in the affirmative, adding quietly, 'perhaps even a little better'.

On 27 May 1901, Sir James, by now an officer in the 11th Hussars, returned from fighting in the Boer War. His route from the railway station was decked with flowers, and by the South Lodge entrance had been erected an evergreen arch from which hung a golden M for Manderston (and Miller) framed by tulips. Here the horses were uncoupled and the carriage pulled triumphantly up the beech-lined drive by a team of his tenants led by members of the Volunteer Band from Duns, the nearby small town. Looking afresh at his rather modest home and mindful of his promise, Sir James set about making his boast to his father-in-law a reality. The next month he engaged the services of one of Scotland's foremost architects, John Kinross, the son of a Stirling coach builder who had served part of his apprenticeship with an Edinburgh firm, Wardrop and Reid, which specialized in Scottish baronial homes.

When he was twenty-five, Kinross had borrowed £250 from his mother and set off for Italy, where he spent two years studying Renaissance architecture and immersing himself in Italian culture, life and language. It was here that he acquired a cosmopolitan outlook that he was never to lose, and his 'inherent aristocracy of taste' flourished.[25] On his return, Kinross paid back his mother (with interest) and published a limited edition of a distillation of his Italian architectural education, *Details from Italian Buildings Chiefly Renaissance* in 1882. This volume bought Kinross to the attention of the eccentric third Marquess of Bute, a scholar, linguist, devout Catholic and one of the richest men in Britain, who owned some 117,000 acres. At only eighteen years of age, Bute had become the patron of the architect William Burges, the foremost exponent of the Gothic Revival in Britain and designer of Cardiff Castle and Castell Coch. Burges died in 1881 and Bute transferred his patronage to Kinross, providing him with commissions for the next fifteen years, including the restoration of a priory, an abbey, a friary, and of Falkland Palace which was unfinished on Bute's death in 1900.

In 1901, a year after his patron's death, came the commission from Sir James Miller's to rebuild Manderston. Miller knew Kinross already. The architect had built a neo-baroque house for the baronet's sister at nearby Thurston in the 1890s, then was commissioned to design a boathouse at the edge of the lake at Manderston to celebrate the marriage of James and Eveline; and in 1895 he had designed a palatial stable block for the Manderston horses. Before starting the new work, Miller sent Kinross to Kedleston to see what he had in mind. When Kinross returned with his sketches, he began to draw up plans to transform the rather austere Georgian mansion into a neo-classical masterpiece to rival – if not surpass – his client's father-in-law's home (though on a smaller scale). It was to be grand enough for formal entertaining and large enough for the small army of servants that such lavish hospitality required. There was sufficient space for twenty-two live-in servants, and others would have been brought in for special occasions. To Kinross's enquiry about what the budget for the rebuilding was to be, Sir James replied airily, 'It doesn't really matter.'[26] It must have seemed the ideal brief for an ambitious architect – but could have been a disaster of excess in less sensitive hands.

The house was to be in the Georgian style, in tune with the fashion of the time as well as in imitation of Adam's Kedleston, and it was also influenced by French neo-classicism. Kinross removed the 1870s additions and built in the style of the eighteenth century. In effect, he combined 'scholarship and eclecticism to make something new',[27] producing an Edwardian version of a Georgian house for Sir James. It 'perfectly represents', as J. Mordaunt Crook has written, 'the Classicizing (or socializing) of new money'.[28] The whole main part of the house was reconstructed: one room was added, others enlarged; a new wing was added for gentlemen with 'bachelors' bedrooms', a gun room and office; the old stables to the west of the house were converted into a laundry and servants' quarters; and the attic storey (also for servants' accommodation) was rebuilt. The original south front overlooking the garden remained but was refaced, while the north entrance façade was demolished and the roof removed and rebuilt to deepen the house.[29] The coat of arms of the Miller family is over the main entrance door. It bears the family motto *Omne Bonum Superne* – All good comes from above – which, as the guide book points out, is a generous acknowledgement, since the fortune that allowed for this building came from herring caught in the deep.

The interior of Manderston owes a great deal to the Adam revival, too – though the arrangement of the rooms was specified for Edwardian entertainment rather than for Georgian verisimilitude, with a ballroom and drawing room of identical size adjacent so that the double doors between them could be flung open for dancing. The

Sir James Miller who gave his architect, John Kinross, a free rein – and an open cheque book – to rebuild his country house heritage.

walls of both were covered in primrose and white, the racing colours under which Sir James's horse, Sainfoin, won the Derby in 1890 – at odds of 25 to one. Rock Sand, sired by Sainfoin won the Triple Crown (the Two Thousand Guineas, Derby and St Leger) in 1903 – the year that the rebuilding of Manderston had started. The entrance hall was lined in marble, as was the much larger hall at Kedleston, and the pattern on the marble floor was identical. The ceilings in particular were in the style of Adam, the most magnificent of which adorned the drawing room, the ballroom (a replica of the dining room ceiling at Kedleston) and the dining room. Much of the furniture is a quotation from Robert Adam's designs, from the heroic busts adorning the bookcases in the library to the soaring organ pipes in the hall, while the frieze in the hall was derived from Adam's design for the entrance hall at Syon House in Middlesex. Indeed, so indebted to Kedleston was Manderston (albeit constructed on a more modest scale) that when Lady Miller's brother, Lord Curzon, was recovering from a motoring accident, he elected to spend his six-month convalescence at Manderston, and gave his sister an old English well – which she sited in the formal Japanese garden – in thanks.[30]

As the eighteenth century gave a 'civilizing' lexicon to *nouveau riche* British taste, so too did a European aesthetic. This was absorbed both from the art and architecture of Renaissance Italy, a stop on the Grand Tour that young aristocrats undertook to complete their education, or the excesses of *Ancien Régime* France, and both styles are found at Manderston. Kinross, of course, had his own particular portfolio of Italian Renaissance influences. The circular morning room, with its views of the

*The funeral of Sir James Miller (1906). The wealthy owner of Manderston left
a year's salary in his will to all his servants and employees.*

Cheviot Hills, is probably modelled on a similar room in the Palazzo Massimo Colonne in Rome by Peruzzi; the radiator grilles in the dining room and below the organ case are copied from Verrochio's Medici tomb in the church of San Lorenzo in Florence; and the large, translucent alabaster vases set in the arches outside the dining room, placed to reflect the setting sun, reprise the blind, semicircular archways of San Miniato al Monte (also in Florence). It was, however, from pre-revolutionary France that Kinross took his most flamboyant reference, and one that trumpeted Sir James's lack of concern with budgetary constraints. The cantilevered silver (plated) staircase that leads from the marble hall to the first-floor bedrooms is an almost carbon copy of the staircase in the Petit Trianon at Versailles planned by Madame de Pompadour, the courtesan and mistress of Louis XV.

But sadly, Sir James did not have long to enjoy his splendid new house: just three months after Manderston's completion, he caught a chill travelling from London to Scotland on the overnight sleeper, insisted on hunting the next day, the chill turned to pneumonia, and he died aged forty-one in January 1906.

In 2001 it was Manderston that Caroline Ross Pirie, the series producer and director from Wall to Wall, chose as the laboratory for the great 'Edwardian experience' to be filmed for Channel 4. In the two earlier series, *The 1900 House* and *The 1940s House*, when modern-day families 'lived history' by bringing their twenty-first-century experience and sensibilities to the material conditions of the past, Channel 4 had purchased the houses to be used, and experts had restored them to the original condition of the period, buying contemporaneous furniture, equipment and artefacts before the Bowlers moved into the 1900 house in Charlton in South London, and the Hymers to the 1940s house in West Wickham, Kent.

With Manderston it would be different. Manderston is a stately house that is open to the public to view as it was when it was rebuilt in 1905: the decoration is as it was when John Kinross had finished, the furniture and works of art as they were when Sir James and Lady Miller selected them. But it is also a home, lived in by descendants of Sir James Miller, Lord Palmer (of the biscuit-manufacturing family Huntley and Palmer), his wife Cornelia and their three children, who vivify the Edwardian setting. The task for Wall to Wall was thus one of assemblage. They would be using only part of the house for the programme to make it a feasible proposition for the 'servants' who were to be employed, yet the production designer, Maggie Gray, was able to plunder the whole 109-roomed house for the things she needed to recreate Manderston exactly as it would have been in 1905, sourcing extras that had long ago disappeared like a silver phonograph in the ballroom and hip baths for the servants' ablutions.

The social historian and curator of the Armley Mills Museum in Leeds, Daru Rooke, who had advised on the 1900 house and who had recommended Manderston, travelled to Scotland to help Maggie and the chief researcher on the project, Mark Ball, reconstruct artefacts and plan the layout of the interiors of rooms that had long fallen out of use, such as the ice room for storing blocks of ice before gas and electric refrigerators, and renovate the huge coal, and wood-burning cooking range that had long been superseded by modern stoves. Daru cast his historian's eye over what was being used in the house today and banished vacuum cleaners (unusual before the First World War), replacing them with bristle brushes and Ewbank carpet sweepers; he insisted that detergent and scouring powder should be binned, and poured away washing-up liquid, replacing such modern materials with soda crystals and Monkey Brand soap which contained sand and was used instead of scouring powder; this was too harsh for washing clothes, for which soft green soap was to be used. Plate powder and tins of Brasso were imported for the endless tasks of cleaning cutlery, condiments and ornaments, and boxes of matches, candles and tapers stacked up, though Manderston had electric light in 1905.

Sadly, the great drying racks in the basement laundry were damaged beyond repair, so it was decided that the dirty clothes and household linen would be packed in wicker laundry baskets and sent

The upstairs family: Sir John and Lady Olliff-Cooper seated with Master Guy.
Behind the sofa stand Miss Anson and Mr Jonathan.

out to a local laundry as would have happened in many Edwardian houses. Maggie was delighted to find piles of linen – sheets, pillow cases and tablecloths – stacked neatly in a linen cupboard off 'pug's parlour', though much of it was yellowing and too fragile for the robust wear that three months' daily use would subject it to, and had to be replaced. Crystal glasses for wine, port, champagne, aperitifs and digestifs were supplied from the Stuart Crystal company's collection and lined up by size in the housekeeper's pantry. Fine china for the upstairs table was supplied by the china manufacturers Wedgwood – Rococco for daily use, and Madeleine for grand occasions – and white earthenware crockery selected for the servants' daily use. Houseplants popular in Edwardian times were placed in urns and cachepots. There were palms for upstairs while downstairs wide-leafed aspidistras were a particular favourite, and were hardy enough to survive the gloomy rooms in the basement.

This was the habitat that the Olliff-Cooper's, a busy, professional family from Hampshire, was to 'inherit' and inhabit for three months. It was not simply the house and all the accoutrements, the grounds, the stables, the dairy, the gardener's house – they were to assume the lifestyle of a very wealthy Edwardian family. They would wear the clothes of the era, eat the food that would have been served, and be constrained by what would have been available, whether for washing their hair, medicating minor illnesses, or attending to personal hygiene and appearance. The novels that they would find in the house would be only those popular at the time. They would navigate the wider world with the help of early-twentieth-century magazines and newspapers. The family would have a fast learning curve of Edwardian social etiquette, and given the wealth and status they had acquired (Mr Olliff-Cooper was elevated to the baronetcy for the duration) and a house run by servants, their social relations would be calibrated entirely differently from the ways they were when the family first arrived at Manderston. The Olliff-Coopers would move differently, talk in different voices and of other topics, their recreations and amusements would be entirely changed and their responsibilities of another order altogether. They would have obligations to themselves, to each other, to their household and to the local community that would frame their time in the Edwardian Country House.

But it was not just the 'future' from which the Olliff-Coopers had been transported, it was also from the past. If the Edwardian period seems in so many ways like another country to us at the start of the next century, it seemed something of a new terrain for those living through it, cut off in style, manner, mores and expectations from the decades that had preceded the accession of Edward VII. Indeed, it was the last time a historical period has become known by the name of its monarch. There has been no second Georgian age and the 'new Elizabethan Age' never caught currency. We name later times as decades – the twenties, the thirties, the sixties.

Manderston epitomized the Edwardian era. It was built for it. The great house was again to host a leisured, privileged, gracious life that has now passed. And this was the world that the Olliff-Coopers were to inhabit for three months. How would the family translate to a century ago? How would they find living in one of the grandest houses in Scotland? How would three over-busy adults and two fully occupied young people fill their days with none of the imperatives and pressures of their daily lives in the twenty-first century? How would they manage with the clothes, the food, the social expectations of a wealthy Edwardian family? And above all, in a time of cheap labour when the luxury of one class was made possible by the work of others – 'hands' in factories and servants in domestic establishments – how would *they* find living with servants? Would they find it embarrassing to be waited on hand and foot? To expect their every whim to be met, their orders obeyed instantly by people whom, if they met them in their ordinary lives, they would recognize as equals? Or would they find it all too easy to slip into a master/ or mistress/servant relationship?

CHAPTER TWO

Below Stairs

week before the Olliff-Coopers swept up the drive to the Edwardian Country House, a horse-drawn wagonette had bumped through the North Gate and made its way towards the house. Sitting on the slatted wooden seats were three 'servants' arriving to take up their positions in the 'big house'. As they clutched the boxes that contained their worldly possessions in one hand and hung on to the sides of their jolting transport with the other, the maids craned for their first glimpse of the house that was to be their home for the next three months. As they rounded a bend, the imposing façade of Manderston hove into view. 'It's *huge,*' gasped Jessica, who had come to take up an appointment as second housemaid. It was exactly the same reaction that Lady Olliff-Cooper was to have at her first sight of Manderston, but then Jessica added, 'And we've got to clean all that!'

Below stairs at the Edwardian Country House. The servants assemble in order of status: the upper servants, the butler, lady's maid, housekeeper and the chef, at the front, the lower servants ranged behind.

As if to emphasize the difference that the house represented to those 'upstairs' and those 'downstairs', the wagonette sheered sharply right away from the raked gravel drive that led to the porticoed front entrance, and drove under an arch to clatter through the brick courtyard. It drew up in front of the plain wooden door that led down a flight of stone steps to the basement: the servants' quarters.

The footmen, Rob and Charlie, hurried out to help the maids clamber down. Smoothing down their skirts and cramming on their bonnets, Antonia, the kitchen maid, Becky, the first housemaid, and Jessica gazed around the courtyard, glimpsing marble statuary through an upstairs window, before following Rob and Charlie down the stairs to the gloom of their new habitat.

Just like the Olliff-Coopers upstairs, those downstairs at Manderston had been among almost 7,000 people who had seen the advertisement calling for volunteers for the Edwardian Country House and sent for further information – and suprisingly far more had wanted to try life below

Dressing the part: the second footman, Rob, adjusts the bow tie of the first footman, Charlie.

stairs than above. They had been attracted not by a life of luxury and leisure, but by curiosity about one that held out the prospect of unremitting hard work, of discipline, and of learning a new vocabulary of service and obedience. According to the 1901 census, the servant class was among the largest group of the total population of some 32 million in Britain, and of these over 100,000 were aged between ten and fifteen years,[1] the youngest being the age of Master Guy.

In his account of domestic service, Frank Dawes quotes the example of the Duke of Portland who, at the beginning of the twentieth century, had an establishment that comprised a steward, wine butler, under butler, groom of chambers, four footmen, two steward room's footmen, master of the servants' hall, two pageboys, head chef, second chef, head baker, second baker, head kitchen maid, two under kitchen maids, sundry vegetable maids and scullery maids, head stillroom maid, hall porter, two hall boys, kitchen porter, and six odd-job men. He also employed a head housekeeper, a valet, a personal maid for the Duchess and another for his daughter, head nursery governess, French governess, schoolroom footman, and fourteen housemaids; and there was a head window cleaner and two under window cleaners. Outside, some thirty servants were employed in the stables and the same number were at work in the newly installed garage, while other servants worked in the grounds, the laundry, the home farm and the gymnasium. The steam-heating plant and electricity generator required a staff of six engineers and four firemen, and the newly installed telephone exchange in the house required a telephone clerk and assistant plus a telegrapher. The whole empire was guarded by three nightwatchmen.[2]

Such an establishment was at the summit of the servant-employing class, and few households matched such a vast number of servants, or such a specialized calibration of roles. Indeed, the majority of servants were likely to be employed in middle-class villas where a cook, a maid and a scullery maid

The housekeeper

Jean Davies, who is sixty, learned her housekeeping skills growing up during the Second World War. She is an enthusiastic cook, gardener and poultry-, goat- and donkey-keeper. For a time she and her husband, Peter, ran a silver service restaurant but now they specialize in 'living history', going round to primary schools showing children all about life in nineteenth-century England. She felt that taking the job of an Edwardian housekeeper would be 'a fantastic experience'. Peter too was interested, and had applied to be butler at Manderston – though such a couple would be unusual in an Edwardian household. She did not relish their separation, but it would be worth it, she kept reminding herself in the first few days when it all seemed very strange and she felt extremely homesick. 'It will be an opportunity for a total immersion in the Edwardian experience.'

Mrs Davies was unfazed by the size of Manderston – 'It reminds me very much of Tatton Park near us in Cheshire, where Peter and I have done demonstrations' – but 'I *am* rather daunted about all the work that's going to be involved.' She had also heard that the chef was French and she knew all about French temperaments in the kitchen from her days in the restaurant business. She wondered how she would get on with the butler – would he be domineering? And then there was the question of discipline, which, for the female staff, was firmly in her domain. 'The young people are going to find it very hard, but that's how it was in Edwardian times. My goodness, I'll keep them busy. But I hope that I can be a person the young ones can turn to if they are in any sort of trouble, or want some advice.'

would be the most the family could afford. Employment was most sought after in the grandest establishments, though. It was not simply the prestige of the name and how it would look on a servant's 'character' (reference). It was the opportunity to work in often beautiful surroundings and to enjoy the camaraderie of a downstairs colony, rather than the intense loneliness of a 'maid of all work' or 'cook general' in a lower-middle-class household.

On arrival at the Edwardian Country House, the maids' first duty was an interview with the housekeeper, Mrs Davies. As housekeeper, 'the sole management of the female servants rests with [her]: it is her duty to engage and dismiss them, with the exception of the nurse, lady's maid and cook, whom the mistress of the house herself engages'.[3] A housekeeper was required 'to have methodical habits, to be firm and impartial in her dealings with under servants, although strictly exacting respecting the due performance of their duties, as she, in all respects, represents her mistress, and is invested with her authority'. The interview was conducted in Mrs Davies's downstairs sitting room, which was known as 'pug's parlour' (since an upper servant was irreverently called a 'pug' by the lower servants) and occupied a prime location in the bow of the house just below the morning room.

It is a pleasant room, large enough to entertain visitors, an abode befitting the 'upper servant' who was second only to the butler in the below stairs hierarchy, and in charge of all the female servants in the house. It is richly furnished in crimsons and dark greens, with a deeply padded sofa and horsehair-stuffed armchairs, and a fire burning in the grate against the late summer chill. (The fire had not been easy to achieve, as the chimney had not been swept for over forty years – two chimney sweep's poles were broken in the attempt and a jackdaw's nest landed on the hearth.) Mrs Davies had brought a number of framed photographs of her Edwardian ancestors to hang in her parlour. A chenille cloth-covered table stands in the centre of the room and it is here that the upper servants proceed in strict order of precedence, with the housekeeper following the butler into her 'own' room, to eat pudding and take cheese after lunch or dinner in the servants' hall. It was here too that Mrs Davies could sit and talk to her fellow upper servants, the butler, Mr Edgar, and the lady's maid, Miss Morrison, in the evening when the work of the house was finally done. She might well be busy, though, with some household mending as the small party gossiped and speculated about life upstairs.

To one side of the room is a desk where the housekeeper prepares for her daily meeting with the lady of the house to receive her instructions for the day, checks the household accounts (which her mistress may wish to see), oversees the orders for supplies of meat, fish, fruit and vegetables and dry goods from the kitchen, tots up the invoices sent in by local tradesmen and deals with any staffing matters that arise, just as her Edwardian counterpart would have done. On a shelf are ranged cookery books such as *Mrs Beeton's Book of Household Management* (an 'entirely new, revised and greatly enlarged' edition of the original 1861 version had been published in 1901); Eliza Acton's cookery books; *Domestic Cookery* by Mrs Rundell; *Warne's Model Cookery and Housekeeping Book*; advice

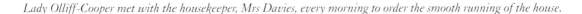

Lady Olliff-Cooper met with the housekeeper, Mrs Davies, every morning to order the smooth running of the house.

manuals such as *Cassell's Household Guide: Being a Complete Encyclopaedia of Domestic and Social Economy, and Forming a Guide to Every Department of Practical Life* (c. 1900–11); *Everywoman's Encyclopaedia* (8 volumes, 1910); and *The Housewife's Friend: A Treasury for Every Household to which is added hints for domestic servants.* Mrs Davies had been informed when she arrived, in words taken from an Edwardian manual for servants, 'As housekeeper you must be accountant, diplomat and task master all rolled into one.' And as another manual warned, 'The office of housekeeper is no sinecure, more especially in the country, when the heads of establishments entertain largely, and when the house is, during the winter months, more or less full of guests.'[4]

The tentacles of status reached down to the linen cupboard where family and servant's table linen was strictly separated.

The room also serves as the housekeeper's storeroom. The walls are lined with floor-to-ceiling cabinets housing the family's finest china and porcelain. The china closet is the responsibility of the housekeeper and she must oversee the washing, drying and replacement of all the china in the closet after meals, checking for breakages or any damage. Hers is also the responsibility for distributing the household linen from the airing cupboards for making up beds and laying tables.

Additionally, the housekeeper has the task of ordering and doling out household supplies such as candles, matches, soap, cleaning materials, polishes and waxes, and toiletries from a small room off the parlour. An Edwardian housekeeper would also have had herbs such as thyme, rosemary and sage dried in the oven to be kept corked in glass bottles; made pot-pourri to make the rooms fragrant by drying rosebuds and petals, violets, orange blossom, jasmine, lavender and orris root, and maybe including a clove-studded orange;[5] she would have distilled rose water of dark, damask roses, made lavender water, and stuffed small muslin bags with rose leaves, cloves, cinnamon, coriander seeds and mace to perfume linen and underwear. She would have dispensed medicine to the servants, such as lozenges for sore throats, inhalations for chesty coughs and healing balms and ointments, and made up her own remedies on occasions, maybe applying a small bag of heated salt to relieve neuralgia as recommended by *The Servant's Own Paper,* or dripping chloroform on to cotton wool to ease earache, handing out spoonfuls of castor oil, recommending a warm mustard bath for chilblains and the application of a bruised poppy leaf for wasp stings. In short, her aim should be to earn the Edwardian accolade that approves:

No better keeper of our store
Did ever enter at our door.
She knew and pandered to our taste
Allowed no want and yet no waste.

It was the housekeeper's task to prepare tea to be taken in the drawing room. This was often a sociable occasion, served when ladies in the neighbourhood paid an afternoon call. She would cut dainty sandwiches and bake scones, fancy cakes and biscuits. Mrs Davies found that her cherry or sultana fruit scones served with jam and her Scottish shortbread were the family's favourites, while the servants were particularly fond of her oat flapjacks which she had to make almost daily.

When visitors came to stay, the housekeeper would take charge of the arrangements, organizing the disposition of bedrooms – in consultation with her mistress, since in Edwardian times this could be a delicate matter, particularly among the bed-hopping 'fast set' that surrounded the King.

Above all, as housekeeper, Mrs Davies's role was to ensure the smooth running of the household and to maintain discipline among the female servants. But she could expect status and service as well as responsibility and hard work. In a house the size of Manderston in 1905, Mrs Davies could have expected an annual salary of some £50 with 'all found', and she would have privileges to match her responsibilities not enjoyed by those lower down the servants' ladder. Apart from the luxury of her own sitting room, the lower servants would wait on her to an extent – a bell pull hangs by the fireplace in her parlour and this peals one of the fifty-six bells in the corridor outside. (Indeed, it was through waiting on the upper servants that the lower were supposed to learn their trade and be pronounced fit to serve the family upstairs.) In common with her fellow upper servants, the housekeeper would not be expected to do any dirty or menial work. Her life would be much more self-regulated than those who were below her in the rigid hierarchy that pertained below stairs, and whose lives she effectively ruled in conjunction with the butler. The housekeeper could arrange her own time off – providing this in no way incommoded the smooth running of the household – and the time at which she retired to bed was her own concern and not prescribed as it was for the lower servants. As housekeeper, she would have been accorded the courtesy title of 'Mrs' regardless of her marital status.

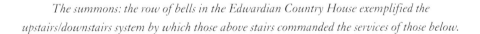

The summons: the row of bells in the Edwardian Country House exemplified the
upstairs/downstairs system by which those above stairs commanded the services of those below.

There was no time for reflection on their new surroundings for Antonia, Becky and Jess: the family were expected in less than a week, and there was a great deal to be done in preparation for their arrival. At Manderston in 1905 there had been thirteen female servants: three laundry maids, six housemaids, three scullery maids and a cook.[7] The re-creation of the Edwardian Country House in 2001 had shut off a large number of rooms so that the servants' task of cleaning the house and looking after the family, though demanding, was possible given that their number matched the number of rooms in use, and the relatively small size of the 'upstairs' family. The present-day female staff consisted of a housekeeper, a lady's maid, two housemaids, a kitchen maid, and a scullery maid (who had not yet arrived), and later a third housemaid was appointed.

First the maids climbed the four, long flights of stone stairs – ninety-seven in all, as they soon came to realize – to their attic bedrooms to leave their luggage. The servants were segregated in their sleeping arrangements, and as much as possible in their household duties too. It used to be accepted that there was a general stiffening in moral rectitude in the Victorian era after the relative licence of the eighteenth century, and the endorsement of a strict moral code of family values meant that extramarital sexual congress of any sort was made as difficult as possible. But historians now are more likely to emphasize the fact that extramarital sex was likely to lead to marriage, and this is why employers, anxious not to lose a good servant to wedlock and motherhood, were strict in their policing of their servants' sexual activities. Followers were forbidden and as many obstacles were put in the way of one of the footmen seducing one of the maids – or any other possible permutation that below stairs life might suggest.[8] 'If one of the menservants was ever found anywhere in the women's section after they had retired for the night, he was instantly dismissed without a reference,' wrote Margaret Powell, who had been a housemaid in Hove in Sussex. [9]

All the female staff slept upstairs in small rooms under the eaves. The housekeeper had a bed-sitting room with a fire, small table and comfortable chair where she could sit in the evening if she chose, rather than downstairs in 'pug's parlour'. Unlike the lower servants, the housekeeper would be free to take a bath whenever she wished in the upper female servants' bathroom (since the rebuilding had provided Manderston with indoor plumbing and sanitation and these had been extended to the servants' quarters – which was not always the case). She shared this bathroom with Miss Morrison, Lady Olliff-Cooper's maid, whose rooms were along the corridor. Miss Morrison had a sitting room and workroom combined where she could attend to her mistress's clothes, ironing, sewing, darning and mending by her fire, and a small bedroom.

The maids' rooms might seem cramped by modern standards, with sloping ceilings and small

At ease: the kitchen maid, Antonia, and the first footman, Charlie.

Jess, the second housemaid, dresses in her attic bedroom for her day's work.

windows, but by Edwardian working-class standards they were positively spacious, and a housemaid used to sleeping three or four (or more) to a bed at home would have felt privileged indeed to share a room – rather than a bed – with only one other person, or even have her very own room as Antonia, Jess and Becky did at Manderston (until Becky and Jess decided it was more companionable to share). The rooms had not been used for years now that Manderston survives with only a caretaker couple, plus help from the estate on big occasions. They were covered with years of grime and cobwebs which had to be cleared away so that the furniture appropriate for Edwardian servants could be collected from the mass of stuff piled up in every storeroom. Local women who worked at the house were employed to help, and soon the rooms were ready for their new occupants. In accordance with the times, they had been plainly furnished with a simple wooden chest (if a maid was lucky; if not, she would keep her meagre possessions in the tin trunk she had arrived with), a hanging cupboard, a single, narrow iron bed with a ticking-covered horsehair or flocking mattress and a cotton coverlet.

The furniture in a servant's room accorded to his or her status in the household: the more elevated the servant, the better quality his or her furniture was and the more likely the washbowl and jug were to match rather than being odd, cracked pieces. The furniture would be second-hand articles that had seen service in the main part of the house, while a strip of thin, worn carpet often failed to cover the wooden floorboards. In most households the small fireplace would probably have been lit only if the maid was ill, but in Edwardian times Manderston had been renowned for providing each servant with a bucket of coal every day. In imitation, the maids in the Edwardian Country House sometimes used to light a fire in one of their rooms, and all would sit up there to talk in the chilly Scottish evenings when they wanted to get away from the eagle eye of the butler in the servants' hall.

There was a washstand with a china basin and jug standing ready for morning ablutions (and evening if the maid didn't fall into bed exhausted without attending to her toiletries). An improving thought or biblical quotation would be framed on the wall, and a small table or chair stood by the bed for a candle (in fact Manderston had electric light installed when it was rebuilt, though it could be erratic in the early days) and a Bible or other improving book – not that there promised to be much time to read. And under each spartan bed stood a chamber pot since 'water closets should not be used during the night'.

It was the servants' quarters that had proved a key factor in the choice of Manderston for the Edwardian Country House programmes: they were – and remain – a superb example of the sophisticated domestic arrangements of an Edwardian country house. Stretching almost the entire length and breadth of the house, they are almost exactly the same now as they were when the rebuilding of Manderston was completed in 1905. Despite their size, it was intended that the servants' quarters should be as 'invisible' as the servants themselves. At Manderston, the basement – which literally functioned to 'underpin' life upstairs – was not visible either when approaching the front entrance, or when looking back from the gardens. Robert Kerr, who was Professor of the Arts of Construction at King's College, London, and himself an architect (though with a not very successful practice), advised in his influential work *The Gentleman's House, or how to plan English residences from the Parsonage to the Palace* (published in 1864), that the first step in building a country house should be to work out how many servants the clients could afford and then plan from that basis, and at Manderston in 1905 that had meant twenty-two.

Then: an Edwardian kitchen maid prepares food at Manderston.

A wide, white-tiled corridor runs the length of the house and from it open the kitchens, storerooms, larders, an ice room (the forerunner of the modern-day fridge and essential in summer), the still room, the servants' hall, the housekeeper's parlour, and the butler's rooms and his pantry, plus sleeping accommodation and washing facilities for the single male servants and any men servants brought by visitors to the house.

The kitchens were also designed by John Kinross: they have black and white ceramic tiled floors, and the ceiling beams are painted with a plaited ribbon pattern which continues into the scullery. Pride of place in the kitchen goes to the state of the (Edwardian) art cooking range housed in a separate unit in the centre of the room. Made by G. Drouet of the Ateliers Briffault in Paris, it provided four ovens of varying temperature as well as a hot plate on top, an open fire for spit roasting and a bread oven. An underground flue leads from the range to a chimney in the boiler house at the other end of the house. Learning the vagaries of this massive furnace would be one of the main tasks of the *chef de cuisine*, M. Dubiard, and keeping it alight would be the round-the-clock (or so it seemed) duty of the scullery maid – of whom there were to be several in the course of the 'Edwardian experiment'.

…And now: the chef, M. Dubiard tackles the Edwardian Country House cooking range.

The kitchen at Manderston is large, with high ceilings and a floor space that seemed like a cricket pitch to tired servants and entailed a great deal of walking during the course of a working day. But a cavernous kitchen was recommended, since the heat and steam and vapour could be overpowering, largely emanating from the range which was a challenging and demanding appliance, but not necessarily a very efficient one. A large range could easily burn a hundredweight of coal a day, but at the beginning of the twentieth century coal was cheap at around £1 a ton and regulations governing pollution non-existent. As late as 1920 it was estimated that only about 3 per cent of the heat generated from the coals was used to heat food, while another 7 per cent went to produce hot water. Of the remaining heat, 35 per cent was absorbed in the brickwork, 25 per cent was lost in flue gases, and at least 30 per cent went into heating the kitchen – all year round.[10]

Deliveries to the house had been well planned. There was a telephone on a hook in a small kiosk in the corridor – something of a novelty in 1905 – from where Mrs Davies would place orders for the house with local suppliers after consultation with the chef over menus. Tradesmen had a separate entrance and a separate corridor, and when the scullery maid heard the bell ring, she would open the door by pulling a lever outside the scullery, which saved her a long walk. She would then direct food

CHAPTER THREE

The Butler's Pantry

his is the first day that we are together and I must impress on the staff that there is going to be no idle chatter at table. The servants are there to eat their meal and they should only speak when spoken to,' explained the butler, reflecting on the first lunch that the servants had taken together in the house.

The housemaid, Becky, thought that it 'was the worst meal time that I have had in my entire life. You could have cut the atmosphere with a knife. I was so scared.'

'All I could think of was "What question might he ask me?"' added Jess. 'His look is definitely scary. It could turn you into a block of salt. I addressed him as "Sir" and apparently that was wrong. He said that it should have been "Mr Edgar". It's very confusing. He is in charge and I am really scared of him and the silence as everyone eats is just unnatural. I am a gobby person and having to be quiet all through the meal was just so abnormal.'

'I realize that the staff are probably all saying "this man is quite awful",' admitted Hugh Edgar, 'but I lived like that myself. When I used to go to tea with my grandfather, he would sit at the head

The servants at table: dinner presided over by Mr Edgar, with Mrs Davies at the other end,
and the rest of the servants seated according to rank.

The butler

Hugh Edgar, a consultant architect who advises on cultural projects, was brought up in Edinburgh and now lives in Surrey. He has worked all over the world, including for the Hashemite royal family, and has built a mausoleum mosque for the late wife of King Hussein of Jordan.

'I am very interested in how Edwardian society worked,' he said. 'I am interested in class and how it operated. I am fascinated by a society in which the boundaries were so clearly defined, when everyone knew their place and knew what was expected of them, and in a way I think that made life easier. I have some experience of Edwardian life because my grandfather was very much an Edwardian and for him discipline was all-important.

Mr Edgar knew that the lower servants would not find the hard work and the long hours easy, and that 'I will have to establish my authority from the start. I am going to see that we run the Edwardian Country House as near as possible to how it would have been run then.' He was also apprehensive about his relationship with his master: would they establish a bond? He was delighted to find that after a time, 'Sir John and I sometimes find ourselves talking man to man, though I never forget that he is the master and I am the servant.' He stoutly maintained that 'Our job here is to serve the family. There is no other reason for our being here,' and was rewarded when Sir John referred to his sixty-five-year-old butler as 'a tower of strength'. At the conclusion of the Edwardian experiment, Mr Edgar reflected: 'This was an era when everything became bigger and more extravagant – and the Edwardian Country House reflected that. Gambling became a craze upstairs and downstairs and then when the war came in 1914, that was a terrible gamble too!'

of the table at tea time and insist "children should be seen and not heard". And that's how it was. All you would hear was "Would you pass the bread and butter, please?" Apart from that, the meal was eaten in total silence. No doubt as time goes by we may be able to relax here in the Edwardian Country House and allow some chatter. But I have to set a standard. If one evening I tell someone that they have to keep quiet, I mean it and it doesn't matter why. I am at the head of the table and so I'm the one who determines who will speak, how much will be said and what will not be said. I appreciate that sounds harsh, but how else do you establish your authority with new staff in a new house? We have to start as we mean to go on. Sir John and his family will be arriving in a few days, so there will be a lot of pressure from the family, there'll be no time for chatter. We will need to have our meal as quickly as possible and then get on with the task in hand.

'I presume that is where my grandfather was coming from in his day. He died when he was eighty-four and he was a very busy man – he worked up to his dying day, he simply had no time for fripperies at teatime. He'd be polite and ask how I was getting on at school. And I'd reply, "All right,

*The trio known as the 'upper ten', the butler, Mr Edgar, the lady's maid, Miss Morrison (centre),
and the housekeeper, Mrs Davies, confer.*

Grandpa" and that was it. He'd recognized that I was at the table, but that's all he'd done. My father
told us that he really loved us children, but frankly I was terrified of him.'

'The office of butler is…one of very great trust in a household,' wrote Isabella Beeton in her
Book of Household Management, which first appeared in thirty threepenny monthly supplements to
the *Englishwoman's Domestic Management Magazine* run by her husband, Sam. The work began in
1859, when Mrs Beeton was just twenty-three, and took her 'four years of incessant labour'. It was
published as a 1,000-page book in 1861 – the most comprehensive work on domestic affairs ever to
be attempted. The encyclopedic book was an immediate best-seller, running to many editions after
Mrs Beeton's death in 1865 from puerperal fever following the birth of her fourth child; she was
only twenty-eight. Her book's value as a domestic *vade mecum* persisted in many households until the
First World War – and beyond. [1]

Mr Edgar was to assume his role with the utmost gravity, always aware of his position and mindful
of his responsibilities. A slim, wiry man who walks everywhere at an extremely brisk pace, breaking
into a trot when matters appear urgent, he had shaved off his customary beard in keeping with the
times and perennially appeared neat and dapper in his black trousers, black tailcoat, starched white

shirt, stiff white wing collar and black bow tie. It was essential that he should always appear formal, but some households preferred that the butler should commit some sartorial solecism – maybe the wrong trousers for the coat he was wearing – to make sure no one mistook him for a gentleman.[2]

As butler, Mr Edgar was the highest-ranking household servant: he was in charge of all the male servants, as the housekeeper was of the female staff, and he took precedence over Mrs Davies at table and in the 'pug's parade' to her sitting room after meals. She would defer to him in other matters, too. He had taken to heart the dictates of the ex-butler to the 'Duke of Romsey' (a pseudonym to disguise the employer's true identity), who had written a guidebook for his fellow servants that they might profit from his experience:

> In all establishments, it is [the butler's] duty to rule. In large establishments it will be greatly required; for under-servants are never even comfortable, much less happy, under lax management. Order in this sense means mutual comfort. What the butler has to do and avoid to secure this object must be determined by himself; but one thing he must never fail to do, viz., to notice faults on their occurrence, and after a firm caution, if the fault is repeated, to bring the culprit before the notice of the head of the house. Let the butler neglect this, and farewell to his rule.[3]

The butler was the person who had most to do with the family 'upstairs'; it was an important and complex relationship. As the anonymous author of *The Servants' Practical Guide* published in 1880 laid down, 'A butler who knows his duties, and performs them with zeal, integrity and ability, cannot be too highly prized by judicious heads of families.'[4] On the butler's ability above and below stairs rested the good order of the household, the comfort of the family and also, to no small degree, its social reputation.

Butlers were expected to be bachelors without the distractions and temptations of a family of their own, and Mr Edgar (or Edgar as he was called by the family) might even be addressed as 'Olliff-Cooper' below stairs should he accompany the family on a visit to another great house, so completely was his identity sunk into theirs. The butler's suite of rooms was positioned as near as possible for access to the principal rooms, particularly the dining room, so that when about his regular duties, or when summoned by bells, he could bound up the stairs to appear in minutes. The butler acted as valet to the master of the house in an establishment the size of Manderston, laying out Sir John's clothes for the day, brushing and

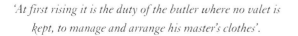

'At first rising it is the duty of the butler where no valet is kept, to manage and arrange his master's clothes'.

sponging them when necessary, polishing his shoes and shaving his master with an open cut-throat razor which he would strop on a leather strap. Safety razors had been available since the 1880s but were still looked on as a bit cissy, and not capable of giving such a close shave. As Mrs Beeton pointed out, 'gentlemen are sometimes indifferent as to their clothes and appearance'[5] – not that this was the case with Sir John – and should this be the case, it was the valet's duty to keep his master 'up to snuff', ensuring that he was neatly, and correctly, dressed for every occasion. An untidy master reflected badly on his servant.

The butler's location near the stairs from the basement to the ground floor indicated that he had easy access to supervise the laying of tables and the serving of meals, and to open the front door to visitors and announce their presence, or accept a visiting card if the family was 'not at home' or chose to pretend that it was not.

Mr Edgar's personal domain included an office that was the hub of the organization of the household, where he implemented the plans and activities of the day that he had discussed with Sir John at their daily morning meeting. It was here, peering through sometimes two pairs of gold-rimmed spectacles, and using his draughtsman's skills and neat, spidery handwriting, he drew up detailed timetables for all the staff, specified special duties for the day for the footmen, pored over seating plans for lunch and dinner, and orchestrated major social events such as fêtes, balls, weekend shooting parties and the like. On his walls a butler would be likely to have an improving tract, framed, or perhaps a discreet watercolour. On his shelves would be lined up the essential works of reference for his position:

Edwardian multi-tasking. Mr Edgar in his role as valet gives Sir John his morning shave (left) and in his capacity of butler, polishes a silver tray from the safe.

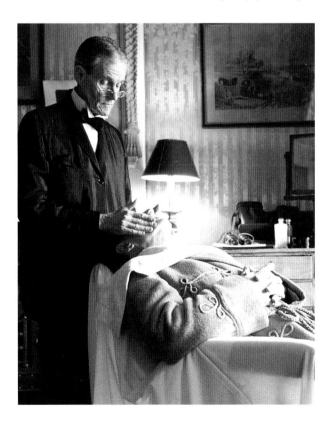

a copy of the Bible, the Book of Common Prayer, manuals with advice for the efficient running of a house and the proper conduct of servants, a last-year's copy of *Burke's Peerage* (since the current one would be in use upstairs) for when visitors came, and probably a copy of *Bradshaw's Railway Guide* for those occasions when his master wished to venture to London, or visit relations or friends a steam train journey distant. It was here that the butler interviewed new male staff, enquiring about their previous experience and often about the occupation of their father, as well as reading the 'character' supplied by their previous employer and noting their personal appearance and mien. It was to this room that he would summon the household servants to lecture them with little homilies, discipline or, in extreme instances of transgression or insubordination, dismiss them. The grave remark 'I will see you in my room later' sent a tremor down the spine of a lower servant – as it was intended to.

The butler would also have been in charge of the cellar – this had been his primary function in earlier times; indeed, Mrs Beeton considered that 'the real duties of the butler are in the wine cellar: there he should be competent to advise his master as to the price and quality of the wine to be laid in'.[6]

A gentleman's gentleman: Mr Edgar discusses household matters with Sir John at their regular morning meeting.

He would ensure that the cellar was properly stocked with bottles of fine wine, champagne, port, 'malt liquors', sherry, brandy and any other fashionable liqueurs that took the family's fancy. He would store the bottles in the correctly labelled bins and, in consultation with the master of the house, decide on the wines to be served at lunch and dinner and carefully note in his cellar notebook those bottles drunk. Traditionally, empty wine bottles (and no doubt the few inches left in the bottom) were the perquisites (or perks) of the butler, who could sell them for pin money. The butler's responsibility for the wine cellar made it imperative that a master should satisfy himself of the man's good habits on appointment, since 'insobriety is a very common failing among butlers…and the inconvenience to which a master and mistress are subjected when they are unfortunate enough to engage a butler addicted to drink, is of a serious nature'.[7] And indeed the temptations offered by the wine cellar were adduced as another reason why it was not a good idea to employ a married man in the position of butler. Should the butler's wife be 'ailing and very much in need of strengthening things…half bottles of wine and whole bottles of wine are under such circumstances not unlikely to find their way to the butler's home; while he justifies himself for this lapse of trust by the specious reasoning that a bottle or two of wine can make no possible difference to a master whose cellars are so bountifully stocked, while to his wife it makes all the difference in the matter of regaining health and strength'.[8]

A plainly furnished (and always impeccably tidy) bedroom led off one end of Mr Edgar's office and adjacent to his rooms was the butler's pantry where silver and plate were washed and polished. Next to that, tucked away with no access from the servants' corridor, was the silver vault where the valuables were stored and to which only the butler had a key. At Manderston, the butler had been the best-paid of all the servants (as would have been the case in all but the largest houses where a steward would have been employed). The leatherbound *Servants' Book* from the house reveals that William Tait, a thirty-five-year-old butler who left the Millers' service to work for Lord Kinross in August 1903, had received an annual salary of £60. Often a butler, at the top of his professional tree, would be 'suited' for life, a stalwart of the household, 'as solid and reliable as the Bank of England',[9] but this does not appear to have always been the case at Manderston. In December 1909 George Smith (who by this time was paid £65 a year) seems to have left after only two days, and his successor, Frank Ricketts, 'went abroad' after only two months, though it looks as if the unnamed butler who came next stayed right through the First World War, when the entries cease.

Folding clothes

'A valet's duty,' warned Mrs Beeton's guide in 1901, 'leads them to wait on those who are, from sheer wealth, station and education, more polished, and consequently more susceptible of annoyance.' To avoid any possibility of this, Mr Edgar, who acted as Sir John's valet as well as his butler, copied out copious notes on how to fold his master's clothes in the correct manner.

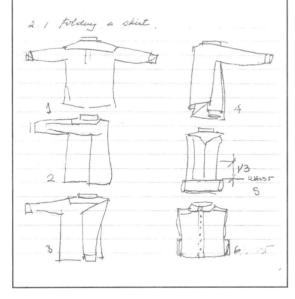

He rises as late as possible, he exerts himself as little as he need; he declines to take up the governess's supper or to clean her boots…several times a day he partakes freely of nourishing food, including a surprising quantity of beer…a jolly, magnificent fellow is the flunkey,' wrote Lady Violet Greville in an article on 'Men-Servants in England' published in the *National Review*.[10] For 'governess' read 'tutor', and could Lady Greville's description fit the case of Charlie and Rob, the two footmen in the Edwardian Country House? Both were aged twenty-three and both thought that being a footman for three months might be 'a bit of a laugh'.

Rob had worked for a time in a hotel in Torquay, where he learned all about silver service waiting – a useful apprenticeship for his Edwardian Country House role. He admits to being 'something of a peacock – I have been known to strut', which again was a quality not unimportant in the lexicon of footmanly skills. As well as having to work hard downstairs under the direction of the butler, footmen had an ornamental role upstairs, serving at table, assisting guests, riding at the back of the carriage in imitation of their forebears who would run alongside their master's vehicle, partly for security, largely for display. On top of this, Rob carried out the duties of a valet for Master Guy while Charlie performed the same function for Mr Jonathan and any visiting gentlemen staying at the house.

The speeding footman: Rob hurries along the interminable corridors and flights of stairs to get food from the kitchen to the dining room upstairs.

The footmen

Charlie Clay, the first footman, expected life in an Edwardian Country House to be like his public school. A former area salesman, the twenty-three-year-old from Nottingham has spent some time travelling around America and hasn't entirely lost his wanderlust. He is not reticent about his charms. 'I've done some modelling, and I rather like to be the centre of attention,' he confessed engagingly. Like most of the younger servants he wondered how he would get on without clubs and bars, but reckoned that he could provide some entertainments for his fellow below stairs staff. Taking orders, though, was not his strong suit. It had got him into trouble at school – how would he adapt to Edwardian discipline? In fact, Charlie soon became quite a favourite with the butler, who thought of him as 'confidant'.

Rob Daly, the second footman, who is also twenty-three, has a degree in genetics from London University, but he hasn't quite found his vocation. Born and brought up in south Devon, he too admits to a liking for attention. He had been looking forward to the Edwardian experience, and was certainly prepared for hard work. Nearing the end of his spell of servitude, Rob reckoned that Sir John 'thinks that we footmen do our jobs well because we want to impress the family, but I am not sure that's the case. We do our menial tasks to the best of our ability because it is the only way of maintaining our self-respect. In an odd way the hierarchy and the restrictions are liberating. You don't have choices and you don't have to make decisions. It takes away a lot of responsibility.'

He concluded, '"Rob the footman" will always be with me' – and Charlie agreed that whatever he did in later life, his Edwardian persona would forever be part of him too.

Footmen brought prestige to the families they worked for. As Pamela Sambrook explains, 'being waited on at dinner by a manservant carried higher status than a mere parlour maid'.[11] A tall, handsome, liveried footman, his posture erect, his hair powdered on grand occasions, who was confident in the rules of etiquette and served adroitly but with something of a theatrical flourish at table, brought glamour to a household. So it was not surprising that when Mr Edgar first interviewed the two young men, he was mentally comparing their height, assessing the set of their jaw and the curve of their calves. In his survey of *Life and Labour of the People in London* conducted in the 1890s, Charles Booth reported that a footman's wages were related to his height: a first footman who stood 5ft 6in would earn from £20 to £22, whereas one who could draw himself up to 5ft 10in, or even attain 6ft, could command from £32 to £40.[12] For aesthetic reasons, footmen of very similar height were preferred to present a pleasing symmetry at table.[13] The livery they wore was intended to indicate to visitors how far they were removed from any connotation of menial work (which is not how it felt to Rob and Charlie), since their braided, gilt-buttoned, eighteenth-century-style jacket, breeches and white gloves would have been entirely unsuitable. Furthermore, his employer invariably provided a footman's livery whereas the maids had to purchase their own uniform. It was another example of the gender difference whereby male servants were paid more than their female equivalents, and, since their roles made them visible to the family and guests, were more individualized and enjoyed a higher status than the 'invisible' servants who laboured to help produce what the footmen served and clean where they served it.

Finally the butler pronounced: Charlie, who had done some modelling and engagingly confessed that he rather liked to be centre stage, would be appointed first footman. 'I think Charlie's a bit of a perfectionist, like me,' Mr Edgar assessed. Rob would be second footman – a post that entailed, among other things, taking charge of Mr Edgar's chamber pot.

As well as the ceremony, there was the skivvying. As Mrs Beeton pointed out, 'the footman…is expected to make himself generally useful…his life is no sinecure; and a methodological arrangement of his time will be necessary, in order to perform his many duties with any satisfaction to himself or his master'.[14] Charlie and Rob's 'many duties' below stairs, which necessitated 'rising early to get through all the dirty work before the family are stirring', included a considerable amount of menial work. Coal had to be carried upstairs for the fires and blocks of ice manhandled into the storeroom; and although pots and pans and the servants' crockery and cutlery were scoured by the scullery maid

Dressing for dinner: Rob stands in for Charlie as Mr Jonathan's valet.

CHAPTER FOUR

Up to Snuff

T he first dinner party,' wrote Lady Greville in her work of information and exhortation, *The Gentlewoman in Society*,[1] 'causes a tremor to the stoutest heart. No really first class entertaining can be done where money *is* an object. It is not necessary to be ostentatious or lavish, but all perfection must be paid for and requires a great deal of care and forethought. How few are the really good dinners we can look back to with satisfaction at the end of the season! Two or three perhaps; for where the food was excellent and well served, the company often proved tiresome. It does not lie in everyone's capacity to organize a really successful dinner…'

There were, she explained, several kinds of dinner parties, ranging from the large dinners or banquets to private dinners, which fell into two categories. 'The spreads…given on strictly reciprocal principles or "cutlet for cutlet" as a great lady of my acquaintance once called them. Here, again, no enjoyment is expected or received: a duty to Society is simply fulfilled. So many people have dined or danced you; so many people must be dined in return.' On such occasions, Lady Greville writes:

> There will be a profusion of retainers dressed in the traditional costume of satin breeches and silk stockings with powdered hair…Dinner tables now resemble either flower gardens and hothouses, a jeweller's emporium, or a window in Liberty's shop with silks of all colours freely and tastefully displayed. The exact proportion in which floral and silver decorations should be used is known only to the elect souls…A few prefer baskets of lovely fruit only…[though] too much conventionality still prevails on all these points where individual taste and feeling only should decide. Large dinners generally break up early; the hostess and her friends respectively feel they have done their duty.[2]

Then there are 'small dinners [which] require even greater care in their management, but when properly carried out are perfection. It has often been said that the numbers at table ought never to exceed that of the muses' (nine), but Lady Greville was inclined to 'extend the number to twelve who can be well seated at a round table'. The guests at 'a *diner intime*, as the French call it, require to be even more carefully chosen than the *menu*…the women must be pretty and agreeable; the men, noted in some way…'[3]

Vita Sackville-West described the syndrome in her novel *The Edwardians*.[4] 'Those meals! Those endless extravagant meals in which they indulged all year round,' sighed Sebastian, 'the darkly handsome…patrician adolescent' master of Chevron, the hero of the novel. Chevron stands in for Knole, the great Elizabethan house in Kent with its reputed 365 rooms, one for every day of the year, and the 'self-contained little town' of servants needed to sustain it. Knole was the central passion of Vita's life, the house that, under its terms of settlement, she as a woman could never inherit.

> How strange, Sebastian mused, that eating should play so important a part in social life! They were eating quails and cracking jokes. That particular dish of the Chevron chef was famous: an ortolan within the quail, a truffle within the ortolan, and *pâté de foie gras* within the truffle…From his place at the head of the table, Sebastian watched the jaws going up and down…they were all people whose names were familiar to every reader of the society titbits in the papers…he was obliged to admit that they were very ornamental. They seemed so perfectly concordant with their setting, as though they had not a care in the world.[5]

Sir William Miller MP, the father of the man who had rebuilt Manderston, had been given a baronetcy for his service to politics by the Liberal leader and four times Prime Minister, William Gladstone, in his dissolution honours in 1874. His honour, however, came not as a reward for his political activities in the House of Commons, for it is said that he never once spoke in the chamber. Rather, it was for what would today be called networking: the grand political dinners Sir William gave with the intention of consolidating support for the Liberal Party in the Borders, winning converts to Gladstone's causes. These causes were financial liberalism, a commitment to parliamentary reform, and a vehement denunciation of the 'forward' foreign policy in the Balkans and Afghanistan of his Conservative partner in the musical chairs of late Victorian politics, Disraeli. This was to reach a moral crescendo during Gladstone's 'pilgrimages of passion' against 'Beaconsfieldism' in the nearby seat of Midlothian in the 1879–80 election campaign, which the Liberals decisively won.

At such dinners the food and wine would have been of the finest quality and likewise the guests chosen – and placed – with great regard for their status and their influence. Status was the pivot on which much of Edwardian high society turned, for in many cases its membership was no longer burnished with the patina of age. Since the middle of the nineteenth century the old British aristocracy of birth and land had been gradually giving way to a new aristocracy of money: the Edwardian plutocracy. It no longer 'took three generations to make a gentleman': it took wealth to live like one. The process had been noted by *Punch* in its monthly series 'The Side Scenes of Society' which chronicled

Social setting: the dining room with its depiction of Mars, God of War on the plasterwork ceiling.
The portraits hanging on the wall were acquired to give the impression of a distinguished ancestry.

the doings of the Spangle-Lacquers, a *nouveau riche* family who had made their fortune from 'soap, gin, tallow, rags or something equally interesting, by a process of alchemy which leaves all the old philosophies far behind'. The Spangle-Lacquers' friends were much the same: 'you can assign [them] no fixed position in society [since they are generally met with] in places where distinction was acquired by paying for it'.[6]

This was not a new situation: all 'old money' had been new once and from medieval times the ranks of the British landed classes were sustained with new recruits, and anyone who made a sufficient fortune would try to buy an estate or build a country seat in order to stake their claim to a position of power in the upper echelons of society. In the 1860s, Lady Stanley of Alderley encapsulated such social mobility in a terse comment: 'Half the peerage have no grandfathers.' It was the acceleration of this tendency after the agricultural depression of the mid 1870s that was so striking. The price of land fell alarmingly (between 1875 and 1897 the value of agricultural land had fallen from £54 to £19 an acre) and the fusion between land and commerce increased. By 1900 'the new rich were setting up in country houses, being given titles and continuing to take the train up to their offices in order to deal in newspapers, ships, tobacco, coal, gold or linoleum'.[7]

The architectural historian Joe Mordaunt Crook writes: 'By the end of the First World War, in London, in the shires, the ascendancy of money was indisputable. A new type of élite had been established…the Edwardian period was the age *par excellence* of the *arriviste*.'[8] It was an unsettling experience: Lady Dorothy Nevill, who had been at court, wrote in 1910 regretting that when she had first known London society it was 'more like a large family than anything else':

> Everyone knew who everyone else was…mere wealth was no passport…in the [eighteen] forties none of the millionaires had yet appeared. There were rumours of Hudson, the railway king, and his wife, but they were never in Society…[but] very soon the old social privileges of birth and breeding were swept aside by the mob of plebeian wealth which surged into the drawing rooms, the portals of which had up till then been so jealously guarded. Since that time not a few of the mob have themselves obtained titles, and now quite honestly believe that they are the old aristocracy.[9]

'The advance of new money can be measured even more clearly by the dramatic spread of the Edwardian baronetage,' wrote Mordaunt Crook. There had been Victorian baronets with a background in trade, but in the Edwardian period the baubles rained down on new money. In 1905, eight millionaires were nominated, their wealth made from lace, cotton, coal, US property, banking and shipping.

The 'mere wealth' of this 'new aristocracy' was remarkable. The word 'millionaire' was a nineteenth-century coinage – or rather import from France – and was used to label those who had made their fortunes in the Industrial Revolution, but between 1809 and 1858 only ten non-landed millionaires were recorded: wealth was still in land. Just after the First World War the balance had tipped decisively. Between 1860 and 1920, 188 non-landed millionaires had died and these men represented 'new money'. When income tax was eight pence in the pound they left their legacies in cash, shares and bonds rather than land. Of the very richest who left over £5 million, Charles Morrison was a warehouseman and merchant banker, Henry O. Wills was a tobacco magnate, and Alfred Beit and Sir Julius Wernher were both gold and diamond magnates, though the Dukes of Derby and Westminster – traditional aristocrats whose money was in land and property – also got in above the £5 million wire.[10]

With their new riches, the men who had not made it from land determined to buy land and build houses on it to emulate the landed aristocracy, or surpass them in the size and grandeur of their homes. It was, as the economic historian W. D. Rubinstein has written, the respect wealth paid to status.[11] Of those one hundred or so new peers created from non-landed backgrounds between 1886 and 1914, about a third had 'compensated for their origins by buying big estates', in Mordaunt Crook's words.[12] Land was traditionally regarded as 'safe': 'It was impossible for land to burn down, or be stolen, or blow up, or sink at sea,' writes Mark Girouard.[13] Land was reliable, it was prestigious and it gave a fellow a permanent stake in the country. It was not, however, the best return on investment for most of the nineteenth century, and by the 1880s it turned out not to be safe at all.

With declining agricultural prices, due largely to the influx of cheap corn from the US and to falling rents, and trumped by the introduction of graduated death duties which rose to a maximum of 8 per cent on fortunes in excess of a million by the Liberal Chancellor of the Exchequer Sir William Harcourt in his 1894 budget, confidence in the land among those who had traditionally owned it was dramatically eroded.[14] In the words of Oscar Wilde's Lady Bracknell: 'What with the duties expected of one during one's lifetime and the duties exacted from one after one's death, land has ceased to be either a profit or a pleasure. It gives one a position, and prevents one from keeping it up. That's all that can be said about land.'[15] Though this view of the effects of death duties and other forms of taxation was greatly exaggerated prior to Lloyd George's 'people's budget' in 1909, squeezed between a world economy that was distinctly to their disadvantage and a government that seemed distinctly unwilling to make concessions, all but the super rich among the aristocracy found it necessary to retrench, curtail spending and sell off land, art – and houses. In the years between the accession of Edward VII and the First World War, Holbeins, Rembrandts, Raphaels, Canalettos, Gainsboroughs and works by lesser artists from private aristocratic collections all went under the hammer, as did silver, gold, china, furniture, books and jewels. From the 1880s landed families sold off their town houses, their subsidiary land, and often their houses on the land too. Wings that had been added in the golden age of Victorian optimism and prosperity were demolished – and sometimes whole houses too. Between 1879 and 1914 some seventy-nine great houses were destroyed and the figure continued to rise after the First World War.[16] By 1914 around 80,000 acres of English land had changed hands for some £20 million including large tracts belonging to the Duke of Bedford. As the *Estates Gazette* noted, 'the unanimity of large English landlords in selling their estates clearly points to some great change in the condition of affairs in this country', with 'the slicing off of large portions of ancestral

'A fabulous animal having the head and wings of an eagle and the body and hind quarters of a lion'. The Griffin gate at Manderston.

and extensive domains'.[17] It was much the same in Scotland: the Marquess of Queensbury sold half his holdings of land in Dumfriesshire in 1897; the Duke of Argyll disposed of the Island of Tiree; the Duke of Fife sold off vast tracts of his land between 1880 and 1889; and the Duke of Sutherland put 330,000 of his Scottish acres on the market.[18]

If they did not sell their houses, then – strapped for cash – the landed gentry were increasingly unable or reluctant to extend their existing residences, or build new ones. Well over half the large houses that had been built between 1835 and 1874 were at their behest, but from 1875 to 1914 the proportion fell to less than one-fifth.[19] A number of great houses did find buyers among the new plutocracy. Sir Julius Wernher bought Luton Hoo, designed by Robert Adam and built for the 3rd Earl of Bute, Prime Minister to George III, in 1767, the gardens laid out by 'Capability' Brown; the Guinness family bought Elveden Hall in Suffolk (from a wealthy – and extravagant – Indian maharajah); the soap-boiler Joseph Watson bought Compton Verney from the 19th Baron Willoughby de Broke; in 1904 Apethorpe Hall near Peterborough was sold to the grandson of the railway contractor Sir Thomas Brassey; and the heir to the Glasgow chemical manufacturer, Sir Charles Tennant, whose hydrochloric-acid belching chimney rose above the city 'higher than the campanile at Cremona',[20] commissioned Lutyens to build him a house at Rolveden in Kent

Lady Miller's London house, 45 Grosvenor Square in Mayfair, decorated for the coronation of George V in 1911.

(1907–1909).[21] The hugely wealthy American plutocrat, William Waldorf Astor, whose wife Nancy Astor would become the first woman to take her seat in House of Commons, bought two: in 1893 he acquired Cliveden on the Thames in Buckinghamshire, which had been rebuilt to the design of the architect Sir Charles Barry by the fabulously wealthy Duke of Sutherland in 1850–1; and in 1903 the thirteenth-century Hever Castle in Kent, the childhood home of Anne Boleyn.[22]

But in many cases the new 'super wealthy', or even the very rich, did not buy the seats of those above them on the social ladder: they purchased part of the estate of the landed gentry and built, or rebuilt, their own houses. 'Turning to the present time,' wrote an architect (and future President of the Royal Institute of British Architects) in 1908, 'probably more country houses are being built and more money and thought expended on them, than at any time since the days of the Stuarts.'[23] The houses represented notable commercial success and the consolidation of this success through investment in land – or rather the countryside. The town house enabled the pursuit of business and the participation in the London season, which ran from the start of the new parliamentary session in

February (or April or May if a family had no contact with political life) to late July when there was a general exodus to the sea – yachting at Cowes, maybe, or a *séjour* on the French Riviera – the country and the grouse moors followed by a spot of partridge shooting, and then the hunting season began.

Sir James Miller owned a house at 45 Grosvenor Square in Mayfair in addition to Manderston. The country house was intended for leisure, the semblance of a rural life to enable country pursuits like hunting, fishing and shooting. Such houses usually stood in fairly extensive grounds but were ornaments on the land rather than deriving an income from it, as aristocratic landed families had in earlier times. In the Edwardian period, the country houses of the *nouveaux riches* were devoted to pleasure and conspicuous consumption: they were set up for entertaining. Who knows, one day Edward VII and the smart set that eddied around him (many of them such as the tea king, Sir Thomas Lipton, and the financier Sir Ernest Cassel were very notably 'new money' men themselves) might include such a house on their social peregrinations. In 1896, the then Princess of Wales for the first time ever stayed in a commoner's home, West Dean Park in Sussex. The magazine *World* noted this social landmark: 'Until this surprising "end of the century" not even a Prince had stayed in any but the most important houses. At one time the visit of a monarch or an heir apparent made the greatest of great ladies, great statesmen or great courtiers, greater. But by degrees the line has been drawn lower and still lower, until at last of very few rich people can it be said that they have never had royalty under their roofs.'[24]

The carriage driver, Tristan, stands at the front door to assist a dinner-party guest to alight from a horseless carriage.

With its 109 rooms, its commanding position, its imposing façade, its 56 acres of formal gardens with manicured lawns, a sinuous lake, and pleasant garden walks – only the distant Cheviots on the horizon look wild and untidy – Manderston is a paradigm of such an Edwardian monument to money and the pleasures it can buy. Inside, the impression is reinforced to the power of ten. It did not need the sociologist Thorstein Veblen, writing in 1899, to point out how precisely material goods were coming to represent the status of their owners, or, the hopes of their owners, the correlation between emulation and consumption.[25] Anyone could read the alphabet of aspiration from Sir James Miller's essay in Classicism in the hallway with its vistas of marble. It was a hallway for show whose use was redundant from its construction, since the introduction of bells throughout the house did away with the necessity for servants to lurk permanently in that grand space. But it was floored with a magnificent roundel of inlaid marble (based on the one at Kedleston Hall) and housed a marble statue of Miriam and the infant Moses by Franco Barzaghe, and from it rose the famed silver staircase with crystal stair rods leading to the first floor where a silver-plated bath reposed in the master bedroom suite. There were Adam-style plastered ceilings and Wedgwood bas-reliefs, solid rosewood doors and then there were the furnishings. '[Manderston] arguably contains the most extravagant and best-preserved examples of Edwardian upholstery in Britain,' conceded *Country Life*, which first appeared in 1897 to feed the British (and overseas) romanticism about the countryside in general, and the house in the country in particular. It is where 'luxury and opulence are matched by quality in every detail'.[26]

Dinner party guests entering the dining room, the entrance to which is flanked by the two impassive-looking footmen in Charles and Robin mode.

The furnishings and decoration of Manderston had been placed in the capable hands of the fashionable London firm of Charles Meillier & Co., the company that had completely redecorated Sir James's Grosvenor Square house in 1897.[27] The firm was probably established in the 1860s and continued in business until the 1930s. At the time of Manderston's rebuilding, smart money had a taste for Louis XV- and Louis XVI-style interiors, and this is what Meillier provided for Sir James's country seat. They also provided the high-quality reproduction furniture – chosen not on the grounds of cost (or if so, inversely so), since for example a reproduction Louis XV Régence cupboard with marquetry inlay was for sale in 1905 for £2,400. Meiller & Co. provided floor plans, drawn to scale, to show how they expected their furniture to be displayed. For example, the highly formal furniture – chairs, small tables, commodes and screens – that furnishes the living room was to be disposed around the room with an insouciant disregard for symmetry and an almost minimalist approach in comparison to the over-stuffed rooms of the high Victorian period less than a decade or so earlier. The curtains in the ballroom were woven with gold and silver thread, which sparkled under the huge crystal chandelier, while the wall hangings there and in the ballroom were 'an immense extravagance',[28] made of brocatelle (a more dramatic – and expensive – fabric than damask) figured in white satin, and cut velvet, with the exceptionally large repeat patterns that were so fashionable in the Edwardian era, replete with draped valances, flounces and tassels, all hung from heavy brass poles, while the Louis Seize chairs in the drawing room and ballroom were covered in rich silk and brocade.

With its impressive exterior and awe-inducing interior, its eighteen bedrooms for family and guests, and including a 'bachelors' corridor' (a self-contained little colony of four bedrooms with their own bathrooms for unmarried men whose late-night revelry and strong cigarettes were shut off

'Dinner stands alone as an institution sacred to the highest rites of hospitality'. Sir John braces himself for the ordeal.

from the rest of the house), it was hardly surprising that Sir John Olliff-Cooper, the temporary legatee of Manderston, should wish to show off 'his' house. Some three weeks into the family's stay at Manderston, Sir John decided that the time had come for him to host a political dinner party for what he called 'the great and the good' among his Scottish neighbours, and invite political opinion-formers from across the border too.

A book of *Etiquette, Rules and Usages of the Best Society* published in 1886 instructed that 'those invited should be of the same standing in society. They need not necessarily be friends, nor even acquaintances, but, at dinner, as people come into closer contact than at a dance, or any other kind of party, those only should be invited to meet one another who move in the same class of circles.'[29]

It's an absolute minefield,' Lady Olliff-Cooper sighed as she sat at her desk wrestling with whom to invite, and how to seat them, writing names on small cards and inserting and reinserting them into a red velvet simulacrum of the oval-shaped Manderston dining table. At her elbow lay an open copy of *Burke's Peerage*. Invitations should be sent out 'from two to ten days in advance', insisted one contemporary guide to etiquette (which seems rather short notice for anyone with an active Edwardian social life). Another, written by Mrs Humphry (who, as 'Madge', was the guru of the magazine *Truth*, and a contributor to *Everywoman's Encyclopaedia*), advised:

> The usual length of an invitation to dinner is three weeks, but this is by no means a fixed rule. In the height of the season it may be abridged or extended, according to circumstances. Sometimes a hastily got up dinner might be given for someone who is passing through London, or visiting some provincial town. Foolish indeed, and inexperienced in the ways of the great world, would be the person who would take exception to a short invitation in these circumstances. In the same way a distant date is sometimes fixed at a time when everyone may be supposed to be fully engaged for several weeks to come and a dinner invitation has been received as much as six weeks in advance of the date fixed. This is, of course, very exceptional.[30]

Informal invitations ran along the lines of 'Dear Mrs Green, Will you and Mr Green dine with us in a friendly way on Tuesday, 9th July at eight o'clock?'[31] This easy spontaneity, however, was not permitted for formal invitations, which could be written 'on notepaper of the small size known to stationers as "invitation notes". Or they could be cards: 'the usual size is 4½ by 3½ inches, and the printed characters are copperplate'. They are 'issued in the name of the gentleman and lady of the house:[32] 'Sir John and Lady Olliff-Cooper request the pleasure of the company of…' Mrs Humphry

'The man of "perfect manners" is he who is calmly courteous in all circumstances'. Lord Steel arrives at the political dinner party.

points out that 'it will be seen that the only items to be filled in are the name or names of the guests, the date and hour. Sometimes "honour" is used rather than "pleasure" and occasionally the "R.S.V.P" is replaced by "An answer will oblige", an ungrammatical sentence which some persons prefer to the initial letters of the French phrase,' sniffed the etiquette-meister. 'The form of invitation cards varies slightly,' she prescribed, 'but the simplest are those used by persons of the highest rank. Those who do not care to copy the customs of the aristocracy often have their crests in gilding on their invitation card' and, she added with disdain, 'I have even seen two crests ornamenting one card.'

Clearly, there was no question of that: the Edwardian Country House might not be a ducal seat but there would be no vulgarity in any communications that issued from *its* portals. The requisite-sized, simple cards were ordered in raised, black copperplate. They could, after all, be used for the variety of social events that were envisaged for the coming months by filling in 'dinner', 'ball', 'fête' or 'shoot', to indicate precisely at which function a guest's pleasure (or honour) was requested.

Receipt of such an invitation placed a complex social responsibility on the invitee too. 'An answer should be returned at once, so that if the invitation is declined the hostess may modify her arrangements accordingly. The mode of replying is regulated by that of the invitation. It would be a great mistake to answer a friendly note with a formal one, and though not nearly so heinous a crime, replying to a formal card by a note in the first person is sometimes misunderstood.'[33] Acceptance was simple: to decline posed a trickier problem. The excuse should be couched in the third person, something along the lines of 'Mr Anstruther regrets very much that he will not be able to accept Sir John and Lady Olliff-Cooper's kind invitation for the 7th as he will not be in the country, having previously arranged to spend a week with friends in Monte Carlo' should be acceptable. The commonplace 'owing to a previous engagement' was considered to be so overused as to constitute an example of 'studied incivility', other than in the 'most formal cases, or where the acquaintance is very slight' when presumably the inviter would be uninterested in the minutiae of the invitee's daily round.

How to invite, and *when* had now been established. But *who* to invite was no easier. The general guidelines were clear: 'A host and hostess generally judge of the success of a dinner by the manner in which conversation has been sustained. If it has flagged often, it is considered proof that the guests have not been congenial; but if a steady stream of talk has been kept up, it shows that they have smoothly

'It is not *correct' instructed an etiquette manual 'to forget that if dinner is the important meal of the day in the matters of food and wine, so it is in courtesy, conversation and geniality'.*

amalgamated, as a whole.'[34] It was all a question, as Mrs Beeton sagely remarked, of 'care being taken by the hostess, in the selection of invited guests, that they should be suited to each other'.[35]

The Edwardian Country House was to host a political dinner, so it would be politicians around whom the event would revolve, interspersed by local people of note and interest to ensure a lively, but not contentious, evening of good conversation. The oval mahogany table in the Manderston dining room could be extended to seat twenty people with ease, and so, counting the family as four, Sir John and Lady Olliff-Cooper, Miss Anson and Mr Jonathan (Master Guy would certainly not have been included, as no one under fourteen would be seen at the dinner table), that meant drawing up a list of sixteen people to invite – with a handful of names in reserve in case some on the A list were 'otherwise engaged'. Soon invitations were written and posted, and prompt replies received.

Sir David Steel, ex-leader of the Liberal party, was coming, with his wife. He had been a Westminster MP for border constituencies from 1965 to 1997, and is now a Liberal Democrat Scottish MP, and the Scottish Parliament's first presiding officer. The MP for Berwick-upon-Tweed and deputy leader of the Liberal Democrat party, Alan Beith, and his wife, Baroness Maddock (herself a former Lib-Dem MP), had accepted, as had Lord Deedes, a grand old man of British politics and journalism who was born in 1913. From a landed Kentish family, Deedes, a former editor of the *Daily Telegraph* and a Conservative MP for twenty-four years, was both the supposed model for Evelyn Waugh's intrepid Boot, and the recipient of the 'Dear Bill' spoof letters from Denis Thatcher that enjoyed such success in *Private Eye*. The final politician was David Mellor, once in the House as Conservative member for Putney; he had put his various political and personal vicissitudes behind him and is now a broadcaster, sports columnist, chairman of the government's task force on football, and a sought-after guest in political salons. In addition to the political contingent, Lady Chelsea, who is herself a modern-day authority on etiquette, would be coming (and would be eagle-eyed in noticing if the parvenus were 'up to snuff' in their first major social test in the Edwardian Country House). Some local guests had been invited, including Mr Liddell Grainger and Lady De La Rue, from nearby Ayton Castle which the Olliff-Coopers had visited, along with personal friends of the Olliff-Coopers, including Baron Bentinck and his wife, who were travelling up from Hampshire for the occasion, and Mr Jonathan had been allowed to invite a friend of his own age.

Lady Olliff-Cooper carefully copied the names of the guests on to small place cards – and then began the delicate business of constructing a table plan. It wasn't just common-sense courtesies like seating people next to those with whom they were likely to have something in common, yet not know so well that they would have nothing new to say. Husband and wife combinations were, of course, to be avoided, and the sexes interspersed. In addition there were the rules of rank and precedence and these were labyrinthine. Manuals for butlers and footmen would have routinely printed tables of precedence, and familiarity with these would have been expected in the competent servant. This was no easy task in the Edwardian period. In the reign of Edward VII the annual number of new barons quintupled from that of his mother, Queen Victoria, within a generation. And the creations were overwhelmingly *nouveau riche*. In 1905, for example, the Tory government nominated eight millionaires for elevation.[36] To help anxious hostesses cope with the influx of newcomers (of which they themselves might be one) to high society, Burke (of *Peerage* fame) published a *Book of Precedence* in 1881 which contained an alphabetical list with a key number by each entry. These 'indicate at a glance the position of the various grades in society',[37] for those for whom such information had not been imbibed with their mother's (or possibly wet nurse's) milk.

The greatest complexity lay in the fact that protocol of precedence had to be maintained within each hierarchical institution, and problems could arise when these cut across aristocratic definitions of place.[38] Gwen Raverat, a granddaughter of Charles Darwin and thus a member of the 'aristocracy of intellect', recalled the difficulties of a Cambridge dinner party:

> The guests were seated according to the Protocol, the Heads of Houses
> ranking by dates of the foundations of their colleges, except that the Vice-
> Chancellor would come first of all. After the Masters came the Regius
> Professors in the order of their subjects, Divinity first; and then the
> other Professors according to the dates of the foundations of their
> chairs, and so on down all the steps of the hierarchy. It was better not to
> invite too many important people at the same time, or the complications
> became insoluble to hosts of ordinary culture. How could they tell if
> Hebrew or Greek took precedence, of two professorships founded in the
> same year? And some of the grandees were very touchy about their rights,
> and their wives were even more easily offended.[39]

It was unlikely that a sister of Lord Curzon would have been so rigid in her *placements* at Manderston, but as newcomers the Olliff-Coopers were determined to play by the book and, according to their manuals, some rules were immutable: the principal female guest – 'the lady to whom [the host] wishes to pay most attention' according to Mrs Beeton, 'either on account of her age, position, or from her being the greatest stranger to the party'[40] – would be seated on the right of the host (and be led into dinner by him), while her husband (if she had one and he was present) would escort the hostess into dinner and sit himself on her right. So Lady Chelsea sat to Sir John's right and, since she was unaccompanied, Lord Steel was to Lady Olliff-Cooper's right, Lord Deedes on the other side while Lady Steel was placed to the left of Sir John. The rest of the company are seated 'as specified by the master and the mistress of the house, according to their rank and other circumstances which may be known to the host and hostess'.[41]

'A lord takes precedence over a baron, doesn't he?' pondered Lady Olliff-Cooper (though in Britain the titles are interchangeable). 'But what if he's a foreign baron?' she wondered further, thinking of the Dutch Baron Bentinck. 'Then Lord Deedes fought in the Second World War and Jonty knows quite a bit about the military from his time in the Cadet Force at Winchester, so it might be nice to seat those two together. And then Jonty is going up to Oxford to read history, and hopes to take some politics too, so maybe he could have Alan Beith on his other side?'

Lady Greville reminded hostesses that 'though the viands are good, they are but accessories; it is especially the bringing together of congenial spirits that is aimed at. A man must not be too great a talker, nor a woman too much taken up with herself; each must contribute his share to the general fund of conversation, and each must come with the determination to appear at his very best and brightest.'[42] But Lady Olliff-Cooper was 'not quite sure yet who's who in that respect. And now I've got two women sitting next to each other and that'll never do. I'll have to start all over again,' she said, pulling all the cards out.

Then there were decisions to be made about what food and wine to serve. Wearily, she reached across her now cluttered desk and rang for the chef.

t is,' explained a new edition of *Mrs Beeton's Household Management* published in 1888, 'in the large establishments of princes, noblemen and very affluent families alone that the man-cook is found in this country,' and indeed Queen Victoria had had a male chef, M. Menager, who was a very superior person himself, living in a smart London house, travelling to work by hansom and coining £500 a year (roughly £32,500 in today's terms), when an apprentice cook could expect to earn about £15 per annum.[43] She also employed a number of sous-chefs, an Italian confectioner and an Indian cook for the curries.

By the Edwardian age, a French (or at least French-trained) chef was what 'very affluent' families aspired to. France suggested Paris and that suggested Second Empire luxuries such as truffles, oysters, game, patisseries, fine chocolates and champagne. There was great cachet in a French menu, and dinner guests would be impressed to hear that it was not just the ingredients that had been imported, but the man to prepare them as well. After all, 'the art of cookery, or *gourmanderie*, is reduced to a regular science in France, where an egg may be cooked half a hundred

The chef

M. Denis Dubiard, the French chef in the Edwardian Country House, was taught to cook by his grandmothers, who both lived in rural France. His grandfather was also a truffle hunter, who managed to find truffles without the help of either pigs or dogs snorting out the delicacies. 'My grandfather just used his nose. He would go out early in the morning and come back laden with truffles. It was amazing.'

It was from his grandmothers that M. Dubiard inherited his instinct for food and his love of cooking, and learned the rudiments of his craft – including cooking on an open coal fire. 'I love cooking traditional dishes, slowly on an open hearth. That is one of the reasons why I wanted to come to cook in an Edwardian house. I am fed up with modern technology, I wanted to come to the countryside and cook in the old ways again, taking ingredients from nature. I have already found

game, pigeons, chickens and lots of rabbits and a plentiful supply of herbs and vegetables.'

M. Dubiard, who is thirty-eight, now lives on the edge of London with his wife and two small sons. He was born in Paris and trained at the famous Maxim's restaurant, and since then has worked in some of the finest restaurants in London.

In the vast Edwardian kitchen, he had to learn the intricacies of the range – and persuade or bully others to share the task of keeping it alight. The Olliff-Coopers had a steady stream of guests and were proud to show off their French chef's culinary prowess with elaborate dinners, plus breakfasts and lunches. And as well as cooking, M. Dubiard ministered to the servants when they were sick, compiling recipes of infusions and poultices that were 'guaranteed' to cure anything from a common cold to heartache.

ways, so those who can afford large families of servants, and give frequent entertainments, consider a man-cook as economical, because [in theory] he produces an inexhaustible variety without any waste of materials, and that elegance and piquancy of flavours which are necessary to stimulate the appetites of the luxurious'.[44] When the Olliff-Coopers arrived at Manderston, they found to their delight that they had just such a master craftsman in their own kitchen. M. Denis Dubiard was trained at Maxim's in Paris, in the tradition of the great French chefs, Escoffier and Carême, and he has subsequently worked in the finest London restaurants and various private houses.

A chef's pay varied from house to house but *The Servant's Practical Guide: a Handbook to Duties and Rules* published in 1880 gives a male cook's earnings at between £100 and £150 a year (and that did not include perks), which compared with around £60 for the butler and was higher than a female cook could have commanded. The cooks employed at Manderston appear all to have been women between 1901 and 1914, and their wages ranged from £40 to £50 a year, depending presumably on their experience and former positions. And of course there would be fierce competition for the services of a fine French chef, and the master and mistress of the house would have no desire to see their star performer lured away by higher wages and better conditions offered elsewhere.

Food served at the Edwardian dining table not only had to taste delicious, it had to look enchanting too. Snowy, damask-clothed tables, glittering with silver and crystal, would display pheasants dressed with their tail feathers, fish in aspic primped with herbs, a glazed and decorated boar's head, hocks of breadcrumbed and clove-

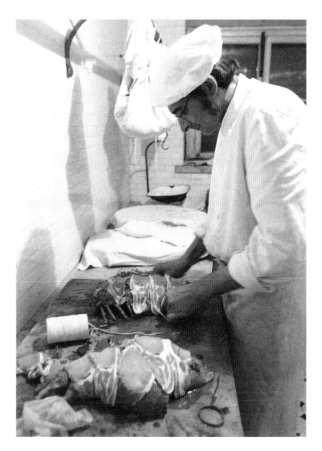

M. Dubiard prepares meat for dinner in the pantry set aside specifically for such a task.

studded ham, candied fruits or frosted grapes piled high on *tasses* (stemmed dishes), small hillocks of bonbons and sugar-spun confectioneries, cream gâteaux decorated with curls of bitter chocolate and candied violets, epergnes filled with exotic fruits or marzipan *petits fours*. There would be raised meat pies, the pastry glazed with egg, the edges crimped and decorated with pastry leaves; jellies turned out from elaborate copper moulds that made them look like shimmering, translucent castles, some with the different flavours layered in jewel-like layers of ruby, emerald and amber, others with perfect nasturtiums or pelargoniums encased in the gelatine, or with creams or fruit piled in a hollow centre; tiny pastry *bateaux* filled with raspberries or wild strawberries in season; asparagus wrapped in damask napkins and laid on silver platters; lobsters decorated with seaweed; silver lattice baskets of perfect, darkly speckled quail's eggs; and, on the grandest of occasions, a centrepiece carved from a block of ice – swans were particularly favoured.

Jellies

'Take some fine soaked and blanched calves' feet,
and set them to cook in one and three-quarters pints of water apiece.
Skim as thoroughly as possible; cover, and then cook very gently
for seven hours,' instructed the great French chef, Escoffier,
in the 1907 version of his Guide to Modern Cookery.

This method would produce the gelatine required for making the fruit and savoury jellies that were so much a feature of the Edwardian dinner table. But the 1901 edition of *Mrs Beeton's Book of Household Management* suggested that 'calves' feet are very rarely used now for the making of stock for jellies. By means of Swinborne's Patent Refined Isinglass, jelly may be made with the greatest facility in a few minutes, possessing the nutriments of calves' feet without the impurities.'

Fruit and wine syrup

Makes approximately 2 pints (around a litre).

  1 pint (450ml) water
  1lb 4oz (550g) granulated sugar or loaf sugar
  $\frac{1}{2}$ lemon and $\frac{1}{2}$ orange
  2 star anis
  4 cloves
  20 coriander seeds
  2 sprigs of mint and a sprig of thyme or lavender
  $\frac{1}{2}$ vanilla pod
  $\frac{1}{2}$ cinnamon stick
  1 pint (450ml) dry white wine

Put the water and sugar in a pan, slice the lemon and orange thinly and add to the water with the remaining ingredients (except the wine). Bring to the boil, turn down the heat and allow to simmer for about 20 minutes. Add the wine and bring back to simmering point for a further 5 minutes, before removing from the heat. Leave to cool while the flavours infuse.

Strain the syrup through a fine sieve.

Pineapple and mint jelly

M. Dubiard's recipe for this jelly was highly acclaimed by the Olliff-Coopers and their guests.

  $\frac{1}{2}$ peeled ripe pineapple
  About 15 mint leaves
  1 pint (450ml) cold water
  $\frac{1}{4}$ pint (125ml) M. Dubiard's fruit and wine syrup
  $\frac{1}{2}$ oz (10g) powdered gelatine
  A little crystallized ginger, finely chopped
  Green food colouring
  Peppermint food flavouring

Cut the pineapple into cubes, and place them in a saucepan with the mint leaves and cold water. Heat this, and simmer for about 10 minutes. Then add the syrup, and simmer for a further 10 minutes.

Leave it to cool and infuse before straining. Add the gelatine to the strained mixture, whisking as you do so. Put the pan on a moderate heat to dissolve the gelatine, carrying on whisking gently. Remove the pan from the heat when it reaches simmering point.

To make a layered jelly, pour the mixture into two separate bowls; add the crystallized ginger to one, and a few drops of the green food colouring and peppermint food flavouring to the other.

Pour a layer of one coloured jelly in the bottom of a copper or china jelly mould, which has been rinsed in cold water. Wait until it has just set and pour on a second layer of the contrasting jelly. Continue with alternate layers until the mould is full. Put into the fridge to set completely.

Table flowers

*'Hostesses in the season vie with each other as to whose table
shall be the most elegant, and are ready to spend almost, if not
quite, as much upon the flowers as upon the food itself,
employing for the floral arrangement people who devote their time
to this pleasant occupation,' proclaimed the 1901 edition of
Mrs Beeton's Book of Household Management.*

The containers were important: some people 'prefer low decorations, others high ones, but there is one rule that should always be in force, and that is that the flowers and their receptacles should never interfere with the line of vision…the great objection to epergnes …was that they hid the guests from one another.'

For the political dinner party, the flowers were chosen to complement Lady Olliff-Cooper's dress. The containers were wicker baskets painted gold then rubbed with silver leaf and burnished with graphite so they looked suitably old; they blended well with the soft pink and reds of the chosen roses – full-blown Bourbon and Gallicia variety. Fronds of asparagus fern were studded between the roses, and the baskets were edged with *Alchemilla mollis* in three different shades of pink, while swathes of small-leaved tree ivy trailed across the table. Any small gaps were covered with damp moss and the arrangement placed on a glass plate to protect both the mahogany table and the white damask cloth. It would also have been usual to use fruit – pineapples or waxy apples or velvet-like peaches – which would have been wired into containers with flowers.

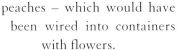

In Edwardian times, the flowers would have been secured by tying small bundles of rosemary or lavender twigs with raffia and packing them into the container vertically. Individual stems and foliage would then be pushed in between the twigs to keep them upright, and water poured in to the container.

In country houses, the gardener would have been in charge of tending the flowers and cutting blooms to decorate the table every day. For a dinner party, the head gardener would be informed of what colour flowers were required and either he, or someone skilled in floral arts, would make up the arrangements in the greenhouse or potting shed. The finished decorations would be carried in through the servants' entrance for the butler or footmen to place where required.

For very grand occasions, when the whole house was to be decorated with flowers, a team of gardeners would arrive at the crack of dawn to ensure that all was ready before the master and mistress came downstairs.

CHAPTER FIVE

Dressing
for Dinner

Morrison had a solution: she had read that an Edwardian maid would nightly collect the loose hair from her lady's hairbrush and form this into rolls to bulk out the elegant hairstyle she was creating. These elaborate styles provided the ideal platform for the elegant picture hats that are so redolent an image of the Edwardian period. These were huge, often anchored by vicious-looking hat pins with jewelled or enamelled ends; decorated with lavish trimmings such as osprey or ostrich feathers, they could cost as much as 50 guineas (around £3,000 at today's prices). Miss Anson had a modern, short, layered hairstyle, which defied any attempt to fashion it into a credible Edwardian coiffure, so she wore a wig, and the care and styling of that fell to Miss Morrison too.

Washing hair was a problem in the Edwardian Country House: at first Miss Morrison had followed a recipe for shampoo that involved lemon juice and egg yolk but, far from conditioning the hair, it made it dull and sticky. Further experiments adding vinegar were more successful and Sir John was happy with that. But Lady Olliff-Cooper disliked the smell of vinegar about her person, and contented herself with Miss Morrison's 'dry shampoo' method – talcum powder rubbed into the hair and then brushed vigorously out again every four or five days.

For grand occasions, a maid might dress her mistress's hair with a tiara, or, for slightly less formal occasions, a jewel-studded comb, or maybe she would weave lace or ribbons or artificial leaves into the hair. One night when Lady Olliff-Cooper set off for the opera in nearby Berwick-upon-Tweed, Miss

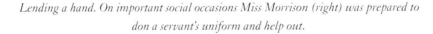

Lending a hand. On important social occasions Miss Morrison (right) was prepared to don a servant's uniform and help out.

'Everything does up at the back!' Miss Morrison helps Lady Olliff-Cooper dress.

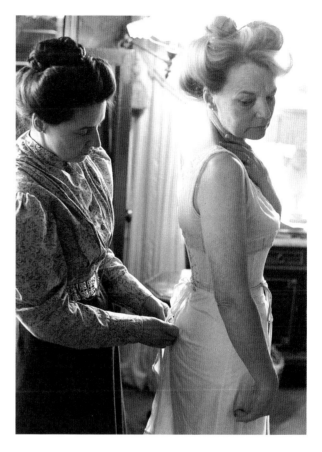

Morrison stood just inside the front door and proudly watched her mistress get into her carriage wearing a marabou-trimmed pink taffeta cape over her dress, with a 'fascinator' in her hair consisting of a spray of osprey feathers, to complete the elegant outfit.

A lady's maid needed nimble fingers for hairdressing and sewing, and also to do up all the hooks on the corsets and the dresses and high-necked blouses that Edwardian women wore, for these did up at the back, making the wearer entirely dependent on help in getting dressed. Miss Morrison would lace Lady Olliff-Cooper's corset, pulling in the waist as tight as was bearable on formal occasions, since in Edwardian times a curvaceous figure was much admired. A new design of corset introduced in 1900 was intended to be more 'natural' and 'healthy' than Victorian ones that exerted great pressure on the waist and diaphragm. It produced an S-shaped figure by forcing the bust forward and the derrière out. But in more Junoesque women the effect was rather more a 'kangaroo stance' with an overhanging 'balcony bust' which was a good foot ahead of the rest of the body.[3] The earliest memory of the photographer Cecil Beaton (who was born in 1904) was of ladies 'laced into corsets that gave them pouter-pigeon bosoms and protruding posteriors'.[4]

New technologies made it more possible to mould women to this much-coveted sinuousness in the Edwardian period than it would have been a century earlier. The corsets were extra-long and flat fronted and the metal hooks could be subjected to what amounted to almost mechanical force, and metal eyelets allowed laces to be yanked in much further than had been the case with stitched silk eyelets.[5] Vita Sackville-West described the elaborate process:

> Buttons [the lady's maid] knelt before her, carefully drawing the silk stockings on to her feet and smoothing them nicely up her leg. Then [the Duchess] would rise, and, standing in her chemise, would allow the maid to fit the long stays of pink coutil [a strong cotton fabric], heavily boned, around her hips and slender figure, fastening the busk down the front, after many adjustments; then the suspenders would be clipped to the stockings; then lacing would follow, beginning at the waist and travelling gradually up and down, until the necessary proportions had been achieved. The silk laces and their tags would fly in and out, under the maid's deft fingers with the flick of the skilled worker mending a net. Then the pads of pink satin would be brought and fastened into place on the hips and under the arms still further to accentuate the smallness of the waist. [6]

Hair ornaments

By the reign of Edward VII, Society women's hats
had reached almost ridiculous proportions on some occasions.
Massive creations perched on top of elaborate hairstyles and were
weighed down with feathers, braid, lace, artificial flowers and fruit
and were sometimes kept on with a long chiffon scarf that
tied under the chin.

No Edwardian lady would have ventured outside without a hat, and since hats were so decorative and also so hard to put on, they were frequently worn indoors on social occasions – including at the lunch table. Even young girls would never go out bare-headed.

These elaborate hats were usually secured by beautiful, though lethal-looking hat pins made of steel anchored through non-too clean hair (since freshly-washed hair was too soft and floppy to provide a satisfactory base) and with decorative ends made of jet, pearl or lacquered enamel.

However, for evenings, when hats were not worn, a decoration of feathers or ribbons might be worn in the hair. The elaborate hairstyles of the Edwardian era meant that it was easy to secure such decorations with wire, but with today's less formal styles, they can be attached to hair combs or to 'scrunchie' bands used to tie hair into a bunch.

Ostrich, peacock, marabou or pheasant feathers can be wired on, as can small bunches of tiny fabric flowers, while adhesive face and body 'tattoos', or paste diamante can be glued on to combs.

Despite the popularity of feathers on millinery and hair decorations, and on the bodices of dresses sometimes, there was a movement against the mass slaughter of birds in order to provide decoration for the heads of society women which was already gaining momentum. In 1889, various 'fur and feather' groups (in this context, fur meant down rather than animal skins) came together to form the Society for the Protection of Birds, which received a Royal Charter from the game-shooting Edward VII in 1904. As a result of the society's lobbying, the Importation of Plumage (Prohibition) Bill was introduced in 1908, but did not become law until 1921.

In the Edwardian Country House, the women found that tight lacing placed restrictions on breathing and movement – and women's magazines were loud in their condemnation of this practice. 'It is a great mistake to think it is ever necessary to tight-lace,' fulminated *Woman's Life* in 1906. 'It is always undesirable and always inartistic. More ruined digestions, more red noses, more weak hearts, more agonies of pain…have been caused by this than anything.'

'I can only perch on hard chairs, I certainly can't relax into sofas or armchairs and I can hardly bend down to cuddle Guy, my corset is so constricting,' Lady Olliff-Cooper regretted, while the whalebone stays chafed so unmercifully that she would slip a fine cotton or silk vest next to her skin. Edwardian underwear was made of cotton – and was saucy in that the bloomers were crutchless to make it possible to use the loo without a major production, though some had a buttoned flap (or trapdoor) for the same purpose. Silk stockings would be fastened on to the corset's suspenders and next came cotton petticoats, usually trimmed with Brussels or Honiton lace in the case of the 'upstairs' contingent, then an underskirt. It was then time to put on the dress, or blouse and skirt if it was to be a quiet day without visitors. If the maid was dressing her mistress for a grand dinner or ball, precious jewellery would be fetched from the safe in the butler's room, but otherwise appropriate pieces would be chosen from the casket on milady's dressing table. The lady of the house was then ready for breakfast, and she swept downstairs, while her maid would tidy her dressing table and collect any

'A [lady's] maid who wishes to make herself useful', suggested Mrs Beeton,
'will study the fashion-books with attention, so as to be able to aid her mistress's judgment
in dressing according to the prevailing fashion'.

dirty clothes for washing. She would gather up the shoes for polishing, check that any outdoor clothes needed brushing or sponging, and gather up the garments that needed running repairs or alterations.

Then it was back to her room, with armfuls of flounces, and the Edwardian lady's maid started her daily round of washing, mending and sewing in her work room. At Manderston, Miss Morrison was fortunate to have a walled balcony with a wonderful view of the grounds: the formal rose gardens, the lawn fringed by the lake and the view framed by the purple haze of the Cheviots. She had rigged up some clotheslines on this balcony so that she could hang the clean, white bloomers and petticoats to blow dry in the wind, hidden from view of anyone walking in the grounds below – she hoped. She would rinse out the vests and silk stockings, using some Lux soap flakes that Mr Edgar had found in the house and given to her. She might have to wash the ladies' corsets too, which could be a major job, scrubbing the fabric with a nail brush and then having to twist and ease the stays back into shape. Then she would wash the cotton garments using carbolic soap, rinse them and then add some Reckitts blue to the water to brighten the whites before wringing the clothes out by hand and hanging them on the line. 'I get real satisfaction from seeing the clothes blowing on the line on a good drying day – and you get a lot of wind in Scotland – so you know that the clothes are really fresh. It's somehow more rewarding than just shoving clothes into an automatic washing machine.'

Miss Morrison's heavy irons were kept hot on a small iron stove in the fireplace which she kept burning all day. She would use them in rotation every time she needed to iron – which was frequently. She also had a small iron heated by methylated spirits, but once she had got the hang of getting her 'iron stove' really hot, she preferred to use this. She would hang fine chiffons, silks and velvets in the steam of a kettle to get the creases out, but that still left piles of cotton

How to wash corsets

Corsets loomed large in the lives of the female members of the Edwardian Country household, and laundering these unlovely garments presented Miss Morrison with something of a challenge. She copied down instructions in the back of the journal she kept:

First, take out the laces and wash them. Lie the corset on a flat surface, and scrub thoroughly with a small brush using soft green soap (or white if you have it) and tepid water. When clean, rinse repeatedly under cold running water and pull into shape lengthways. Lie flat to dry, pulling into shape at regular intervals. When the corset is dry, rethread the laces. Do not iron.

and linen from Lady Olliff-Cooper and Miss Anson to iron every day and all the frills and pleats and ruffles, of which there were many, needed the attention of a goffering iron. Miss Anson had a particular fondness for linen clothes which were a devil to iron, until Miss Morrison remembered one of the tips that her grandmother, who had been in service herself, had passed on: 'Sprinkle the fabric with water, roll it up tightly, and then it'll be much easier to iron.'

Alterations and trimmings seemed to take a lot of her time, particularly those of Miss Anson, who would want a collar changed here, a sleeve altered there, even her bloomers made more streamlined on one occasion – 'She has alterations on alterations,' sighed Morrison. And in order to give variety to the outfits, Morrison experimented with making new belts and trimming blouses and dresses with different ribbon or lace, adding feathers and stitching net and artificial flowers to hats. She had intended to run up some new clothes for her mistress herself, but found that in all the time she was in the house, she only ever had time to make one skirt. As soon as she sat down at her sewing machine (a revolutionarily useful

'The lady's maid should be properly qualified for her situation...particularly in needlework'.

machine with its ability to 'tuck, frill, gather, quilt, braid and embroider' – as well as stitch – first introduced in Britain in the 1850s), the bell that she had placed at the bottom of the staircase leading from the Olliff-Coopers' floor would ring. She would hurry down the stairs to find that Lady Olliff-Cooper needed to change her clothes again, perhaps to receive a visitor, pay a call or go riding. Her corset needed to be relaced to suit whatever clothes she was wearing, and her hair redone.

If Lady Olliff-Cooper was calling on a nearby country house, Miss Morrison would be expected to accompany her in the carriage, to carry any small gifts she might want to take, arrange her clothes and help her on and off with her outer garments. Miss Morrison's Edwardian counterpart would have welcomed these excursions as much as she did, since they got her out of the house and provided an opportunity to meet and talk with other ladies' maids in the houses she visited.

A lady's maid worked long days, and for this reason (and for the dexterity of their fingers) younger women were often preferred. A lady's maid was at the beck and call of her mistress until the mistress retired for the night: she would have helped her dress for dinner and have waited for the summons to undress her, plait her hair, make sure that her nightwear was aired, and help her into bed at the end of the day, and this could be well past midnight if the family was entertaining or attending a function.

In addition to her duties as hairdresser, seamstress, dresser and escort, a lady's maid would have been expected to be a mine of information about medical matters, beauty aids – and stain removal. She would have made her own potions using lemon juice to whiten hands, known a recipe for a pomade for removing wrinkles with onion juice, honey and wax, be confident about how to get rid of ink stains as well as brightening tarnished pearls, banishing moths (camphor bags or turpentine soap wrapped in brown paper) and a host of other useful things.

Inevitably a degree of trust and closeness developed between a lady and her maid: it is hard to attend to the intimate toiletries of a person without getting to know them fairly well. Lady Olliff-Cooper was no exception: 'My maid Morrison is a truly wonderful person. She is teaching me all manner of useful things and she has a delightful sense of humour. She is a real treasure. I have come to value her greatly. And I think that Morrison is thoroughly enjoying serving me, and takes as much pride in turning me out as a cook would take pride in turning out a wonderful meringue gâteau, or something like that.' Most ladies' maids became the confidantes of their mistresses, sharing not only snippets about clothes and beauty, but gossip, excitements, anxieties and heartaches too. Miss Morrison was privy to Lady Olliff-Cooper's anxieties about how she was coping with her new world, listened to her concerns about Guy, and was discreet about the fact that on many nights Sir John did not sleep in his own bedroom down the corridor, but spent the night in his wife's bed. A lady's maid was expected to be discreet, and sometimes wise beyond her years, yet never forget her station. She could give advice when asked but never proffer it uncalled for.

In the eighteenth and early nineteenth centuries, French maids (like French chefs) had been considered the pinnacle of elegance with their supposed insider knowledge of Parisian haute couture, and their 'charming' broken accents, though Germans and Swiss were recognized as being more practical. But during and after the Napoleonic wars it was considered unpatriotic – and maybe a little risky – to employ a French maid in such a close capacity. In Frances Hodgson Burnett's novel *The Making of a Marchioness*, published in 1901, Lady Maria Bayne, the mentor of the heroine, Emily Fox-Seton, advises her: '[Jane – who had applied to be Miss Fox-Seton's maid] would probably be worth half a dozen French minxes who would amuse themselves by getting up to intrigues with your footmen. Send her to a French hairdresser to take a course of lessons, and she will be worth anything. To turn you out properly will be her life's ambition.'[7] In any case, Miss Morrison was indignant at the very idea: 'French maids! I'll show them that there are no maids finer than Scottish maids,' she asserted stoutly.

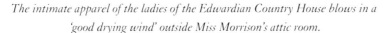

*The intimate apparel of the ladies of the Edwardian Country House blows in a
'good drying wind' outside Miss Morrison's attic room.*

Dressed in style for the races: Sir John and Lady Olliff-Cooper.

Lady Olliff-Copper was soon to find that she was no exception to this interest in modish dress. 'My family are a bit puzzled by me and say I am turning into a mindless doll, though Jonty kindly indulges me by saying that I am just getting in touch with the female side of my personality. They see me taking an interest in female sorts of pursuits, which is not my normal role at all. I had no idea how much time one *could* spend thinking about dresses, what colours go best with what, what trimmings to add, what jewellery to wear,' marvelled the modern-day casualty doctor. 'I don't spend much time on my appearance at home, and my clothes by and large come from charity shops because I think they're good value, and I get quite a kick out of searching for things and making the best of them. But here I think my husband is quite overwhelmed by seeing me dressed up like that. He keeps saying "you look so beautiful" – in tones of slight surprise, actually. It's not quite so flattering but there you are, and I think he feels it reflects on him. I imagine it was like that in Edwardian times too. Men dressed up their wives as much as possible to reflect their status. That was the wife's role. I feel that I am living in a Mills & Boon romantic novel. It's a woman's fantasy of beautiful clothes, and jewels and carriages, and judging by my husband's reaction it's a man's fantasy too, corsets and crotchless underwear and suspenders.'

Mrs Humphry decreed: 'The object of a fashionable woman in dressing, is to make herself distinctive without becoming conspicuous – to excel by her union of graceful outline and fidelity to the fashion of the moment (no easy task), and while offering no striking contrast to those around her. So to individualize herself that she is one of the few who remain in the memory, when the crowd of well-dressed women is recalled only as an indistinguishable mass.'[22] It was hardly surprising that women spent time poring over the plethora of illustrated magazines that were available – and which disseminated high fashion beyond the realm of the very rich. Between 1880 and 1900, forty-eight new titles appeared. Sam (widower of Isabella) Beeton's monthly *Englishwoman's Domestic Magazine*, the blueprint of modern-day women's magazines, had ceased publication in 1879, to re-emerge in 1881 *as Milliner, Dress-maker and Draper*, while another of Beeton's titles, *The Queen*, merged with another magazine in 1863 to become *Queen, the Ladies' Newspaper*. From the 1880s a series of new magazines emerged, aimed at 'women of taste' who had an interest in society – royalty in particular – fashion, home and family. *The Lady's Pictorial* (which Oscar Wilde complained was devoted to 'mere millinery and trimmings')[23] ran from 1881 to 1921. *The Lady*, subtitled 'A Journal for Gentlewomen', was first published in 1885, but it was not until 1894 that its circulation took off when an ex-nanny introduced a small-ads section and soon the magazine had become what it remains today – 'a sort of *Exchange and Mart* for nannies'.[24] Then there were the penny (as opposed to sixpenny) weeklies, *Forget Me Not* and

Home Sweet Home, both launched in 1893, and the hugely popular *Woman at Home* merged with the mass circulation penny paper *Home Notes* which started publication in 1894 and eventually became *Woman's Own* in 1957. *Home Chats*, which was unlikely to have graced the Manderston bedside table since it was aimed at 'women who actually did some, if not all, their own domestic work',[25] thrived from 1894 until 1957, while *Woman's Weekly*, with its knitting and sewing patterns and romantic fiction, first appeared in 1911, and the similar *My Weekly* the previous year.

'I think it's a tribute to how much we have become involved in the project that I have become really interested in women's magazines of the period,' said Lady Olliff-Cooper. 'I have just been sent a copy of *Weldon's Ladies' Journal* for 1910 and I am scanning the pages for new ideas for dresses and hairstyles and hats. The Edwardians were obviously very keen on wearing bits of animals, feathers – osprey feathers, ostrich fathers – and masses of furs which were very *à la mode* in 1910. But what I need now clearly, is half a seagull. Half a seagull was a real fashion statement in 1910. They are simply everywhere.'

As well as gazing at fashion plates in magazines, a well-to-do Edwardian woman could have attended one of the newly popular fashion shows, window-gazed – or simply have gone on a shopping expedition to one of the many department stores that were particularly instrumental in extending fashion's domain to the middle classes. The fashionable shopping hours were between two and four in the afternoon. Omnibuses mingled with hansoms, and shop delivery vans, instructed to move at a snail's pace so that passers-by could read their advertising slogans plastered on their sides,[26] clogged up the London streets packed with ladies intent on a day's shopping in the new department stores. It was a similar story in Manchester, Birmingham and Edinburgh.

'Half a seagull is quite the thing.' A sampler of New Year fashions from Weldon's Ladies Journal *(1910).*

Mr Edgar flung open the heavy rosewood doors and Lady Olliff-Cooper drew in her breath when she saw how beautifully the staff had laid the table with a fine white damask cloth, a battery of crystal glasses and regimented silver cutlery, placed just so, in order that plates and bowls could be put directly in front of each diner without having to rearrange the cutlery between courses. The mahogany table had been wound apart by brass handles and extra leaves slotted in to accommodate the twenty diners. A napkin, folded into an elaborate mitre shape by Rob and Charlie (or Robin and Charles as Sir John had decided they should be known above stairs), stood by each place 'making an ornament to the table'. Silver condiment sets for salt, pepper and mustard were placed at regular intervals along the table. Heavy silver candelabras burned softly at either end of the table, wound round with ivy and small flowers. The three footmen (Kenny the hall boy had been dragooned into service for the evening – and renamed Kenneth for the occasion), wearing livery, their hair powdered, their patent, buckled slippers gleaming, stepped silently forward to pull out the chairs and seat the guests at table, Sir John, as host, sat at the head of the table with his back to the fireplace. It is to be hoped that the female guests would have remembered that 'gloves are kept on till the wearer seats herself at table. They may or may not be resumed after dinner, though usually the right-hand glove is put on previous to hand-shakings and goodbyes before the party breaks up. At very formal houses where the hostess is a dragon of social etiquette, one dares not relax the slightest rule…'[35]

Dinner was to be *à la russe*, a style first introduced in the 1820s which remained the fashion in the Edwardian era. As Mrs Beeton explained, 'It differs from dinners in the mode of serving the various dishes. In dinner *à la russe*, the dishes are cut up on a sideboard, and handed round the guests, and each dish may be considered a course…a menu or bill of fare should be laid by the side of each guest'.[36] Before that innovation, dinners were usually served *à la française*; the host had carved at table and two large courses, each with a great variety of dishes, were put on the table one after the other. A gentleman would help himself and offer his neighbour dishes that were within his reach, and ask for other dishes to be passed either by another diner or a footman. A soup and a fish course would have been on the table at the same time and would have been removed when the entrées (cutlets, fricassées, boudins, sweetbreads or pâtés) were served followed by the roast. The new style was

Table napkins

As ever, Mrs Beeton had advice for this area of etiquette and decoration. 'In ordinary family use,' she wrote, table napkins or serviettes 'are sometimes folded smoothly and slipped through "napkin rings" made of bone, ivory or silver…each member of the family having his or her own ring.' Those required for dinner parties and other formal occasions, however, 'should be neatly and prettily folded'. The napkins need to 'be slightly starched and smoothly ironed…a small dinner-roll…should be placed in each napkin, and such patterns as "Mitre", the "Neapolitan" or the "Rose" and the "Star" are convenient shapes, [and] the appearance of the dinner table will be greatly improved by putting a flower or small bouquet in each napkin.'

THE MITRE

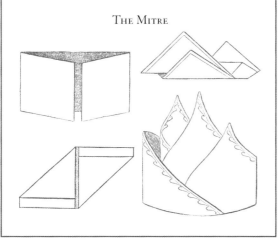

recommended since 'it gives an opportunity for more profuse ornamentation of the table, which, as the meal progresses, does not become encumbered with partially empty dishes and platters'.[37]

By 1905 meals were simpler, but the Olliff-Coopers' political dinner still consisted of eight courses, all to be expertly served by tyro footmen serving soup from a solid silver tureen and handing round vegetables in solid silver dishes (since at the last moment the chef's aesthetic had revolted at the prospect of china, and silver had had to be fetched from Edinburgh). The plates were Wedgwood in Madeleine design, and each footman was assigned to a particular section of the table, in a plan carefully drawn up in advance by Mr Edgar, so there would be neither collisions nor guests left waiting to be served.

As was correct according to Mrs Beeton, 'the master of the house should be answerable for the quality of his wines and liqueurs' and Sir John, mindful of his responsibility, and of the impression he was anxious to make, had consulted with a St James's wine merchant that had been founded in 1698. 'I think you should serve champagne with the oysters – Ruinhart champagne was very popular with the Edwardians and it's beginning to make a comeback,' Simon Berry advised. 'Then a Riesling

Mr Edgar carefully ladles out soup in the dining room.

with the fish would be appropriate. The Edwardians drank far more German wines than we do today, though Chablis was on our list in 1910 if you prefer that. To do justice to the venison, how about one of the great reds – a Brane-Contenac perhaps, a claret from the Margaux region?' But the real *pièce de resistance* came when Mr Berry produced from his cellars a genuine 1905 bottle of Tokay (or Tokjai as it is now usually known), a legendary wine that was supposed to have anointed the lips of the dying Tsars and rulers of the Ottoman Empire. 'It comes from Hungary, and was expensive since it's the essence of the grape. They are not crushed, the juice is extracted by force of gravity. Tokay wasn't imported into Britain until the beginning of the twentieth century, but because it has a high sugar concentrate, it is one of the few bottles of wine that was laid down in 1876 that is still drinkable today. I *think* I could let you have a couple of bottles.'

Sir John's eyes gleamed. 'We'll treat it like port and serve it when the ladies have left the table,' he decided.

In Vita Sackville-West's novel, the heir of Chevron describes a dinner party there: 'The jewels of [the guests] glittered, the shirt-fronts glistened; the servants came and went, handing dishes and pouring wine in the light of the many candles. The trails of smilax wreathed greenly in and out among the heavy candelabra and the dishes of grapes and peaches.'[38]

The first formal dinner was a taxing occasion for the Edwardian Country House footman, who should 'wear thin-soled shoes that their steps may be noiseless, and if they should use napkins in

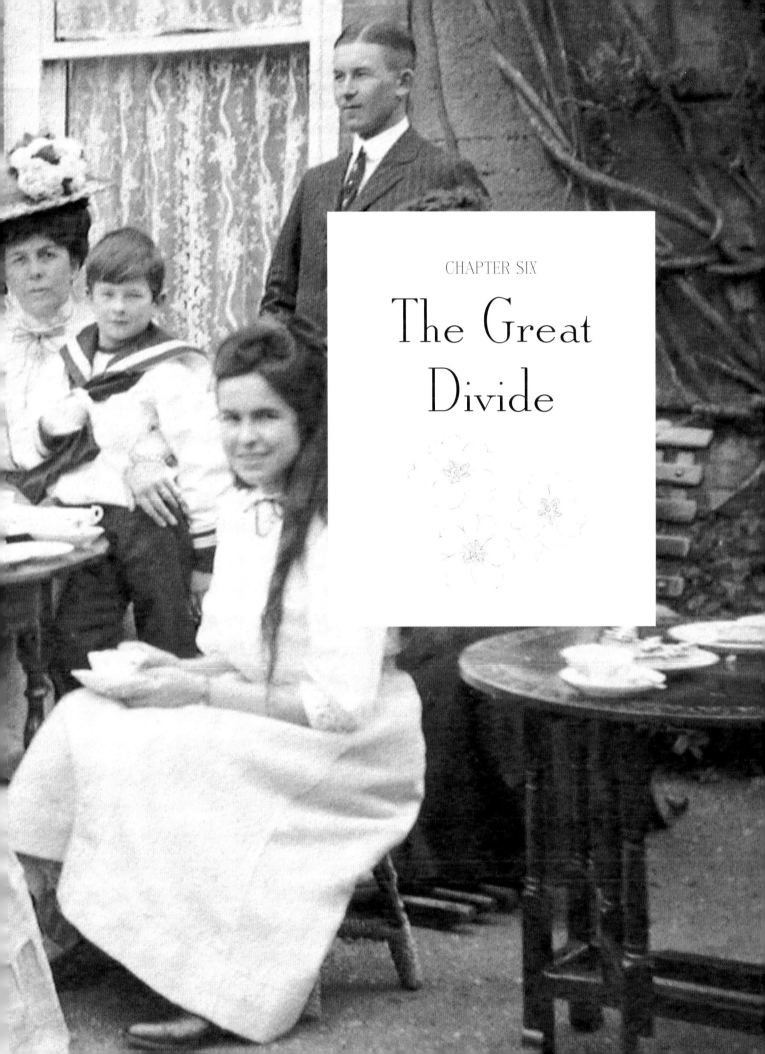

CHAPTER SIX

The Great Divide

In an Edwardian country house, the architect Robert Kerr insisted, 'the family constitute one community; the servants another. Whatever may be their mutual regard as dwellers under one roof, each class is entitled to shut its doors upon the other, and be alone…what passes on either side of the boundary shall be invisible and inaudible on the other.'[1] This social segregation was planned into the very fabric of the house, with the servants' quarters layered around those of the owners, their children and their guests. The 'family' occupied the ground and first floors; the servants worked below them in the basement and slept above them in the attics. Just as boundaries were never to be blurred in social behaviour, so there were to be no spatial ambiguities. Those who lived above stairs did not venture below. The master and mistress of an Edwardian country house almost never set foot in the kitchens that produced their food, or the laundry that did all their washing, and knew only by report the conditions in which their servants lived. Upper servants such as the butler, housekeeper, the lady's maid and the chef would appear in the family's quarters only when summoned, or for pre-arranged meetings. Apart from the footmen who ushered in guests and served at table, the lower servants would rarely have had any direct contact with the family at all.

The respectful distance that the servants were required to keep was evident in many ways, but it was particularly exemplified in one small act. If a letter arrived for a member of the family, or a visitor left a calling card, the butler or a footman would take it to the appropriate person, but he would not make physical contact by handing it over from his gloved hand to his master or mistress. Rather, he would put the object on a small silver salver kept expressly for the purpose, and the addressee would take it from the tray to read and place any answering communication on the tray.[2] No contamination between the world of work associated with grease and grime (though not a speck would have been present on the footman's impeccable uniform) and that of the fragrant, leisured classes would have occurred. Other servants would be expected to be as invisible and as inaudible as possible. 'Always move quietly about the house, and do not let your voice be heard by the family unless necessary. Never sing or whistle at your work where the family would be likely to hear you,' advised a manual for servants published in 1901. 'Should you be required to walk with a lady or gentleman, in order to carry a parcel, or otherwise, always keep a few paces behind…'[3]

It was in the nineteenth century that this stratification of the domestic community, had formalized the situation of the previous century where family, children, guests and servants had been more likely to have been jumbled together as part of the informal, organic whole, into one in which roles were rigidly defined and hierarchies firmly adhered to. With the social changes of the late century, when unpropertied wealth rather than land and pedigree became the indices of status among many of the new country house owners, these distinctions were maintained, even calcified, by a class that, in many cases, was only the first or second generation to live to the manor born. While there can be no single model for how a country house was organized, the most appropriate description in many instances in Edwardian times was less of the household as a community than as a well-oiled machine with its specialized functions separated, each 'cog' meshing smoothly to ensure that the whole 'ran like clockwork'.

The country house way of life could not exist without a raft of servants. Staff were needed to cook, clean, garden, valet, and look after the children and the horses in these commodious establishments. The number of rooms, the cluttered, fussy style of furnishings, and the intensely social way of life made country houses extremely labour-intensive to run. Standards of housekeeping were high; meals were extensive, elaborate and frequent. The family changed clothes several times a day – six was not unusual for the women – and became accustomed to a gilded bubble of gracious living, cosseted with fresh flowers everywhere, their whims answered at the ring of a bell, their newspapers ironed and sometimes even their coins washed.[4] The country house way of life of conspicuous consumption required an appreciative rotating audience of guests partaking in a series of events – dinners, shoots, parties, balls, weekend house parties – all of which added greatly to the work of the servants. And the servants themselves created work, needing to be cooked for, washed up after, and their laundry dealt with. The suburban middle classes might have kept a maid-of-all-work; the aristocracy of money kept an establishment of specialists where duties were strictly defined and compartmentalized – and demarcation was rigorous. It was not solely the work to be done that dictated the number of retainers, however. An Edwardian country house was not simply required to

'I am having a really good time horse riding. I've learned a lot and I really enjoy it,' enthused Mr Jonathan.

be run with discreet efficiency; it needed to advertise its wealth through display – including the display of servants. This entailed a full 'front of house' cast, consisting of a distinguished butler, liveried footmen and coachmen, a range of personal servants – ladies' maids and valets – and, when needed, nannies, nursery maids, governesses or tutors for the children.

Rank and income influenced how many servants a family might keep, and manuals gave advice on this to those new to employing servants; the criterion was less the size of their houses, and thus the work that needed to be done, than the size of their incomes. In general, it was considered that around 12 per cent of income should go on servants' wages with an additional 10 per cent required if horses and carriages were kept and servants needed for those duties.[5] This total would have been increased by the wages paid for casual staff recruited locally to help out on special occasions – a wedding or a christening, a large ball, a shooting party or a servants' ball – or for specific tasks of maintenance and repair around the house or seasonal work in the grounds.

Writing on how to plan *The Gentleman's House* in 1864, the architect and academic Robert Kerr suggested the first task should be to work out how many servants the client could afford, not, as one might have expected, what work needed to be done and therefore how many servants would need to be employed to do it.[6] So the planning of the 'domestic offices', in his view, did not start from the desire to make work as labour-saving as possible, but rather to accommodate a given number of servants and allow them adequate space to carry out their duties. This arrangement was possible because labour was in plentiful supply, and thus cheap – more so in the country than in town. Domestic servants were largely drawn from rural areas.

The Edwardian housemaids' routine: Becky sweeps a rug with a dustpan and brush

It is sometimes difficult to build up an accurate picture of life below stairs since few servants wrote their memoirs, or left any written record, though those who did have left an illuminating and poignant legacy. A vivid picture has also been built up in recent decades from oral sources, historians and journalists interviewing those who were in service in the late Victorian and Edwardian period, and beyond. Further insights can be gleaned from the numerous manuals that were produced for the instruction of servants, from comments from employers in memoirs, diaries and letters, from recipe books, contemporary novels, magazines and newspapers. For accurate statistical information, the census returns are an invaluable source of information about the conditions of domestic service. The census was taken every decade and it was a criminal offence not to make a return. However, because of the nature of the material revealed and the possibility of identifying the respondents, census returns are confidential for a hundred years. The 1901 census was taken in March that year, only weeks after Edward VII had been proclaimed king. It went online in January 2002, but the work of analysing the data and establishing patterns of the very start of the Edwardian period will take time.

...while Erika dusts the dressing table and polishes the bedstead.

Employment categories changed to some extent after the 1871 census and it is much harder to extricate precise information about domestic servants after that date. Doubt has also increasingly been thrown on the census enumerators' returns: some enumerators tended to interchange the words 'housekeeper' and 'housewife', and women's part-time work was frequently not entered in the returns.[7] It is possible to use the 1871 census material as a basis and add to this the various surveys of domestic service – both governmental and by other organizations – published between then and the First World War. The 1871 census showed that 79 per cent of all those working in domestic service came from rural areas,[8] though as the rural population shifted to cities and towns this became less the case and has been advanced by historians as one of the reasons for the slow decline of those entering domestic service. However, employers tended to prefer country lasses (and lads) who they believed to be healthier and stronger, with better morals and more willing to take orders. There were, of course, far fewer job opportunities in the country than in towns and cities, and there would be a tradition of service in the neighbourhood 'big houses'. A son might well serve where his father had, and employees frequently recommended their relatives when a vacancy came up where they were working.

Domestic service provided training, and a career structure of sorts. For girls it encouraged housewifely skills (though these were likely to be in excess of the abilities needed to run their own modest homes when they married) and for both sexes a form of apprenticeship. Mary Russell Mitford,

The kitchen maid

The kitchen maid in the Edwardian Country House has a very responsible job in 'real' life. Antonia Dawson works as a Police Control Room Officer responding to 999 calls in central Nottingham police station. Fortunately for those below stairs, she also has a qualification in catering and hotel management. 'I live a very modern lifestyle. I've got my own house, my own car and I look after myself. So it would be really interesting to see what it would have been like for a woman living in the Edwardian period – to be told what to do, how to talk to people. I know that if I *had* been born then, this is the sort of job I probably would have done, given my class. I imagine that I would have considered myself very lucky to be employed in a grand house like this. I'm thirty now and that's quite old not to be married – or it certainly was then – so I'd be hoping for promotion to a cook, or something like that.'

writing about life in the Berkshire countryside in the nineteenth century, recalls how farmers' daughters went 'into service at fourteen and stayed till they married, learning there lessons of neatness, domestic skill and respect for quality of all kinds'. In this regard, things had not changed much in the countryside in the Edwardian period – except that education had been made compulsory until the age of thirteen in 1880 (raised to fourteen in 1918), though there were many exemptions for child workers and in general girls did not enter service until they were sixteen or seventeen.[9] In 1901, of 4 million women in employment, nearly half were in domestic service[10] and they formed around 11 per cent of the total work force.[11] In 1912 Lady Willoughby de Broke was still valiantly commending domestic service in terms that 'a well-trained domestic servant is of real value to the nation, she makes the best possible wife and mother, as she has acquired a good knowledge of housewifery and habits of cleanliness, punctuality, and, to some extent, hygiene'.[12]

A scullery maid might have been expected to achieve the position of a housemaid by the time she was twenty, and a hall boy who had failed to achieve the status of footman by the time he was twenty 'was destined to remain a lower-class servant',[13] whereas it is likely that he would not have attained the maturity and experience necessary to be a butler before his thirties. The 1871 census revealed that less than 10 per cent of ladies' maids were over forty. The majority of female servants would hope to 'marry out' before they were thirty, or, if not, have attained the respectable status of housekeeper. Such a woman might hope to remain in this position until she was too old to work, and then, if she was fortunate, be looked after in her infirmity by a grateful family; if not, the workhouse loomed. Almost all female servants were single: the census recorded only 3 per cent who admitted they were married, and a number of these were living apart from their husbands. Very occasionally a husband and wife might be employed as butler and housekeeper, and widows were sometimes hired as housekeepers, governesses or nurses.

The housemaids would have their work planned so that they would open the shutters, set the fires, sweep, dust and polish the living rooms before the family was up in the morning. As soon as the family had gone downstairs for breakfast, the housemaids would tidy and clean the bedrooms and bathrooms, making sure that they had finished before anyone returned upstairs. Should a maid encounter a member of the family in the corridors or on the stairs, she would lower her eyes to the ground, or even turn her face to the wall, so that there was no possibility that she would have to be acknowledged by an employer who chose to think of his or her lower servants as household functionaries rather than sentient beings helping the family.

'She knows that I work for her,' sighed Becky, duster in hand, shrinking into the shadows as Lady Olliff-Cooper came expectedly out of her room and swept down the silver staircase to the morning room. 'She could at least acknowledge my presence. How does she think everything gets done if she never sees any of us working?' But if one metaphor that describes the Edwardian country house is that of a smoothly running machine, another is of a gliding swan: the elegant serenity of upstairs made possible only thanks to the frantic, but unseen, footwork going on below. The world below stairs was separated as effectively as possible from that above and the separation was made apparent in every material detail. It would have been perfectly possible to visit most large country houses, and Manderston was no exception, without ever being aware that there *was* a 'downstairs' and certainly not what went on in those nether regions, while enjoying the distillation of all that effort. Heavy mahogany doors sealed the basement off from the ground floor, and while the side that faced the family's part of the house was elaborately carved, the reverse side that the servants saw was plain and functional, in some houses covered in green baize to further muffle sound from below.

Charlie, wearing white gloves so as not to mark the silver, lays the table for dinner with the precision expected of a first footman of quality.

The domestic offices were planned to immure the family from reality, to nurture the illusion of effortless production. The tradesmen's entrance at Manderston was set back and to the side of the house so that no one glancing out of the window in the main house need ever catch sight of the delivery of food destined for their table or the carting away of detritus generated by their luxurious consumption. The self-contained world of downstairs meant that staircases climbed from the basement to the attic floors via ninety-seven stone stairs, entirely bypassing the circulation system of the main house, so that the lower servants would pass their daily lives unseen and unheard by those they served. The bells that jangled incessantly, set off by peremptory pushes and pulls from upstairs, were a one-way communication: the only response possible was a leap to action. The kitchen was situated in the middle of the basement complex so that cooking smells wafting upstairs would be minimized. This was no easy task in days when it was recommended that cabbage should be boiled for half to three quarters of an hour with the lid off, when game was hung until it was so high as to be almost rank (any maggots perished in the cooking), and, without effective refrigeration, keeping milk, cream and cheese from going rancid (particularly in the summer months) was a constant problem – though there was a rather primitive chest ice box at Manderston, which helped.

The arrangement of the kitchen might have partly solved one problem, but it exacerbated another: heavy trays of food had to be carried from the kitchen, along the servants' corridor and up a steep flight of stone stairs where, at the top, stood a butler's tray stand where the trays could be balanced for a moment before Mr Edgar or the footmen pushed open the heavy door and carried the food into the dining room. It was back-breaking work. The food lift in operation when Manderston was rebuilt had

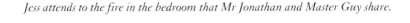

Jess attends to the fire in the bedroom that Mr Jonathan and Master Guy share.

long been removed; neither was there a 'dumb waiter' – a serving duct that ran between floors enabling plates to be loaded on one floor and winched up or down to the next – so sixty-five-year-old Mr Edgar and the footmen had to carry a succession of heavy trays piled with crockery, glasses, cutlery, tureens and serving dishes full of food, up and down stairs for breakfast, lunch, tea, dinner and any other occasion that took upstairs' fancy. In addition it meant that the food was often half cold after its lengthy journey along corridors and up staircases, and then standing outside the dining room until all the dishes had been assembled for serving. This, as with the odours of cooking pervading the house, was a perennial problem. The Prime Minister, Benjamin Disraeli, was reported to have murmured, 'At last, something warm,' as champagne was served at dinner in a country house one evening.

As the material aspects of the house connived at the family's comfort upstairs, so the daily routines of their servants were dictated entirely by the requirements of their master and mistress. The lower down the pile you were, the earlier you were expected to get up. As Kenny went back for a snatched sleep in his hall cupboard bed after stoking up the fire, the scullery maid, up in her attic room, tried to ignore the alarm clock that was insistently ringing – providing she had remembered to wind it up the night before. 'I never rely on the alarm clock,' said Becky, the conscientious first housemaid in her room next door. 'I listen for the grandfather clock chiming on the floor below. If it chimes six, I'm all right, because Jess [the second housemaid] and I are supposed to get up at half past, but if it strikes seven then we're in big trouble.' The female lower servants would get out of bed, feeling for the thin carpet strip with their bare feet, pad along the corridor to fetch water from the tap to fill their pottery jugs and then take them back to their rooms. Then they would pour the water into a bowl

Eyes demurely lowered, Becky hurries along the hall in response to the family's latest request.

for a quick wash of face, hands, underarms and private parts before getting dressed. 'At first it took me ages to get my corset on, but now I'm much quicker,' said Becky, 'and I don't need help any more.'

Each maid had arrived at the house with her uniform in a black tin trunk. Unlike the men servants whose uniforms were supplied by their employer, a girl entering service was required to buy or make her own uniform. She would need to have three sets of clothes – print dresses for the mornings for doing the dirty work, a black dress and a white cap and apron for afternoons, and her own clothes for outdoors and church on Sundays. She would be expected to wear a hat at all times outside and generally to look 'clean and decorous'. An article in *The Girl's Own Annual* in 1890 detailed exactly what 'a young servant's outfit' should consist of and totalled the cost at £3 11s 4¾d – no small

'I was concerned about the servants' behaviour at prayers this morning. I noticed that Antonia was not present and that Kenny had his hands stuffed in his pockets and a smirk on his face.'

'Antonia is unwell, Sir John, and she is in her room. I will make sure to speak to Kenny myself.'

In her workroom Miss Morrison was washing her mistress's clothes and those of her sister before settling down to trim the hat that Lady Olliff-Cooper had decided to wear to the forthcoming fête to be held in the grounds of Manderston, and to wrestle with Miss Anson's wig. 'I learned how to do what was called board work when I was at hairdressing college. It was very tedious at the time, and most people didn't bother to do it. They weren't interested in wigs and thought they'd never need to know about them. But I stuck at it, because you never know when it might come in handy. That was twenty-five years ago, and I'm so glad that I did. It's given me the confidence to tackle these Edwardian wigs here now,' recalled Miss Morrison. But as she worked, her ear was cocked in case the bell at the foot of her stairs summoned her to her ladyship's bedroom.

Miss Morrison interrupts her sewing to respond to a summons from Lady Olliff-Cooper.

On the floor below, Becky was cleaning the bedrooms while the ladies breakfasted. The housemaids swarmed silently in the wake of the family all day: when they left a room, the servants would go in to restore it to its pristine state, tidying papers and anything the family had used, plumping cushions that bore the imprint of their presence, and then slip quietly out again unseen, unacknowledged and unthanked.

Morning cleaning ran to a tight schedule, an almost impossible one if there were several guests occupying the first-floor bedrooms. First Becky opened the windows to air the room. The carpets had to be swept either with a carpet sweeper or with a stiff brush, and the wood surround mopped. The curtains were heavy, as were the wall drapes around the bed, and Becky battled with dust endlessly. She had been advised that if she washed the paintwork with a mixture of vinegar and water this would stop the dust from settling, and she thought that she might try that. Fortunately for her since there were numerous bathrooms on the first floor for family and guests at Manderston – including a priceless silver-lined one in Sir John's bathroom – she did not have to deal with the chamber pots by emptying their contents into a covered slop bucket as happened in the servants' quarters. Ever vigilant for bed bugs that thrived in horsehair, she checked the mattress and finally made the bed (*The Complete Servant* recommended the housemaid should change into a clean apron before doing so, but Becky certainly didn't have time for that), plumping up the pillows and the quilted satin eiderdowns. Then it was the bathrooms to clean, rubbing the porcelain with coarse salt in the absence of scouring powder if scum proved stubborn. Edwardian housemaids would 'turn out' a different room on a rota basis each week, moving the furniture to clean under it.

The hierarchy of servants' tasks was subtly calibrated and unwritten: while Becky would have cleaned and tidied Lady Olliff-Cooper's room, she would not have touched her ladyship's dressing table. That was the privilege of the lady's maid, just as downstairs, while the housemaids would clean the reception rooms, they were forbidden to touch the writing desks which would be dusted by the butler.[16]

Major cleaning in an Edwardian country house would have to wait until the family left for the London season. Then windows would be left open to air the rooms; curtains would be taken down, brushed and sponged; windows cleaned; brocade wall hangings brushed with a soft brush then gently rubbed with tissue paper and a soft silk cloth; and wallpaper blown free of dust with a pair of bellows and then lightly rubbed with a stale loaf of bread torn into pieces. In the days before the invention of the 'puffing billy' vacuum cleaner in 1901 and its slow adoption into British households, tea leaves (or even sand or grass) would be scattered on carpets to absorb the grime before a stiff brushing; wooden floors would be scrubbed with soap or soda and water or dry-scrubbed using sand; paintwork wiped with a mixture of soap and beer, or grated potatoes made into a paste with water if the paint was white, and buffed with a chamois leather; grates would be blacked with powdered blacklead mixed to a paste and then burnished with three separate brushes till it gleamed and the slate hearth polished with hot mutton

Jess dusts the elaborate swirls of the silver staircase.

'Frankly, we've got a bunch of fussy eaters here,' said Antonia. 'Mr Edgar can't eat eggs, cream, butter, milk, rice, potatoes, or meat the majority of the time, but he does like pulses. He'd eat them at every meal. Then Becky is a vegetarian, and I am worried that she is not getting enough to eat, she was thin when she came, but she is stick thin now. Jess doesn't like meat much either, she loves rice and pasta and veggies. Charlie doesn't eat broccoli, cabbage or cauliflower. He has to have a baked potato every day. Kenny will eat any lean meat without fat between two great doorsteps of bread. He'll eat anything between bread, I think he'd eat a spaghetti bolognese sandwich. Tristan doesn't like mushrooms or gravy, he doesn't much care for puddings or fish either and he won't eat hot things, spicy curries and that sort of thing. Rob will eat pretty well anything but he talks so much that it all gets cold and then he doesn't want it. But Ellen is fantastic, she'll eat anything that's put in front of her and Mrs Davies is much the same, but she never makes any comment on my cooking which is a bit scary as she's the housekeeper!'

There was no time to make a pudding: 'We'll have fruit today,' Antonia decided, 'and maybe I'll make a tapioca pudding for tonight.'

Kenny was bringing in the coal and filling the scuttles, sweeping the yard and giving a hand in the kitchen. And Ellen was peeling potatoes in the scullery and waiting for the next load of washing-up to arrive, having just finished scouring the pots she'd had soaking overnight from dinner. Ellen's

Fire drill: Jess watches with satisfaction as the fire in the morning room blazes.

day was largely spent washing up the pots and pans used in the preparation of meals, and then washing up the things used in eating the meals, with some vegetable preparation in between. Maybe she might be told to pluck and dress a grey partridge, a duck or a pheasant: 'To pluck either game or poultry, have a bird upon a board with its head towards you, and pull its feathers away from you, which is the direction they lay in; many persons pull out the feathers in a contrary direction, by which means they are likely to tear the skin to pieces, which would very much disfigure the bird for the table,' advised *The Gastronomic Regenerator*.[17] This didn't worry Ellen too much since she'd lived all her life on a farm, but she knew how excruciating Becky had found it when she'd been asked to help. 'But though she can't bear the idea of meat, and it took her ages, she did it. I really admired her for that.'

The last job of the day for Ellen was to sweep and mop the black and white tiled floors in the kitchen and scullery, which got filthy with all the traffic and food dropped during the day – but they never seemed clean enough for the chef, which was rather dispiriting, Ellen thought. Sometimes Kenny would help her with the washing-up, but he had other jobs to do, Mr Edgar needed his help, and Charlie and Rob called on him to do their bidding in the butler's pantry. But M. Dubiard had promised that he would show her how to make ice-cream. 'I've come here to learn,' insisted Ellen.

After a few days Mr Edgar had relented and allowed conversation at the dinner table providing that it was decorous. If voices were raised or opinions got heated, he would rap out 'Silence, sir', or 'Silence, miss' and that was – usually – sufficient. Although it was the servants' main meal of the day, it was not one to linger over since the family had lunch at 1 p.m. and Mr Edgar, the footmen and of course the kitchen staff were all involved in that.

After lunch, the meal had to be cleared and the washing-up done in the butler's pantry while Ellen washed the servants' crocks in the scullery, then everything had to be put away again. Jess checked on her fires, Miss Morrison obeyed a summons upstairs to help Lady Olliff-Cooper change into her tea gown (which was always a relief since it was loose and flowing and did not require a corset to be worn). Becky went to Miss Anson to help her get ready to go riding, which meant taking off her wig since it would not fit under her hard hat, and lacing up her tight leather boots. Charlie went to help Mr Jonathan get ready for riding too since he was to escort Miss Anson; and down in the stables, Tristan was saddling the horses.

Mrs Davies had probably done a quick tour of the upstairs rooms when she was sure the family was out of the way, as would her Edwardian counterparts, to check that 'her' housemaids had done their work properly – though within a short time she realized that this was no longer necessary: the maids were highly conscientious and efficient. She would also make sure that there was fresh water in the vases and check other small items of household concern. It was standard practice in service for the housekeeper – or the mistress of the house – to test the maid's work by hiding small coins about the rooms, under a chest of drawers, on a picture rail. If they pocketed the money, maids would be sacked for dishonesty: if the coins were not discovered, they would be accused of negligence and severely reprimanded. At first, Becky had suspected that Miss Anson was testing her domestic skills by concealing screwed-up pieces of paper in unlikely places in the Edwardian manner.

After lunch the housekeeper went into the kitchen to start making scones and some 'fancies' for tea in the drawing room. Her cherry or sultana fruit scones with jam were a particular favourite upstairs and Mrs Davies made some most days, while downstairs the servants were particularly partial to her oat flapjacks so they were regularly prepared. This would be the time when she might bottle some fruit, make chutney or jam, usually from produce gathered from the kitchen garden or orchards of the estate.

CHAPTER SEVEN

Sunlit Lawns

While money is poured out lavishly upon questionable luxuries and needless "sport",' reproved the *Berwickshire Advertiser* in 1911,[1] 'sweet charity often has to go begging. Continual effort is necessary to raise the requisite funds to carry on the humane work in which Lady Miller [the mistress of Manderston] is active and earnest.' It went to on to report on a 'garden party held on Tuesday at Manderston' to raise funds for the various local charities in which her ladyship was involved. 'The day was ideal, brilliant sunshine and a cooling breeze; and as the grounds of Lady Miller's home lend themselves to such a function, the event was a great success…and there was a large company present.' But when the reporter tried to describe these grounds, he found the challenge all but impossible: 'to write in adequate terms of the garden is beyond us: it would require one able to describe beauty as Zola is to depict horror, but they are a feast of colour and a banquet of sweet perfume that would never pall the eye nor satiate the appetite'.

Finding herself the chatelaine of this earthly paradise, Lady Olliff-Cooper was mindful of the aristocratic tradition of *noblesse oblige* – the conviction that the right to rule, and the enjoyment of rank, privilege and wealth, carried with them moral obligations of public service and benevolence towards dependants, whose gratitude, deference and submission legitimized the existing social order. In plutocratic imitation of this, she resolved to hold a bazaar at Manderston to raise money for her favourite Border charities. As Lady Tweedsmuir, writing of her own Edwardian childhood, recalled, 'Undeserved sneers have been directed at the Lady of the Manor who blandly dispensed soup and blankets, but it must be admitted by any impartial observer that she was often the one who urged her husband to carry out work on cottages…The Lady of the Manor should have her place of honour in the history of the countryside…she lent her garden for…fêtes and heroically saw the public trampling down her lawns, or her drawing room for church sales, or her dining room for the Sunday School play. It was all part of the pattern of country life that seemed as immutable as the laws of nature.'[2]

Charity work was part of the wider ideal of Christian duty; it was an aspect of women's traditional role as nurturer, and could be seen as the responsibility that the 'big house' owed to the community in which it was situated and from which it drew sustenance in the form of labour, resources and produce. A remnant of the reciprocity inherent in feudalism, it mimicked the model of benevolent patriarchy and hierarchy that ordered the Edwardian country house. It validated, in some eyes, the possession of wealth in the midst of poverty since that wealth could be seen as being put to good use. Bazaars would be regarded as part of the social calendar of the locality. In the straitened circumstances of many traditional landowners and the very different views of societal responsibility held by many of the rich parvenus, the opportunity for the population to visit country houses in the Edwardian years had become much more restricted. The 'privatization' of the country house had led the journalist W. T. Stead to conclude that 'the landed proprietors…prevent public access to their parks, treasure-houses, historical buildings, collections of art and curios in a general way…it cannot be said that any one acts generally as if he considered himself trustee for the public'.[3] Indeed, when a coach party had turned up at Manderston requesting to look round the house, Sir John had sent them away – politely but firmly. Increasingly it was only on such select occasions as a bazaar that the hoi polloi were admitted to the gracious surroundings of the wealthy house in carefully regulated circumstances. It provided the family with an opportunity to show off their fine home and grounds, potent symbols of the unbridgeable distance between the rich and everyone else.

Equally, the money raised for charitable causes such as hospitals, the sick, the old and the needy was vital in the days before the state took financial responsibility for those of its citizens who could no longer support themselves, and the only recourse for the poor or infirm would be to poor law provision and the harsh and degrading conditions of the workhouse. Most charities were run as private committees and access to them – and the agreement to do voluntary work on their behalf – would be in the hands of society ladies. To become part of this network of social patronage had cachet much sought after by the *nouveaux riches*, and provided a worthwhile way for women with time on their hands to spend it doing something useful and beneficial in congenial company.[4] Indeed, 'only as Lady Bountiful', writes Jessica Gerrard, 'did [society women] have opportunities for independent action and unfettered power over the lives of others. Women of intelligence, energy and initiative and a thirst for power, found in philanthropy a socially approved outlet for their talents and needs.'[5] If troops of servants deprived wealthy women of their roles as housewives and, to an extent, as mothers, 'it can hardly be said,' crowed Lady Greville, 'that if the ladies of England [or no doubt Scotland] are wrapped in luxury, they are idle as well'[6] as they 'attempted to transpose the values and relations of domestic service to a wider class of the poor'[7] by ministering to their tenants in time of need, visiting hospitals and workhouses, establishing saving groups, teaching in Sunday Schools, holding educational classes for the

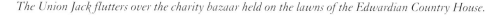

The Union Jack flutters over the charity bazaar held on the lawns of the Edwardian Country House.

Sir John and Mr Edgar confer in the sunshine.

In the centre of the lawns, M. Dubiard, wearing his chef's apparel, was expertly shucking oysters, though there weren't many takers. Mr Edgar in the tea tent wondered just how many cups of tea could be drunk in a single afternoon. Miss Morrison, dressed in sage green – 'one of milady's hand-me-downs, it makes me look less like a servant' – could not be off duty either while the breeze threatened to lift off Lady Olliff-Cooper's large feather-trimmed hat, which her maid had to keep tying on with a chiffon scarf.

Mr Jonathan was running one of the most popular events of the bazaar, 'tip the man off the log', whereby two contestants sitting astride a log tried to knock each other off using bolsters. There was always a queue for this feather-bedded form of wrestling, and quite a few old scores were paid off in ritualized form that afternoon. One of those who joined the contestants several times was Jonty's younger brother Guy, who, dressed in an Eton jacket and pint-sized pinstripe trousers, took part in pretty well every activity going, including watching the Punch and Judy show and entering 'racing the blind horse' which was Tristan's responsibility.

In the largest marquee, Lady Olliff-Copper was talking to the local exhibitors who had entered the various competitions for needlework: there were three categories, quilt, tapestry and 'other'. The entries had already been logged and sorted out by Miss Anson, acting as her sister's secretary. 'To my untutored eye they all looked very good, as though the patchwork and samplers and cross stitch and all the other things had taken several winters of long dark evenings in front of the fire to make.' She had spoken to all the entrants as they delivered their handicrafts so she could put some useful information on the card: something along the lines of 'Mrs…has been a staunch supporter of the Scottish Rural Arts Institute for forty-four years…' that would give her sister something to say to each person as she did her rounds. In categorizing the entries, Miss Anson had been helped by the expert eye of her sister's maid, Miss Morrison, and now the entries were being judged by the lady of the house, herself a skilled lace-maker. 'I took judging the needlework competition very seriously, because it was obvious that people had put a huge amount of effort into the workmanship, which was of a very high standard.' After much deliberation Lady Olliff-Cooper chose what she considered to be the best work, handed out certificates to the winners in each category, and watched the demonstrations of lace-making, elaborate 'Fabergé-style' egg-decoration, millinery and calligraphy that were going on in the tent.

There really was no end to the ingenuity of the Edwardians when it came to organizing competitive fund-raising events. *The Lady's Companion* in January 1911 recommended that 'few things succeed better at Bazaars than simple and amusing competitions, the small outlay necessary for materials being a great recommendation. An entrance fee of 2d should be charged for each competition, outside spectators paying 1d to "view the fun".' It went to suggest such gender stereotypical activities as 'Nail driving competition – Ladies only; Sewing on buttons – Gentlemen only; Sharpening lead pencils – Ladies only; Apple paring – Gentlemen only. Prizes awarded for the largest number of apples correctly peeled, cored and sliced; Millinery competition – Gentlemen to trim hats with crinkled paper and pins. Creations to be judged by a committee of Ladies' – and a range of other 'fun' pursuits that must have had bazaar-goers queuing up two deep on a sunny afternoon to participate in 'Pin sticking – pins to be stuck into a sheet of paper in neat and regular rows – 100 in 5 minutes; Covering books with brown paper – neatest and most workmanlike result takes prize; Match-tying – tying so many matches within a given time on a piece of string; and Candle-lighting – twenty-four candles are fixed in a row, and the successful competitor lights all with a single match'.[9]

Mr Jonathan ensures fair play in the 'tip the man off the log' contest.

Community effort: local people enter into the Edwardian spirit (left)
and Mrs Davies's husband dresses the part (right).

The invitation to visit the Edwardian Country House had been enthusiastically received locally and many of the visitors who flocked to the bazaar were playing the part to the full. Some had journeyed to Newcastle, Edinburgh, or even London to hire Edwardian costumes, while others had rummaged in their attics or got out the sewing machine. The results were impressive: there was a gentle rustle of taffeta on the breeze, smart, laced ankle boots tapped along the paths, large plumed hats obscured women's faces, lace *fichus* tickled their necks and their velvet skirts and cotton petticoats brushed the grass, parasols were twirled and shooting sticks punctured the lawns, hunter watches stretched across ample waistcoated male chests, and children in knickerbockers dodged among the crowds. It was hard to decide who qualified for the title 'best dressed Edwardian' but eventually the prize for the man was awarded to Mrs Davies's husband, Peter, who had at one time thought that he would have rather liked to have taken the role of butler in the house.

The bazaar was an opportunity to sample a range of Edwardian delights: Betty Snow, who lives in Bonkyl Cottage a few miles from Manderston, had a stall selling nothing but home-made jams, pickles and other epicurean delights. She had gooseberry and elderflower jelly, rowan jelly, rose petal jelly, spiced crab apple jelly, rhubarb and ginger jam, tayberry jam – a cross-breed fruit of raspberries and blackberries that had first become popular in the Borders around 1905, she thought. There were jars of lemon and orange curd, rhubarb chutney, brandied raspberries with wild strawberries, bottles of raspberry and blackcurrant vinegar – 'very good for a cold with honey and hot water' – and mixed herb and garlic oil. There was a home-made cake stall with sponges, fruitcakes, scones and dainty butterfly fairy cakes. John Murphy from Heatherslaw Corn Mill, the most northerly mill in England, just over the border, had a stall with a millstone that was used to grind his wheat, all the varieties of which were grown locally. Brenda Leddy was selling clotted cream and butter made from milk from her Jersey cows in Kelso, and Chainbridge honey farm had a stall selling honey and beeswax. There was a produce stall groaning with giant marrows, turnips and cabbages belonging to Jock Bolton from a nearby farm who also supplied the house with vegetables, a plant stall and a stall explaining the work of the Gardeners' Royal Benevolent Society, one of the charities that would benefit from the bazaar. This stall was manned by one of the society's local patrons, Lieutenant Colonel Simon Furness, from a nearby country house of the same period as Manderston, Netherbyres at Eyemouth. He had generously donated the house to the society in 1991, and moved to a smaller property in the grounds.

A particular draw was an apothecary stall of Rose & Co from Haworth in Yorkshire, which displayed a range of typical Edwardian products from the workaday, such as dolly pegs, carbolic soap and bags of Reckitt's blue, which were especially covetable to the female servants with their work-roughened hands, their faces denied creams, their bodies innocent of fragrant lotions and powders. There were tempting lavender lotions, rose water skin freshener, geranium and orange oil for the bath, herbal foot balms and mustard baths, beeswax for lips and rose and glycerine salve for hands and nails, eau de cologne, *papier poudré* 'for busy people', powder puffs and dry shampoos. Miss Morrison resolved to hunt out some recipes and try to concoct something similar from ingredients she had to hand.

And from those days before antibiotics there were medications on the apothecary's stall too: vapour rubs for colds and catarrh, rubbing ointments containing wintergreen and valerian for aches and pains, 'Zam-Buk' ointment to soothe cuts and grazes, sprains and chilblains, sasparillo pastilles for a sore throat. Gazing

Mrs Davies's recipes

The housekeeper, Mrs Davies, made this rich fruitcake for the 'guess the weight of the cake' competition at the Manderston Bazaar.

Fruitcake

8oz (225g) butter
8oz (225 g) caster sugar,
    or soft brown sugar
4 eggs
8oz (225 g) plain flour
4oz (100g) sultanas
4oz (100g) raisins
4oz (100g) currants
2oz (50g) candied peel
2oz (50g) glacé cherries
4oz (100g) chopped almonds

Cream the butter and sugar together. Add the eggs one at a time, and beat well. Add the sieved flour and all the dry ingredients together and mix well. The mixture should fall slowly off a wooden spoon. If it is too stiff, add a little cold milk.

Put the mixture in a deep cake tin that has been buttered and lined with grease-proof paper, and bake in a slow oven (325°F/180°C/gas mark 4) for one to one and a half hours. Leave the cake in the tin until it is cool, and then store in an airtight tin.

(NOTE: in Edwardian times, imperial measures would have used; metric equivalents are given here – for best results, one system only should be used consistently.)

which she did regularly, she would make sure to wear a different hat each time. It was a tonic for the patients to see her. In my view it did them more good than any medicine.'

In the Edwardian period, cottage hospitals were the most usual form of care for the sick in rural areas. These were generally small, and care in them had to be paid for, though charges were generally modest and constituted about one-tenth of the hospital's income, the rest of which came from wealthy landowners and from local fund-raising events – like the Edwardian Country House bazaar. The elderly poor were more likely to be treated in workhouse infirmaries. Until the 1908 Poor Law, the workhouse was the only option for an old person without family or financial support, and probably at this time some 5 per cent of the population over sixty-five would be living in the workhouse – and a high proportion of that total would be those who had been in service and had no family to turn to in their old age, nor legal entitlement to a pension. The 1908 Old Age Pension Act was drafted 'to lift the shadow of the workhouse from the homes of the poor' in Lloyd George's words – though persons did not qualify unless they lived on less than 12 shillings a week (the equivalent today of about £35) and, prior to 1925, until they reached seventy years of age. The workhouse was greatly feared: it was a monotonous, prison-like regimented life, with poor food and the loss of dignity and freedom – including the right to vote.

On the day of the Edwardian Country House bazaar, the Olliff-Coopers were just about half-way through their time there. As she sat listening to the band, the sun warming her back, Lady Olliff-

A page from the Manderston album showing a bazaar at Thurston, the nearby house of Sir James Miller's sister, in 1911. The house was the work of Manderston's architect, John Kinross.

Cooper took stock. 'It feels like a watershed. It has taken us these first six weeks to sort ourselves out, and now it's time to reflect on what we've achieved, what's gone right and what's been wrong.

'I love the house. It's just so beautiful. I still feel it's all totally magical, as if Cinderella is going to the ball,' she reflected. 'I feel that I am almost living a teenage life with all the fun and frippery, the obsession with clothes and with your appearance. But the thing that has really surprised me is how regimented my life is. The whole day seems to be taken up with getting dressed into whatever is appropriate for whatever meal it is next, then eating the meal, then getting changed again for the next meal. We have sometimes three courses for breakfast and then another three courses for lunch and maybe five or six courses for dinner. So that's a lot of time at table. It's getting better because Morrison and I are getting more adroit at getting me dressed, but I don't have nearly as time as I imagined I would to read, and write letters and write my journal and just wander round the grounds. I calculate that about five hours of my day every day is taken up preparing myself for meals and then eating them. I find it hard to relax because of this rigid timetable and the length of meals and all the formal dressing, and it doesn't help that my corset is so tight that I can never sit in comfort. I have to perch on the side of the chairs. I know that I seem to be fussing about meals and dresses, and you could well ask, "Hasn't she got anything better to do than complain? She's hardly got a life of drudgery like the servants below stairs" – and that's certainly true. When I came here I was desperate to get away from my daily life of endless hard work and chores, but of course my life of luxury here is at the expense of other people working very hard. I know that the kitchen staff are getting up at 6 a.m. and are not in bed until 11 at night. It worries me that we will come over as very callous to the people who are serving us, which is not a very nice thought.

'I have never in my entire life had such freedom from chores, yet so many restrictions in other ways. If I'm out riding, for example, and so lunch is delayed, then the schedules of everyone below stairs is thrown completely out of kilter. So you can't have any spontaneity like that at all. Having the servants around all the time is a real block on conversation. I am finding that difficult. I imagine that if you lived like it for long you would end up having practically no contact with anyone unless you made a real effort to drag them off to another room to talk privately. It could be a real emotional desert.

'It's hard for Guy, who is only ten. It's such a formal existence. We are always saying sit still, sit up straight, put that down, don't touch – and he's an ebullient child and he needs to run around and shout, and though he has the rough and tumble of school, it's not easy for him here sometimes.

'I also think that we are *very* conscious of the need to observe all the Edwardian social niceties. As *parvenus* we would have been much more conscious about etiquette than those at the very top of the social ladder who could behave as they liked because they were a duke or something and could simply say, "I'm going to do it my way" and people would accept him because of who he was. But we have to take a lot of trouble over how to behave and how to address people, who takes precedence over whom, and whether you eat jelly with a fork or a spoon, and all that sort of thing.

'But it is a seductive business and both John and I are going to find it very difficult to go back to normality. We have just had a couple of friends of Jonty's to stay and it reminded me how completely effortless entertaining can be in these circumstances. I don't have to change the sheets here or put them in the washing machine or anything. And when it comes to meals, I just tell M. Dubiard that there will be six extra for dinner and that's it. Whereas at home I rarely entertain because it's so tedious trailing round the supermarket and carting all the shopping home in the car and unpacking it and deciding what to cook, and then cooking it and washing up and balancing all that with a career and motherhood. It's far too tiring. When we have dinner parties here I don't even iron my own dress, or do my own hair. It is all done for me. I am completely pampered. All I have to do is to go down and act the part. I can see how a woman of those times, if she was married to a wealthy man, could have a life of total idleness and selfishness. But I *am* conscious that I am at the top of the tree here, and that for other people it may be a much less enjoyable experience.

'I think that having a title helps too. It increases your confidence because people approach you with the attitude that they are privileged to meet you. It makes me feel more confident and more gracious. I no longer attempt to open doors myself, I just stand there until someone opens them for me. I am no longer embarrassed by my "title". In fact after a little while I began to find myself feeling mildly irritated if people didn't address me as m'lady. And Sir John has taken to his title like a duck to water. In fact I think that it has brought out the best in him. John is easily capable of running a large country house like this. He is a man of enormous abilities who would be quite capable of running Blenheim Palace. He would make a very good benevolent landlord, an aristocrat really, he would take a genuine interest in his tenants. He is not the sort of person who is happy being a member of a team. He likes to be captain of the ship, making all the decisions himself. He is a natural autocrat – though he would say he's not, everyone else around him would say that he is. I think he has seen here a lifestyle which would have suited him very well if he had been born a hundred years ago. He would have fitted in perfectly. I am sure that he would have become a much-loved squire.

An Edwardian Punch and Judy show enchants the children at the Manderston bazaar.

'I find it easier to be married in this environment. By and large as a wife you don't have overlapping interests with your husband, you're not in competition with him. We have our separate spheres. It's not like the twenty-first century where the roles are more mixed up and men have to adopt semi-female roles, taking out the rubbish and stuff like that. But here we're not stepping on each other's territory at all, which is very nice. One of the nicest things about this experience is seeing John really happy in his role.' But at that very moment, hairline cracks were beginning to threaten the tranquillity of Lady Olliff-Cooper's Edwardian world. In the far corner of the lawn was a striped tent in which sat a fortune-teller shuffling her tarot cards. In front of her sat Miss Avril Anson, Lady Olliff-Cooper's unmarried sister who lived with the family in the Edwardian Country House. 'You are frustrated,' pronounced the fortune-teller. 'You feel constrained and it simply went on from there…it was all completely relevant to my current situation', Miss Anson confided to her journal. 'She told me that my life was currently stretched like a piece of fabric held

The young master tucks in. Guy Olliff-Cooper at the fête.

together by pins. I had very limited options while this remained the case. It would not last long, but I should use the time *now* to consider what I wanted when my life moves into the next phase. She said that my body is stressed and that I must take care of it (good food, plenty of sleep, etc.) or else I would be quite ill. She warned me of a dark-haired woman who does not have my best interests at heart. Her description of my life at present was spot on, and I am going to monitor how accurate her predictions were.'

In the twenty-first century Dr Avril Anson, a scientist, works as a marketing consultant. She is single, in a long-term relationship, has her own home and an independent lifestyle, though she sees her sister Anna and her family, who live nearby, frequently. But in the Edwardian Country House, Miss Anson's position was less that of an independent sibling equal, and more of a financially dependent unmarried woman. And she found this inhibiting and stressful. 'I realize that Anna and John view me in the role of a poor relation dependent on John's generosity. The etiquette book I was given when I arrived explained that I am a dependent relation:

> As the unmarried sister of the mistress of the house, your status within the household is dependent solely on the good grace and generosity of the master. You should endeavour at all times to be a good companion to your sister, the mistress, and not present any kind of burden to her husband. No task should be too great for you to take on to ensure that the household runs as smoothly as possible and expresses your gratitude to them for providing you with this comfortable life. You should scrupulously examine every aspect of your conduct to make sure that you uphold the family name and position and do nothing to bring it into disrepute.

I don't find this acceptable at all. It makes my position here very difficult.'

Miss Anson

Avril Anson is Anna Olliff-Cooper's younger sister. She has a PhD in microbiology, and was a lecturer at the University of Exeter before moving into marketing. At fifty, she is now a freelance marketing consultant. She is an intrepid overseas traveller, but she was attracted by the idea of some time travel when Anna rang her up to say that she was thinking of applying to take part of the Edwardian Country House project and would she, Avril, be interested? Before she'd even put the phone down, Avril's head was full of images of 'ladies in long dresses playing croquet against the backdrop of a stately house… Everywhere was sunshine, tranquillity and peace. Of *course* I was interested.'

After a few days in the house Avril wrote a letter to her mother in fine Edwardian style: 'I'm being as agreeable as I may to my sister and to her husband, as is proper for a guest who expects to stay for three months in her brother-in-law's home.' But it was by no means easy. She felt that she was trying to reconcile two irreconcilables: her status as an independent, educated, professional twenty-first-century woman, and that of a dependent Edwardian lady of reduced rank and circumstances within the family. She found it particularly hard that despite her education and managerial experience in the 'real world', her role in the Edwardian Country House was to be submissive, obliged to hold back from offering opinions and seek permission from Sir John, as head of the household, for many of her activities. She resolved, 'I want to find out as much as possible about the women's movement at the beginning of the century, and how they managed to change attitudes in society and move forward to take control of their lives.'

It was a battle fought with twenty-first-century sensibilities. Marriage remained the standard experience of women of all classes until the 1960s and this was particularly the case until the First World War. In 1901 nearly 85 per cent of women over forty-five either were married or were widows; in 1911 the figure was 83.2 per cent, and this continued to be the number into the 1960s.[12] The imbalance in the sex ratio, which increased gradually between 1871 and 1911, and dramatically as a result of the First World War, meant that there was a growing number of women who never married.[13] But marriage was regarded as a woman's 'natural destiny', and those who did not achieve it were regarded as 'failures', compared by the novelist George Gissing to 'an odd glove', useless without a partner, 'redundant' to the business of life, which was marriage and motherhood. Unmarried women faced an often lonely and certainly marginalized future, living with their parents or in the household of a male relative, or relative-in-law.

From 1880 elementary education was compulsory for both boys and girls up to the age of thirteen, and while the majority of upper-class girls were educated at home by a governess, increasing numbers of middle-class girls were either attending day schools, or being sent away to boarding school. Girls' grammar schools were established; the Girls' Public Day School Trust was founded in 1906 and by then the number of girls in secondary education had grown, but it was still much smaller than that of boys. It was not exceptional for school to finish at lunch time for girls so that they could spend the afternoon with their mothers at home learning 'domestic arts'.[14] As the journalist Mary Stocks recalls, even after an excellent academic education such as she had received, 'it was counted as no disgrace for a girl to pursue no profession, do no systematic work, and "come out" as a young adult female available for invitations to dances or proposals of marriage'.[15] If she did not receive, or declined to accept, such proposals, her life could be very restricted. Opportunities in higher education were limited: it has been estimated that about 15 per cent of all university students in 1900 were women, but they could not study in the same environment nor for the same qualifications as men. After the First World War, notwithstanding the carnage of actual or potential husbands on the battlefields of France and Flanders, the 'problem' of what to do with unmarried women was eased by the increasing number of opportunities for higher education, training and employment open to women. But before 1914 'excess' women were regarded as a social problem, particularly as the highest number of those 'surplus to requirements' were middle class, and it was estimated that in 1900 about a third of the daughters of peers remained single.

'We are equals and we have a close relationship,' said Anna Oliff-Cooper (left) of her sister, Avril Anson. But the Edwardian Country House experience put it under strain.

CHAPTER EIGHT

Huntin', Shootin' and Fishin'

. P. Herbert wrote the following lines in 1930.[1] But as Phyllida Barstow points out,[2] this would have seemed unacceptable levity about a serious matter in the Edwardian era when plutocrats were emulating aristocrats in aiming to bag as many birds as possible, and when a day out on the moors in the sleeting rain was considered what country house life was *for*.

It's really remarkably pleasant
To wander about in a wood
And kill an occasional pheasant
Provided the motive is good
And one of the jolliest features of killing superfluous game
Is the thought that you are saving the creatures
From a death of dishonour or shame.

Every bird has to die
By-and-by, by-and-by,
And they're lucky to die as they do,
For if they do not
They are probably shot
By someone who's not in Who's Who;
And I give you my word
Any sensitive bird –
A point for our foolish reproaches –
Prefers his career
To be stopped by a peer
And not by unmannerly poachers.

As in so many social matters, it was the King, Edward VII, who led the field. As Prince of Wales he had purchased the 8,000-acre Sandringham estate in Norfolk in 1862 with money accrued from the properties in the Duchy of Cornwall, to give him some independence from his controlling mother, Queen Victoria. The pleasure-loving monarch-to-be had straight away set up his new home as one of the finest hunting lodges in the country, building a railway station at Wolferton, which was two miles away, to bring his guests as near to his estate as possible and planting acres of trees and bushes to give cover to the birds he intended to shoot. Competition between landowners to bag the largest number of birds at a shoot grew intense in the years leading up to an entirely different sort of killing field in 1914. In 1913 Lord Burnham's guests in Buckinghamshire shot nearly 4,000 pheasants in a single day,[3] and Lord de Grey – admittedly a recognized expert shot – bagged 556,813 birds between 1867 and his death in 1923.

The King was not a first-class shot, thought Lord Warwick, but 'he was at least a good one, and was certainly a first-class sportsman'. According to Jonathan Garnier Ruffer, Edward was best at hitting driven partridges, and least good at potting pheasants.[4] His sons, however, were in the top league. The oldest, Prince Eddie (who died in 1892), was excellent, but his younger brother, the future King George V, was even better, and by the beginning of the twentieth century was reckoned to be one of the six top shots in the country.

When the King led a shooting party at Sandringham in November 1905, the nine or ten guns brought down a total of 6,448 birds – 4,135 pheasants, 2,009 partridges, 14 woodcock, 275 wild duck, 12 pigeons and 3 'various', plus 232 hares and 576 rabbits – a total 'bag' of 7,256 in three days.[5] The birds were beaten out of their hiding places towards the guns by the estate gamekeeper, other estate workers and local men recruited for the day's sport. The tweed-suited shooting party would raise their guns and congratulate each other on their skill in bringing down so many of the dense flock that darkened the sky, convinced that it was good 'sport' as another dead weight of feathers thudded to the ground, to be retrieved by gun dogs. A farmer who watched a Sandringham shoot described such an occasion:

> On they come in ever increasing numbers, until they burst in a cloud over the fence…This is the exciting moment, a terrific fusillade ensues, birds dropping down in all directions, wheeling about in confusion between the flags and the guns, the survivors gathering themselves together and escaping into the fields beyond. The shooters then retire to another line of fencing, making themselves comfortable with camp-stools and cigars until the birds are driven up as before, and so through the day, only leaving off for luncheon in a tent brought from Sandringham.[6]

King Edward VII shooting at Sandringham in 1907. The King would keep the clocks in his Norfolk home half an hour fast to ensure extra sport before darkness fell.

41

chauffeurs) who were at the steering wheel. Like Toad in *Wind in the Willows* the new cohort of motor car owners dressed in a vulgar fashion, drove recklessly and made a great deal of noise in doing so. Owning a car meant that distances became paltry and social life was reconfigured, since the distance a horse could travel no longer needed to circumscribe a person's social round. The Edwardian plutocrat's delight, the 'Saturday to Monday' country house party, was one significant result.

But motor-cars were not generally welcomed by the 'horsey community' since they interfered with fox-hunting: the smell of petrol put the hounds off the scent while the cars frightened the horses. More soberly, as David Cannadine points out, the military implications of the combustion engine meant that the cavalry, previously the elite corps, ceded ground to the mechanized infantry in the First World War.[24] But the trend was irreversible. In 1896 the Locomotives and Highway Act abolished the requirement for a man waving a red flag to walk in front of every car, and raised the speed limit on public roads to a dizzying 14 mph. That same year the future Edward VII took his first spin in a motor-car.

There was one advantage at least that cars had over horses, muttered Kenny rebelliously, as he was instructed to clear up the horse dung after the meet had departed. But Mr Edgar saw an opportunity.

'I told Kenny that he would have to clean the forecourt after the meet and he was just about to explode when I said, "And I will come with you to help you." I had two objectives in mind. One was to demonstrate that there is no task that is too menial. It doesn't matter what it is if it needs doing. The other is a more subtle point and that was a lesson in humility that we all need to learn. The minute Kenny saw me take off my white gloves and don an apron over my Sunday best it didn't matter any more that we were collecting horse manure; we were two men together doing a necessary job. So I hope that Kenny had learned that lesson.'

The next few weeks would tell.

Edwardian motoring: the Napier car that the Olliff-Coopers used during their Edwardian séjour, and (inset) fashions for Edwardian lady motorists.

41

CHAPTER NINE

Being
Edwardian

ine. If they want Edwardian, I'll give them Edwardian,' spat M. Dubiard, slamming a large copper pan down on the hot range. The simmering resentment below stairs had come to a head. As befits the *chef de cuisine* in a grand Edwardian country house where entertaining was as much for show as for conviviality, M. Dubiard spent nights poring over recipe books, determined to serve the correct food for the period. With a minimum of three courses at luncheon and five for dinner, frequent guests in the house and a round of dinner parties, it meant a great deal of work.

Before arriving, M. Dubiard had worked his way all through *Larousse Gastronomique* to refresh his memory, and in the house his 'bible' was Escoffier, though he consulted other sources such as Carême, Brillat-Savarin and Duglèré, whom he called 'the Mozart of the kitchen', and Mrs Beeton too, as well as drawing on his own compendious knowledge of French cookery. On their first night in the house, the Olliff-Coopers had been served a consommé followed by a tomato soup with basil and tapioca. The fish course had consisted of a petite croustade of smoked salmon and scrambled eggs; the main course had been Beef Wellington which, according to Escoffier, would have been called an *entrée* since it was 'less voluminous' than a *relévé* (literally 'to relieve' the soup), though he admitted that now that meals were served *à la russe*, rather than *à la française*, the distinction had become somewhat academic. The *entremet* (dessert) was a rhubarb and damson jelly and the meal concluded with tiny pineapple tartlets. Similar meals had followed: upstairs had dined on such delicacies as lobster and asparagus, oysters prepared in a variety of ways, quail, turbot with fennel, veal, langoustines, glazed roast pork, savoury and sweet soufflés, saddle of lamb, lamb cutlets, vegetables *provençales* (without garlic since, to M. Dubiard's irritation, Sir John had decreed that no garlic was to be used in the food served to the family as he was allergic to it), braised oxtail, galantine of duck, roast guinea fowl, sirloin steak. Then there had been a variety of sweet and savoury jellies, custards, sweet omelettes, tarts, pies and ices with praline and sugared violets. The list went on.

FANCY DISHES.

Delicious desserts as suggested by Mrs Beeton.

M. Dubiard checks whether a hare hanging in the game pantry is sufficiently high to serve.

One day the kitchen maid, Antonia, had been taken to see the specially built Manderston dairy, housed in a corbelled tower, the octagonal room designed like a cloister with a vaulted ceiling, its floor, walls and counters fashioned from marble and alabaster 'imported from seven countries'.[1] A carving on the wall depicting a dairymaid milking a cow, which was modelled on an animal in the byre, is reputed to have been removed on the instructions of Sir James Miller when he realized that the dairymaid was sitting on the wrong side of the cow. The solecism corrected, the plaque, which weighs close on half a ton, was rehung. It was in these delightful surroundings that Antonia was taught how to churn butter and how to make clotted cream, and this now featured on the dinner menu to accompany dessert or be taken at tea with scones and jam.

M. Dubiard had noticed that when he had sent up jugged hare, rich in a sauce made from its own blood, the dish had been returned untouched. Likewise when Sir John had shot game, he donated it to the kitchen staff. 'I think they only want bistro food like we eat in the twenty-first century,' the chef fumed. 'They are just not living as an Edwardian family would have done.' Leafing through his recipe books, the chef noticed the incidence of dishes that rarely figure on modern menus such as teal, ptarmigan, widgeon, lark (as a pâté, roast or in a pie), pigeon, capon, fish such as flounder, smelts, eel, pike, squab, dory, and parts of the animal not often consumed at today's table such as heart, sweetbreads, tail and cheek, not to mention sucking pig, pig's trotters and pig's ears. Stroking his chin thoughtfully, M. Dubiard's eyes began to gleam.

The issue of 'being Edwardian' had become wider than one of culinary peccadilloes. The material conditions of an Edwardian existence were clearly in place in the country house: the absence of labour-saving devices ranging from washing machines through vacuum cleaners to detergent and scouring powder; the clothes from corsets and bloomers to laced walking boots, long skirts, large, feathered hats and furs (above stairs), stuff frocks, crisp white caps and aprons (below stairs). The turn of the century was signalled by the absence of commodities too: no proprietary brands of shampoo, no deodorants, tampons, make-up; no instant coffee, sliced bread, tea bags, Coca Cola; no trainers, fleeces, felt-tip pens, video games, television, CD players, mobile phones…

The duties of the servants were spelled out in the book of rules and instructions that they had been handed on arrival, and were expected to read, learn and inwardly digest, and Mr Edgar had drawn up a timetable for everyone so they knew exactly what they should be doing and when. Upstairs the Olliff-Coopers and Miss Anson were likewise supplied with manuals of advice on etiquette, including correct forms of address, rules of precedence and dress codes, while contemporary magazines and newspapers brought the family and servants up to date with news of the outside world as it was lived then.

But 'being Edwardian' was about *living* the Edwardian experience, not just using Edwardiana as a stage set. It was about trying to comprehend the rules of engagement and etiquette of the era in order to get into its prevailing mindset. It was physically hard for the servants to have to rise before the sun, scrub pots and pans all day and be at the beck and call of their employers at all times. But what was much harder intellectually and emotionally was to shed twenty-first-century attitudes and acquire

a servility and unquestioning obedience that would have been required of an Edwardian servant. This did not mean, of course, that our Edwardian forefathers and mothers were accepting, uncritical, uncomplaining beings without sensibilities, unaware of concepts of dignity and respect. During the period before the First World War, increasing numbers of men and women chose not to go into domestic service the moment that other opportunities in factories, offices and shops became available. In his social survey, Charles Booth noted that the reluctance to take up domestic service owed less to meagre pay and poor conditions – for unskilled factory or agricultural workers endured far worse of both – than to the requisite servility. It was increasingly shunned because of the relationship between master and servant which was similar to that between sovereign and subject, demanding 'an all pervading attitude of watchful respect, accompanied by a readiness to respond at once to any gracious advance that may be made'

Master Guy, the only member of the Olliff-Cooper family to feel at home below stairs, jokes with Antonia and Becky.

A television-free zone: Jess reads, Erika plays cards and Tristan talks in the servants' hall.

without ever 'presuming or for a moment "forgetting themselves"'.[2] A butler writing in the magazine *Nineteenth Century* near the end of Victoria's reign regretted that the master of the house often assumed that his position endowed him with an innate superiority, and was likely to forget 'that the servant whom he treats like a dog may have nerves as highly strung, and may feel as acutely as the guest whom he must treat with courtesy'.[3] And most poignantly a footman's memoir cried out against his lack of freedom: 'The life of a gentleman's servant is something like that of a bird shut up in a cage. The bird is well fed and well housed, but is deprived of liberty.'[4] And indeed employers were advised that 'servants, like birds, must be caught when young'.[5]

It took a considerable leap of imagination for the servants to shed twenty-first-century attitudes and climb back into the cage of the Edwardian era. A few days after the family arrived, the first footman, Charlie, was optimistic about things in an inappropriately modern way: 'It's a bit of a "them and us" mentality at the moment because obviously we are waiting on them hand and foot, which is our job after all, but I think that in time Mr Edgar and Rob [the second footman] and I will be a position to bridge the gap. Hopefully in time, we'll be able to have a bit of banter. Well, perhaps not banter,' he conceded, 'but be a bit more light-hearted with Sir John and Lady Olliff-Cooper and the rest of the family. And at the same time we'll keep our links with the rest of the servants and tell them exaggerated stories of what's happening upstairs, I think it'll be a laugh, really.' But it wasn't.

When Charlie, in charge because Mr Edgar was unwell, tried to put in place a modern managerial solution – such as any twenty-first-century human resources consultant would welcome – to the problem of the scullery maid's exhaustion and ennui, he found it wasn't that simple. 'I thought we'd have a sort of a rota. That is, I would take it in turns to do the washing-up for a day a week and that would give Ellen [or Kelly as it was at the time] a break and allow Kenny to take over from me as footman for an evening to give him a bit of variety – and experience – too.' But this was not an acceptable situation as far as Sir John was concerned. He had no desire to know that his personable first footman was in the basement up to his elbows in greasy suds, while it was the untrained hall boy now standing before him in ill-fitting footman's livery.

It had been the same with the staff's request for a rota of regular half-days off, which had finally been granted. 'I will do my best,' Mr Edgar had responded, 'but the needs of the family have to come first, and if any one of us is required to serve them, then he or she cannot have the time off. The sole reason that we are here is to serve the family.'

As far as the Edwardian Country House servants were concerned, the family upstairs had no such constraints. They would have been uncomprehending of Henry James's observation that such Edwardian plutocrats lived lives of 'gilded bondage'. To them, the family was free to indulge its every whim thanks to *their* labour. As far as they could see, the Olliff-Coopers were living for pleasure, enjoying a pampered lifestyle – and they weren't always all that grateful for it. Rob was struck when he had accompanied Lady Olliff-Cooper on a visit to a school in Duns and she had told the children that it had only taken her a couple of days to settle into her Edwardian lifestyle. 'It dawned on me then that if you are given privilege, as they have been given privilege, it's easy to get used to that pretty well straight away. But if you have had privileges, what you deserve, your rights, all taken away as we have below stairs, that's much harder to adjust to.'

But it wasn't all one way. The family upstairs had restraints too; they were hardly ever alone. 'It's got to the point that Jonty has taken to writing an appointment in my diary just to talk to me,' said his mother guiltily. The servants were present at every meal and the presence of Rob and Charlie standing erect, staring impassively into the middle distance as the family ate, was a considerable restraint on conversation. 'Servants have eyes and ears to wag downstairs' one of their etiquette manuals had cautioned. The maids tidied the women's bedrooms when they were downstairs and any intimate secrets could be perused at leisure, journals and letters read if any member of the family was less than vigilant, or one of the housemaids or Miss Morrison proved particularly curious. 'No man is a hero to his valet' was a salutary truth that the male members of the family brought ruefully to mind sometimes, mindful, perhaps, of an inevitable indiscretion or flash of irritability. Though they employed some thirteen below stairs servants, Edwardian etiquette made it improper for the family to venture to the nether regions of their own house, and they suspected that their daily doings were the subject of servant gossip and speculation, criticism and occasional ribald jocularity. Any discontents the staff felt filtered through to the family, while uncertainty about how extensive were the lands of the lord of misrule below stairs must have made for unease on occasions.

The family's activities had to fit into the rigid timetable of the house – meals had to be served at prescribed times or the efficient mechanism of the house would be thrown into disarray. The gong sounded for luncheon, then to dress for dinner, then for dinner itself. If the servants' life was ruled by bells, it seemed to the family that theirs was by gongs. Then there were the restraints of Edwardian etiquette (the word means labelling or ticketing), and this elaborate code grew up from the early nineteenth century to delineate social boundaries. The purpose was to keep those below you at a distance, emphasize 'commensuality' with those who were your social equal, and aim to gain access to the next higher group.[6] The 'system' governed what it was proper to discuss in front of the servants, and what with the servants; the rules of precedence and address; how to start a letter and how to end it; who to invite to your house and how; and the whole fraught business of introductions, being 'at home' and paying calls.

'Inferiors' were introduced to 'superiors', and rank always took precedence over anything else. Servants were not introduced to anyone. Once a lady had been introduced (but not before, unless she was immensely grand) she might call on that person and send in her card. *The Lady* explained this labyrinthine system:

> There is a very strict etiquette in the matter of cards and calls and there is one essential difference between *calling* and *leaving cards*. It is usual on paying a first visit merely to leave cards without inquiring if the mistress of the house is at home. Thus Mrs A. leaves her own card and two of her husband's cards upon Mrs B. Within a week, if possible, certainly within ten days, Mrs B. should return the visit and leave cards on Mrs A. Should Mrs A., however, have 'called' upon Mrs B. and the latter returned it by merely leaving cards, this would be taken as a sign that the latter did not desire the acquaintance to ripen into friendship. Strict etiquette demands that a call should be returned by a call and a card by a card.[7]

Master and servant: Rob stands to attention as Sir John eats his lunch on a fishing expedition.

Lady Olliff-Cooper

*Manderston
Duns*

Once this ritual had been gone through and the notional Mrs (or Lady) A. and Mrs (or Lady) B. actually got together, there were further conventions to be observed. The first visit should be short – around fifteen minutes – and conversation should be light and impersonal; politics and religion were to be eschewed and dogs and children were not appropriate appendages. If the call was a morning one, outdoor clothes should be kept on; in the afternoon a coat or cloak could be shed, but a lady would keep her hat on (partly no doubt because it was such a kerfuffle to fix it on and off with hairpins and hatpins galore). If the initial visit was deemed to have passed off well, a dinner invitation might ensue and the tactics could be deemed to have worked. Should the family leave the area for a period, maybe to go to London for the Season, they would distribute cards marked 'P.P.C.' – Pour Prend Congé) and when they returned the whole intricate game would start up again with maybe some new players to add a little interest.

There is, of course, no entirely homogeneous society that can be simply reconstructed by consulting its manuals of instruction. There were some upper-class Edwardians who chose to ignore these social niceties, either because they had pretensions to be 'bohemian', or simply because they were so grand that they could be insouciant about what others thought of them. Yet as late as 1911 Lady Colin Campbell was quite firm:

> Visits of form of which most people complain and yet to which most people submit, are absolutely necessary – being in fact the basis on which that great structure, society, mainly rests. You cannot invite people to your house, however often you may have met them elsewhere, until you have first called upon them in a formal manner, and they have returned the visit. It is a kind of safeguard against any acquaintances which are thought to be undesirable. If you do not wish to continue the friendship, you discontinue to call, and that is considered an intimation of such intentions, and therefore no further advances are made.[8]

And for those *arrivistes* not born to the purple, such rules served as handrails around the maze that was Edwardian society.

For the Olliff-Coopers, the complexity of the situation was compounded. As newcomers to Edwardian society, not only were they having to navigate a whole atlas of unseen, confusing and sometimes contradictory behavioural maps, they were also having to think themselves back into the dynamics of that terrain. Their task was to unlearn twenty-first-century ways of behaving, speaking and even thinking, and to assume the new and sometimes uncomfortable logic of their situation.

'It is difficult for us to know how far to act as Edwardians and how far to stick to our twenty-first-century principles,' worried Lady Olliff Cooper. 'It's a very difficult, delicate balancing act and sometimes we manage it better than others. Quite a lot of the time we do actually *feel* Edwardian and hence our instinct is to act in ways that the Edwardians would have done, but of course the way that Edwardians acted is perceived nowadays as being callous and indifferent, unkind and unfeeling in many respects. So when we act like that we will appear as callous and uncaring people. And yet the rest of the time we agonize because we know that we are letting our twenty-first-century sensibilities get in the way of historical veracity, the way we *would* have acted, no matter how we might feel about such behaviour now.'

A few weeks into the project, Sir John began to feel that the balance was tilting too far one way. 'There is a natural inclination to get to know people and want them to like you, and in the twenty-first century we think that we get the best from people by having them like and respect us, but we know today that this has to be earned. It's not just there as of right. And that would not have been the Edwardian view. As a family, we have stayed at very high quality hotels, but being waited on in hotels is just not the same as being waited on in your own home by your own servants, though I am not quite sure why there is that difference. I know that I am perfectly capable of running an Edwardian country house as it would have been run in 1905, though obviously I have not been brought up to do so. And that is what I am going to do. The staff is becoming over familiar and we are allowing it to happen. We are finding it hard to detach their twenty-first-century status, the people they are, the jobs they do in the modern world, from their status here now as employees with not much status. I have spoken about this at great length to Edgar and we are both agreed that it is essential to re-establish an absolute understanding of the employer/employee relationship as it would have been before the First World War.'

His wife agreed: 'There was a feeling that people were slipping into an easy twenty-first-century familiarity that was just not authentic and could have turned the whole project into a second-rate costume drama rather than a real social experiment in Edwardian living. So yesterday morning I made a list of some of the things that need to be tightened up around the house on the female side. John has spoken to Edgar and I have spoken to Mrs Davies, and as a result things seem to be running much more efficiently. Our meal was on time last night and it was delicious as usual. I realize that we are going be seen as remarkably haughty and really rather unpleasant if we fully adopt Edwardian attitudes in this way. But that's how it has to be.'

Below stairs Mr Edgar had assembled the servants and told them of the new regime: 'Meals on time on the dot, all the china and glass and silver checked in and out by the housekeeper, a smart appearance at all times, no hands in pockets or lolling around, attendance at prayers and at church compulsory unless I give permission otherwise, no time off without my express agreement, and no familiarity,' he warned. 'This is going to be run as an Edwardian house upstairs and down.'

A person who did know how life in this particular country house had been was Mrs Whinney, who had worked at Manderston seventy years ago in the household of Sir James Miller's widow. Mrs Whinney's name was Betty, but when she had gone to work in a house where the mistress was called Lady Betty, the mistress decided that it was not at all proper that a housemaid should have the same name as she did, so in future the housemaid was always known as Elizabeth above stairs, and Betty below. Mrs Whinney was invited to meet the present-day 'servants' and answer their questions about how it had been in *her* day. She had joined the staff when she was fifteen years old; it was her second position and her wages had been £30 a year, paid quarterly as was usual. By the time she was nineteen she was head housemaid, with three girls working under her, and when she left service in her early thirties her wages had risen to £60 a year. But the servants were always trying to find ways to scrimp and save a little: when the family were away and the servants were paid 'board wages' Mrs Whinney had to buy her own sugar, so she decided that she would learn to drink tea without it.

When she saw Charlie and Rob, it had brought back vivid memories of the footmen she had worked with at Manderston: 'They used to wash their own shirts to save money rather than pay the laundry, and one of them asked me to iron his shirts, and when I refused he pushed me into the safe where the silver was kept, and he locked the door and went off to the pictures leaving me there. Luckily the housekeeper, Mrs Hall, a tall, handsome woman, very strict but very nice, met him and asked where I was and he came back and opened the door and I was lying on the floor unconscious. I suppose it was lack of air.'

Mrs Whinney's memories of the butler were not very warm either: 'He was a bit on the amorous side. One day he made an advance to me when I was cleaning a room and I just took my brush and hit him on the face with it and his cheek bled. He pretended to everyone that he'd cut himself shaving. I think that was partly why I left. I didn't feel comfortable there any more, and I couldn't talk to anyone about him, the only way to deal with it was to move on, so I did.'

A superior life. Sir John and Lady Olliff-Cooper discuss their plans for the day.

But despite that, Mrs Whinney told the servants that she would still recommend domestic service as a job for young people: 'I felt I was quite privileged. If I had gone into a factory it would have been very repetitive work, whereas in service you met a lot of new people. We had a nice place to live, we had good food and though there wasn't much time off we made our own fun. The footmen would put tapioca in between the sheets which made it very uncomfortable to sleep, and it was the devil to get rid of it. When I was promoted to be head housemaid, they used to put flour on my pillow, and I didn't see it, and the next morning I'd wake up and all my hair was white. But you got a useful training in service; you learned to do things properly and if you didn't you'd suffer the consequences because you wouldn't get a reference when you applied for another job. It was good discipline.'

But, as Lady Olliff-Cooper recognized, there were bound to be difficulties in trying to reinstate Edwardian discipline. 'There's a lot of bubbling discontent in the house at the moment,' she recorded. 'If you put nineteen modern-day people together in a house and tell half the people that they are superior and in every way more important than the other half, you are bound to have problems. In the twenty-first century we are brought up to think of everyone as being equal. In the Edwardian era people were brought up thinking that their superiors were superior, and that there was an unbridgeable divide, so you are bound to have problems with twenty-first-century people not wishing to go back to a position of servitude – which is entirely understandable.'

A window on another world. Becky watches guests arrive at the Edwardian Country House.

But the lower servants did not see quite like that. 'I was on my hands and knees one day drying the marble floor in the hall after I had mopped it, and I just felt so Edwardian, because literally not a soul noticed me,' Becky reflected. 'In one room people were playing billiards, and in another Sir John was singing, and another someone was snoring. It was all going on around me. The house was full of guests and people were milling about and it was as if I was invisible, and I thought this is what it was really like to be an Edwardian maid. It was the strangest feeling and yet it was good, because it seemed so authentic. It was what I wanted to experience, to really know what being a maid felt like. I was so tired, my hands were sore, my eyes ached, and my back ached. I had been up and down stairs all day long. I hadn't got to bed until 2 a.m. because there was a ball and we had loads of clearing up to do, and I was up again at 6 a.m., and now there are guests staying in all the rooms. So that's more work.'

The housemaids, the footmen, the hall boy, the groom and the scullery maid felt that they had got Edwardian lock, stock and barrel, whereas upstairs were enjoying Edwardian advantages without signing up for aspects they found distasteful. And matters came to a head over food.

every way, she is just amazing, she's funny, she's clever, she's just ace. We went out for a walk through the woods and we ended up at the South Gate and stood looking over the fields to the Cheviot Hills. It was beautiful evening and we ended up snogging. I didn't think that I was going to get through this Edwardian stuff, but now I think I'm going to just breeze through. I am just so happy it's untrue and I'm feeling very, very lucky.'

The hall boy

'The thought of being able to walk in the footsteps of a person who lived before my time would be a great adventure,' wrote Kenneth Skelton to Mr Edgar in his letter of application to the Edwardian Country House. 'I would love the opportunity to be a member of your staff and I am offering my services as hall boy.' Eighteen-year-old Kenny is a care worker from Stoke on Trent, looking after people with Alzheimer's, Parkinson's and senile dementia. 'It's hard work and can be stressful. The pay's not much but it's very worthwhile.' He soon found that the authentic Edwardian experience could be tough going too. 'I have *never* worked so hard in all my life,' he groaned. Kenny found the below stairs hierarchy and discipline particularly irksome, and was soon in revolt against the privileged lifestyle it was designed to support. But there were compensations. 'I like maids,' he had ventured before he joined the project, and soon there was one in particular…

But the course of true love, Edwardian style, was not a smooth one. It was hard for Ellen and Kenny: 'We haven't really had much of a chance to get to know one another, we don't have any time on our own. We must get on average about half an hour a day when it's just me and Ellen and nobody else. Everybody is always around and Mr Edgar walks in and you can't even sit with your arms around each other.' It wasn't just the jobs they had to do, their long working hours and the fact that their free time hardly ever seemed to coincide that made life difficult for the young couple. It was also that romance below stairs was frowned on, and if discovered usually led to dismissal. Mr Edgar, who was by no means unsympathetic, called Kenny into his office to warn him to make sure that the romance did not interfere with his work, and to remind him that it was essential that he and Ellen were discreet. 'If the mistress gets to hear of it, it'll be Ellen that has to go,' the butler warned.

It was not easy to see how servants would ever marry since so many obstacles were put in the way of the usual progress of courtship. 'Followers' were not permitted, partly because they were a distraction from work and daily routine and partly because they were considered likely to be 'undesirable', careless or even light-fingered with property. The only men that the women servants were likely to meet were their fellow servants, tradesmen who came to the kitchen door or the servants who came to the house with guests and were billeted below stairs for the duration of the visit. The limited time off did not help either and the most a maid might hope for was a wander through country lanes with a suitor during her half day off. In more benevolent families, a female servant might be allowed to invite a young man to tea in the servants' hall, but this was an unusual dispensation from the mistress of the house. As Margaret Powell, herself a housemaid, recalled:

The business of getting a young man was not respectable and one's employers tended to degrade every relationship. It seemed to me one was expected to find husbands under a gooseberry bush. *Their* daughters were debs, and they could meet young men at balls, dances and private parties, but if any of the servants had boyfriends they were known as 'followers'…a degrading term… You had to slink up the area steps and meet on the corner of the road on some pretext like going to post a letter. And on your night out when you came back you couldn't…bring him in to say goodnight to him…he wasn't a young man, he was a 'follower'. They made you feel there was something intrinsically bad in having a member of the opposite sex interested in you at all.[9]

Getting acquainted: Kenny interrupts his firewood chopping to talk to Ellen.

Obviously, not all servant romances became public knowledge – some were kept quiet by an understanding butler or housekeeper, and sometimes employers could show generosity, allowing the couple to marry and remain in their employ, maybe even giving them a cottage on the estate. But as with most Edwardian sexual mores, it was the female servant who suffered. A maid who got pregnant was invariably summarily dismissed, sent packing at once without a reference, to face a grim future. 'I insisted on her [a pregnant kitchen maid] leaving the house at once,' reported an Edwardian country house owner, Henry Polderoy. 'One cannot be too careful or too quick in these matters: a man of my standing must avoid the very shadow of a slur on his reputation or judgement. Although the girl declared that she would be unable to reach her mother's home…on the same day, I would not allow her to remain…It would never do to encourage vice by making things comfortable and easy for the sinner.'[10] And when Sir James Miller's brother-in-law, the urbane and worldly Lord Curzon, discovered that one of his housemaids had allowed a footman to spend the night with her, 'I put the little slut out into the street at a moment's notice,' he wrote to his wife.

Unless she was able to return to her family, which rural poverty made impossible in many cases, the girl's options were extremely limited. At the end of the nineteenth century, the figures told a sad story. In 1900, 60 per cent of all unmarried women applying to have their children admitted to London Foundling hospitals had been in domestic service, and of those 35 per cent were drawn from 'the higher ranks of service'.[11] And it was believed that a large proportion of the prostitutes in London had 'chosen' life on the streets in preference to the only other alternative for the unemployed – and unemployable – domestic servant, the workhouse. Small wonder that any servant who found herself 'in the family way' would resort to desperate measures such as swallowing quinine, penny royal or handfuls of Beecham's pills, taking scalding mustard baths, volunteering to move heavy furniture or clamber up precarious ladders, or throwing herself off tables and down stairs in order to abort her unborn child. The father of the child may well have been another servant or tradesmen, but it was also possible that it could have been the 'young master' – or even the older master – who regarded a comely female servant as his property in sex as in other forms of service. A sexually predatory employer could make a servant's life insupportable since she was likely to be disbelieved and dismissed if she reported him, and she would be sacked if she became pregnant. A pornographic eleven-volume memoir, *My Secret Life*, published in Amsterdam in the decade before Edward VII came to the throne, reveals the extent to which the author considered the servants in his mother's house to be there for his priapic delectation, referring to them as if they were blood stock: 'clean, well fed, full-blooded', 'has not been used, ridden or raced for a week, and is ready for service'. In the now famous case of Arthur J. Munby, a barrister and civil servant, it was revealed when he died in 1910 that he had been secretly married to a parlour maid, Hannah Cullwick, for nearly forty years. Despite the fact that she was his wife, Hannah continued to act as her husband's servant, waiting at table, scrubbing the floors, valeting his wardrobe and addressing him as 'sir' in company, while he delighted in taking photographs of her in this subservient, grimy role.[12] He wrote a poem that expressed his feelings:

> Her strong, bare, sinewy arms and rugged hands
> Blacken'd with labour, and her peasant dress
> Rude, coarse in texture, yet most picturesque,
> And suited to her station and her ways;
> All these, transfigured by that sentiment
> Of lowly contrast to the man she served;
> Grew dignified with beauty and herself
> A noble working woman, not ashamed
> Of what her work had made her.[13]

Standing in for Charlie at lunch one day, Kenny could not help overhearing the conversation at table. 'If you weren't particularly enamoured of your husband you could always seek diversions,' Lady Olliff-Cooper suggested. 'And vice versa,' chipped in a male guest eagerly. 'And that was basically all right because most of these were arranged marriages to an extent,' her ladyship continued doubtfully. 'But of course servants weren't allowed to have relationships with other servants. A footman could not have had a relationship with a maid. Or if they did I imagine they would both have to leave and get married.' 'No,' contradicted Master Guy, 'if they did and the master of the house found out, they'd be chucked out,' he concluded with relish.

It increased Kenny's resentment of his masters and the double standards he felt operated above and below stairs: 'The family came into this project from a wealthy background already – the only difference for them is that they are a bit more pampered with a period twist. Whereas the people downstairs have come from comfortable backgrounds into something which is absolutely disgusting. They have one bath a week, they have horrible food and the Edwardian experience is infinitely more profound for the servants than it is for the family upstairs. I don't see how anyone can make a comparison between our struggle and their struggle because it's just not the same. The ladies upstairs moan about having to wear a corset, but the girls downstairs have to clean fires and mop floors and bend over and scrub out baths in theirs, so how those upstairs can moan about having to sit and eat tea in their corsets is absolutely beyond me. I don't think they have the slightest comprehension of how we live downstairs.'

One night, when the Sir John and Lady Olliff-Cooper had gone to the opera and had taken Mr Edgar, Mr Raj Singh and Miss Morrison as their guests, the young downstairs servants decided to sample life upstairs. Creeping up the backstairs, the uninvited guests burst into the marble hall and hurried from room to room, sampling the delights of gracious living. The lower servants took turns at the billiard table, 'that essential plaything for every Edwardian gentleman', situated in what was originally the library at Manderston until, after Sir James's death in 1906, his widow had been persuaded by her brothers to move in the games table. Schooled in pub pool, the servants potted shots across the seeming acres of green baize – 'the slate bed of a full-sized billiard table measures 12ft by 6ft ½in, and as an allowance of 2in in width must be made for the projection of the cushions, the *playable* bed of a table is 11ft 8in in length and 5ft 9 ½in in width, and consequently is practically double as long as it is wide', explained the chapter 'Games of Skill' in the 1904 edition of *Cassell's Book of Sports and Pastimes*. While declining to get into a discussion about the origin or longevity of the game, the book insisted that 'recent improvements…have so changed its character that, practically speaking, it may be considered a game of modern date'.[14]

They lounged guiltily in the comfortable morning room sofas, while Rob picked out a tune on the piano. The servants peered into the card room before flinging open the double doors to the ballroom and sliding across the highly polished floor as if it were an ice rink, glistening under the crystal chandeliers. 'It was really weird,' said Antonia, for it was a rare chance for her to see how the family she served lived, as it was for Ellen – the kitchen staff neither needed to go nor were invited above stairs other than for daily prayers. 'It was like a dream, or a scene from a novel. It was really, really magic.' They tiptoed up the famous silver staircase and then stood outside Lady Olliff-Cooper's bedroom, before realizing how late it was getting and how far they had strayed beyond their boundaries. The world turned briefly upside-down, the 'lower five' hurried back to the servants' quarters and their narrow iron beds, thin strips of carpet on the floor of their attic or basement rooms, their tin baths and dawn start the next morning.

The upstairs/downstairs divide in the Edwardian Country House found its image in national politics. In 1906, after 'the most exciting general election for years', magic lanterns supplied by Lord Northcliffe's new popular *Daily Mail* projected the results on to massive screens in London's Trafalgar Square and on the Embankment: it was a landslide victory for the Liberals. The Conservative and Unionists had been reduced from 400 to 157 members while the Liberals won 400 seats, including 24 Lib-Labs; there were 83 Irish nationalists and 30 Labour members were returned.[15] With an unshakeable majority and broad, geographically based support, the victorious new government saw itself as poised to 'sweep away the last relics of feudalism' in the name of the politics of 'the People'. In 1908, H. H. Asquith, 'the first non-landed Prime Minister in the nation's history',[16] succeeded Campbell-Bannerman as Prime Minister and appointed the Welsh solicitor turned politician David Lloyd George as Chancellor of the Exchequer.

Lloyd George was a 'political genius who cast spells rather than won debates';[17] his exuberant and exhilarating rhetoric could 'kindle an audience into flame' and the object of his invective and exhortation were the '[upper] classes' as opposed to the 'masses'. His intention was to 'rob the hen roost' of the wealthy to 'raise money to wage implacable warfare against poverty and squalidness'. In 1906

Campbell-Bannerman had promised that Britain would become 'less of a pleasure ground for the rich and more of a treasure house for the nation': in other words, the glaring inequality between rich and poor, which was the subject of so much contemporary comment, was to begin to be redressed. The Old Age Pensions Act of 1908 introduced non-contributory pensions 'as of right' (though it was means tested) by which everyone over seventy years of age was entitled to an income of five shillings a week (at a time when less than half the population lived beyond sixty-five).[18] In the words of the Fabian socialist, Beatrice Webb, it guaranteed 'an enforced minimum of civilized life' for the very old.

In 1911, Lloyd George introduced his proposals for a contributory insurance scheme by which 'the employer and the State should enter into a partnership with the working man in order as far as possible to mitigate the burden [of unemployment and sickness] that falls upon him'. The provisions of the bill covered manual workers, including domestic servants. In the case of female servants this required a contribution of 3d a week from the master or mistress, who was also obliged to collect the servant's contribution which was an equal amount, purchase a National Insurance stamp and stick on the card. In some households this was regarded as an intolerable interference by the state into domestic life. Pamela Horn tells how petitions and demonstrations were organized in opposition to the bill which, in the words of the *Daily Mail* – which was in the forefront of orchestrating the campaign against this 'obnoxious legislation'[19] – 'creates a new tax of 26/- a year for every servant [and] will destroy happy domestic relations in hundreds and thousands of homes'.[20] Despite the protests, the scheme came into force in July 1912. Every insured female worker was entitled to medical care by a

doctor, free treatment in a sanatorium or other institution 'when suffering from tuberculosis', weekly sickness benefit of 7s 6d a week for twenty-six weeks and a disablement benefit of 5 shillings thereafter should she still be unable to work. The provisions were the same for male servants, but the contributions were a penny more and the sickness benefit was 10 shillings.[21]

It is hard to see why numbers of servants also petitioned against the introduction of this Act. It may speak of employer intimidation, or a pragmatic wish on the part of the servant not to displease the master and mistress in whose house he or she lived; it may suggest that such servants were confident of their treatment in sickness as in health; or it may indicate that the model of paternal (or maternal) benevolence that characterized the Edwardian household was deeply embedded in servant as in employer consciousness.

At the same time as they were introducing sweeping social welfare reforms, the Liberals were, with some considerable reluctance, entering into an

Potting the black. Mr Jonathan concentrates on a game of billiards.

Epsom racecourse: The Derby was the greatest national carnival of the Edwardian year - the House of Commons went into recess for the day, and the King only missed the occasion if the Court was in mourning.

escalating naval arms race with Germany. The government finally committed itself to building eighteen new Dreadnought battleships. This costly imperative posed a stark choice: either cut spending on social welfare, or raise taxation. Lloyd George was in no doubt which it should be. He had plans to open Labour Exchanges for the unemployed; the growth in cars necessitated an ambitious road-building and improvement programme; and child allowances were to be introduced. In his so-called 'People's Budget' of 1909 the Chancellor raised duties on spirits and tobacco, the top rate of death duties was increased to 15 per cent, income tax rose from 1 shilling to 1s 2d, and a super tax of sixpence in the pound on incomes over £5,000 was introduced for the first time. Most startling was the direct blow at the landed classes: a capital gains tax on land. Whenever an estate changed hands due to inheritance or sale, a 20 per cent tax was to be levied on the unearned increment (an increase not due to development or investment) of the land's value. And a 10 per cent tax was to be charged on any increase in land value when a lease was transferred or renewed, plus an annual 10 per cent tax on undeveloped land.

In fact, these taxes were not particularly successful revenue-raising initiatives since the value of land was not rising significantly, nor had it been since the 1880s, and the duties were repealed in 1920, but they were symbolic of Lloyd George's assault on the landed classes – and those who had acquired land. And the landed classes and their representatives fought back. Though the budget was passed in the Commons on 4 November 1909 by 379 votes to 149, when the bill came to the Lords, it was thrown out. Lloyd George picked up the gauntlet with alacrity. 'Savage strife between class and class' predicted the young politician Winston Churchill, who was President of the Board of Trade in the Liberal administration. Lloyd George toured the country, denouncing the peers as 'five hundred men chosen accidentally from among the unemployed' pitted against 'millions of people who are engaged in the industry which makes the wealth of the country'. Edward VII was appalled at what he regarded as dangerous rhetoric

CHAPTER TEN

The Fast Set

D eath of the King' proclaimed a black-bordered *Daily Mirror* on 7 May 1910. Edward VII had 'breathed his last' at 11.45 p.m. the previous night in the presence of Her Majesty Queen Alexandra, and their children: the Prince and Princess of Wales, the Princess Royal (the Duchess of Fife), Princess Victoria and Princess Louise (Duchess of Argyll) – all except their daughter Maud, Queen of Norway, who was on her way. 'The Whole World Sorrowing…the nation plunged into mourning…the period of Court mourning will last at least six months,' reported the paper.

Sir John summoned the family and servants to announce the news, and Rob and Charlie removed Edward VII's portrait from the walls of the Edwardian Country House, and reflected on what the news might have meant to them in the early summer of 1910.

The King's body lay in state in Westminster Hall for three days as 250,000 of his subjects filed silently past. Eight kings and an emperor attended the funeral at Windsor, which was held on 20 May. Edward's terrier dog, Caesar, trotted behind the coffin, much to the irritation of the German Kaiser, who was disinclined to yield precedence to a small, rather scruffy, dog.

When Queen Victoria died, commentators had proclaimed the end of an era. 'It will mean great changes in the world,' predicted Lady Battersea, a member of the Rothschild banking family. 'Black garments, crape, black bows on whips – all black!…Black, mourning London, black, mourning England, black, mourning Empire – those facts are text and sermon. The emptiness of the great city without the feeling of the Queen's living presence in her Empire, and the sensation of universal change haunted me.'[1] It seemed significant that Edward should come to the throne at the very dawn of the twentieth century, and court and country waited in anticipation for the metaphorical heavy chenille drapes of Victoria's reign to be flung wide open, for a relaxation in manners and moral codes, a less fussy etiquette and a less rigidly hierarchical society. They were not to be entirely disappointed.

Edward both granted licence to his eponymous era and was perfectly in tune with it. He was a monarch for the plutocracy, surrounding himself with men of money (which he frequently needed) who were invariably from a background in trade or finance and several of whom were Jewish. In the words of George Dangerfield's elegant book *The Strange Death of Liberal England*, 'He represented in a concentrated shape those bourgeois kings whose florid forms and rather dubious escapades were all the industrial world had left of an ancient divinity.'[2] The King practised conspicuous consumption to a fine art at home and abroad (where he particularly favoured the casinos of Biarritz and Monte Carlo). He was 'the first English sovereign of whom it could be fairly said that he knew the world [which was more than could be said for most of his ministers]. King Edward had met the Americans in America, the Indians in India [unlike his mother who as Empress of India had never visited the subcontinent]'; he had travelled in Spain, Italy and Russia; he was at home in Denmark [which was the homeland of his wife] and Germany; he especially enjoyed Austria and he loved Paris and the French'.[3] As Prince of Wales, he had been pro-French and wary of German intentions, and as King liked to see himself as having been instrumental in forging the *entente cordiale* between England and France in 1904.

The king who gave his name and set the style of era that was to linger on for another four years after his death had had a long period of apprenticeship for his brief nine-year tenure of the throne. He was fifty-nine when his mother, Queen Victoria, died on 22 January 1901, the longest reigning monarch in British history. It had been a mortifying time waiting in the wings (perhaps not unlike the situation with the present royal family). The imperious mother had infantilized the wayward son, keeping him at arm's distance from the affairs of state for decades and failing to appreciate the qualities he *did* have of diplomacy, personability, and a modernizing view of his role – whether in revitalizing the dreary mausoleum that Buckingham Palace had become (which he had christened 'the Sepulchre' when he moved there as King), riding round London incognito in 'common' hansom cabs, clamping down on the excessive drinking of the household at Balmoral, or recognizing Britain's place in Europe.

As Prince of Wales, Bertie, as he was known within the family, had the reputation as a playboy, a *bon viveur*, a gambler and something of a *roué*. He was a prince in the most acute contrast to his late father, Victoria's 'beloved Albert', who had been a model of middle-class moral probity, constitutional application and the very personification of the Puritan ethic. His mother used to sigh, 'What will became of the poor country when I die? If Bertie succeeds he would…spend his life in one whirl of amusements.'

'A strong Conservative, and a still stronger Jingo', in the words of the radical Charles Dilke, the King was convinced that the Liberal government's proposed social reforms would destabilize society. Yet he expressed concern for the poverty in which so many of his citizens lived, and, having sat on a Royal Commission concerned with the housing of the working classes, showed sympathy for their

The Coronation of Edward VII, 9th August, 1902. The King's appendicitis had delayed the ceremony by seven weeks and most foreign dignitaries had returned home, but the London crowds were enthusiastic.

then the restless carousel started up again, interspersed by visits to Paris and race meetings at Goodwood and Ascot, the Derby and the Grand National, none of which the Prince was inclined to miss.

Alix, meanwhile, spent rather a lot of her early married life pregnant (the couple were to have five children) and at home with the children she so enjoyed. She swallowed her pride over her husband's deviations from the path of marital fidelity, providing she was not humiliated by them in public (as she felt she was over his long affair with Daisy Brooke – later the Countess of Warwick – in the 1890s), recognized that she could not expect him to be at home from *cinq à sept* (the traditional hours for paying calls), and that he might absent himself from functions and not return home until the small hours. As he grew older the King 'settled down' with a series of sequential 'official' mistresses, who at least did relieve his constant tendency to boredom and assuaged his unpredictable flashes of irritability.

The first was the daughter of the Dean of Jersey, Emily (Lillie) Le Breton, who had married a not terribly satisfactory and not terribly wealthy widower, Edward Langtry. Lillie was heart-stoppingly beautiful and soon *tout Londres* knew it when she was painted first by the artist Frank Miles, and then by John Everett Millais who thought that she was 'quite simply the most beautiful woman on earth' and captured her on canvas holding a species of amaryllis that gave her the epithet 'Jersey Lily'. Edward Burne Jones, Edward Poynter and Whistler painted her too. Photography was a relatively

A record from the Manderston album of a house party held there, signed by the hostess,
Eveline Miller, and her guests.

A leisurely afternoon on the lake: Mr Jonathan rows his aunt and Miss Morrison.

new art, and when likenesses of Mrs Langtry as a 'professional beauty' were printed, they sold like wildfire and the instant celebrity found herself invited to the smartest houses. Oscar Wilde fell in love with her too – in his fashion – admiring her less for her beauty than for her 'charm, her wit, her mind', and was fascinated to meet the *maîtresse en titre* of the Prince of Wales. For on 24 May 1877 Lillie Langtry had met the Prince, who was then thirty-five, at a supper party in London. He was enchanted by her and asked if he might call on her the next afternoon. According to Theo Aronson, this was the accepted courtship by a married man of a married woman since her husband was likely to be out at that time, and, as was the fashion, she would be wearing a tea gown to receive visitors.[9] Tea gowns, as Lady Olliff-Cooper found, were a delight: they were diaphanous, floaty creations, underneath which a lady did not wear a corset. This was not a signal of sexual availability like going naked under a fur coat: women as ultra respectable as the Duchess of York (later Queen Mary) wore a tea gown, as did hundreds of other society ladies, for such apparel represented leisure and tranquillity. It also made illicit sexual congress much easier and quicker with less fumbling.

The Prince's affair was pursued through afternoon calls and country house weekends, and it soon became apparent to hostesses that should the Prince of Wales be invited to dinner or a ball, he would be much more likely to attend if Mrs Langtry was invited too. He showered her with jewels and furs; he arranged for her to be presented at court (which unlocked more social gates including balls at Buckingham Palace), and Princess Alexandra invited her to Marlborough House and Sandringham, and treated her husband's mistress with dignified courtesy and kindness.

The enterprising Mrs Langtry eventually became a successful actress, and though the affair with the Prince of Wales cooled, he remained fond of her, seeing her often and always making a point of attending the first night of her performances, but in 1890 he fell in love again. This time it was with the spirited at innumerable country house parties, in Paris where he shopped with her at the couturiers as she was fitted with spectacular dresses, 'violet velvet', 'gauzy white gowns', 'purple grape-trimmed robes and veils of pearls on white'.[13] He also paid frequent visits to the Brooke home at Easton Lodge near Dunmow in Essex, arriving with a retinue of valets and mounds of luggage, equerries and loaders for his guns.

In December 1893 Daisy Brooke's father-in-law died and she became Countess of Warwick and châtelaine of the magnificent Warwick Castle (where one of her first acts was to design a special suite for visits from her royal lover). Her friend and neighbour, the romantic novelist Elinor Glyn, believed that she had 'never seen [a woman] who was so completely fascinating as Daisy Brooke…hers was the supreme personal; charm which I later described as "It" because it is quite indefinable, and does not depend on beauty or wit, though she possessed both to the highest degree'.[14] But by 1897 the affair between the 'It girl' and the King was effectively over, though again a warm friendship remained for a time, and if Daisy missed anything it was less the King's 'goggle-eyed' devotion which could be 'boresome',[15] and more the status of being royal favourite.

In 1898, the Edward was fifty-six – but still not king. He remained a philanderer and sexual opportunist, but it was in this year that he met the woman who was to become the last of his 'official' mistress, the twenty-nine-year-old Hon Mrs George Keppel. Alice Keppel was sensuous, vivacious and passionate, and spoke with a deep, throaty, mesmerizing voice (she was rarely seen without a long cigarette holder, which epitomized her sophistication). She was also intelligent, articulate, informed, kind, tolerant and tactful and someone once compared her to a Christmas tree 'laden with presents for everyone'. She had been married to the third son of the Earl of Albermarle some seven years before she met the King, and though they had married for love, Alice also had wealthy lovers, which she rather needed in London society, she and her husband having very little money of their own. Indeed, her first daughter, Violet, was probably not her husband's child; she grew up to be a novelist and lover of Vita Sackville-West, the doyenne of Sissinghurst, who so captured the period in her novel, *The Edwardians* in which the character Romola Cheyne is based on Mrs Keppel. Mrs Keppel was the great-grandmother of another royal mistress, Camilla Parker-Bowles.

As befits a royal mistress, the Keppels moved from their house in Knightsbridge to a grander establishment in Portman Square. But it was not very grand because the Keppels were not very rich, and one of the indices by which this could be judged was the ratio of servants they kept. The really wealthy would employ eight or even more indoor servants for each member of the family: the wealthy employed four and the Keppels had two.

In 1901 Queen Victoria died and now Mrs Keppel was the *King's* mistress, '*la favorita*' as she was known, and a leading participant in the lavish hospitality that now transformed the royal round with splendid parties, balls and levées. She stayed with him in the South of France, he called on her frequently at home arriving in a green brougham, played with her two small daughters who curtsied to the portly monarch, sat on his knee and addressed him as 'kingy'. Nancy Astor shrewdly assessed the importance of Alice Keppel: 'She is the medium through which one approaches the King. They say she absolutely rules him. She reigns supreme and is treated with all the dignity of a Pompadour.'[16] But though the liaison was fully accepted by the King's 'fast set'– indeed, the multi-millionaire Sir Ernest Cassel was a great friend, adviser and benefactor of both – the alternative royal couple were not welcome in all the great houses in the land. Lord Salisbury refused to entertain Mrs Keppel at Hatfield, as did the Catholic Duke of Norfolk at Arundel, and the Duke of Portland at Welbeck,[17] but the less traditionally minded landed classes, and above all the *nouveaux riches*, passionately desired the King to grace their house parties. They wanted him to enjoy himself, and if that meant inviting his mistress too, that accorded very well with their understanding of the new spirit of Edwardian society. And on the day of the King's coronation (postponed because of His Majesty's attack of appendicitis) on 9 August 1902, a pew in Westminster Abbey, irreverently referred to as 'the King's loose box', contained a selection of Edward's current and ex-loves including the actress Sarah Bernhardt, Mrs Ronnie Greville and, of course, Mrs Keppel; the Countess of Warwick was there in her own right as a peeress. Meanwhile, splendid in a dress of golden Indian gauze embroidered with diamonds and pearls with an embroidered, ermine-lined train, sat his queen, Alexandra, in a throne adjacent to his.

At the revamped Buckingham Palace life followed a similar pattern to that at Marlborough House, though with far more official entertaining, state business and foreign visits. Edward was not an intellectual; he did not read books, his penchant for music was more Gilbert and Sullivan than Bach, his visual taste was untutored bordering on the tacky, his conversation was hardly discursive and he did not pore over his official boxes in the way that both his parents had, and he was less than assiduous in mastering the intricacies of governance. But the new king had a sharper political sense than his mother and 'more usage of the modern world', so Sir Charles Dilke decided, while Sir Edward Grey, the Foreign Secretary, commended the new King for his rare combination of 'bonhomie and dignity'.

'O for the wings of a dove' ... Lady Olliff-Cooper and Master Guy in harmony.

On his accession Parliament had increased the King's annual income of £100,000 per year to £450,000, which with the £60,000 a year he received from the Duchy of Lancaster totalled over half a million pounds. But it was not enough. The King had expensive tastes and some exceedingly wealthy friends, who were akin to 'a race of gods and goddesses descended from Olympus upon England [living] on a golden cloud, spending their riches as indolently and naturally as the leaves grown green'.[18] His appetites were prodigious, his capricious generosity legendary.

In the Edwardian era, London was the financial capital of the world: between 1890 and 1914 the City controlled almost half the international flow of capital, and in the era when capitalism was moving from its primary stage of production to the secondary one of finance, an axis operated between London, Paris, New York, Johannesburg and Frankfurt. London was an increasingly cosmopolitan city and millionaire

The historian Anthony Allfrey suggests that Sir Ernest Cassel was:

> the last of the new breed of financiers mainly of Jewish and mostly of German origin, who
> played such a pre-eminent part in English social, political and economic life of the Edwardian
> age, a position they owed to the unprejudiced, if not disinterested, patronage of King Edward.
> None contributed more to the flow of capital and diffusion of trade at a time when the industrial
> strength of Great Britain was ebbing: few contributed as much to the giddy social whirl or to the
> delectation of their Prince and King. Without them the short-lived, exotic, agitated and often
> anxious Edwardian era would never have achieved its full flavour and texture.[25]

At the King's insistent request, Mrs Keppel was admitted to his bedroom as he lay dying of bronchitis
and a series of heart attacks, and to their discomfort the King insisted that she and the Queen should
kiss and make their peace before he lapsed into a coma and died at a quarter to midnight on 6 May
1910, aged sixty-eight. Mrs Keppel had to be led away in hysterics, repeating as she went, 'I never did
any harm, there was nothing between us. What is to become of me?' as Princess Victoria, the King's
youngest child, tried to calm her. But she recovered and, invited to the funeral, went, dressed from
head to toe in what might have been construed as 'widow's weeds'. The Queen, though 'unable to
cry…was in a terrible state of despair' and insisted 'he was the whole of my life, and now he is dead,
nothing matters' while his oldest son, soon to be proclaimed King George V, wrote in his diary: 'I
have lost my best friend and the best of fathers. I never had a [cross] word with him in my life. I am
heartbroken and overwhelmed with grief.'

There were the conventional tributes in parliament and the press, and the nation, to whom the
King's death had come as a surprise, wondered what life would be like under the new, almost
unknown George V who, it was rumoured, was a very different man from his father.

But if pieties were to be expected, there were many more for whom Edward's lifestyle did not
serve as a template: it was not only the poor, the working classes or the middle classes who neither
could, nor in many cases had any desire to, emulate the royal round of pleasure. There were landed
establishment figures who considered the King to be a vulgar disgrace, acting like a *parvenu* in a
society of which he was at the summit and supposed to be the supreme exemplar, and there were the
intellectuals and the administrators for whom Edward VII was a disastrous waste of regal space in an
age when so much needed address and redress. The novelist of subtle social observation, Henry James,
disapproved of him as an 'arch vulgarian, Edward the Caresser'. The poet Wilfrid Scawen Blunt
wrote perceptively in his diary:

> Everyone has gone into black for the King's death, and some enthusiasts talk about going into
> mourning for a year. It is all very absurd considering what the poor King was, but the papers
> are crammed with his praises as if he had been a saint of God. All the week since his death has
> been one of storms and tempests attributed to a comet so diminutive that nobody has seen it yet,
> and last night one of the great beech trees was thrown down in the park. I saw it lying uprooted
> on my way to the station this morning, a symbol of the dead King, quite rotten at the root, but
> one half of it clothed with its spring green.[26]

And within two years of the King's death, the authoritative *Dictionary of National Biography* included
an entry written by the editor, a Tudor historian, Sir Sidney Lee, which spoke scathingly of the King
as 'no reader of books. He could not keep his mind upon them…he lacked the intellectual equipment
of a thinker, and showed on occasion an unwillingness to exert mental power'. It charged that the

From the Manderston stable: Sir James Miller owned two Derby winners, Sainfoin (1890) and Rock Sand (1903).

King had had 'no personal control of diplomacy' and had 'no conception of any readjustment of the balance of European power' and even for that diplomatic masterstroke commonly attributed to him, the *entente cordiale*, with France 'no direct responsibility for its initiation or conclusion belonged to him'. Reading the entry, the Labour leader, Keir Hardie, professed to feel duped. 'Now we know that whilst he was supposed to be labouring abroad for the country's good, he was simply enjoying himself as a very amiable, pleasure-loving man of the world, who was bored with politics and had not the capacity to understand foreign relationships.'[27]

Edwardian views of Edward thus mirror the complexities and tensions of his eponymous era. This was at a time when industrial strife was mounting, when it was becoming increasingly obvious that Irish nationalism was unanswerable within the existing frame of nineteenth-century political solutions, when Parliament's hereditary chamber was about to lose some of its power, and when the international situation was growing ever more threatening. Legislation introduced by the Liberal government, the growth of the Labour vote, and the stuttering, uneven advance of trade union power were evidence that the pendulum which had been inexorably swinging since the 1880s was taking an ever wider arc into the lives of the British people. The state was gradually assuming more systematic responsibility for its citizens, and private fiefdoms of money, property and privilege would not be left untouched in this halting progress towards a measure of the redistribution of resources – and thus inroads into a person's freedom to spend entirely as they would what they had or could acquire.

'Yes, sir,' said Kenny, adding, under his breath, 'but not a 20 guinea bet.' Which, considering that Kenny's annual salary was in the region of £12 a year, was hardly surprising.

But those who won – and lost – money on the racecourse usually found other ways to do so too. Indeed, it was while staying at a country house party near Doncaster for the St Leger races that the then Prince of Wales was involved in a serious scandal that threw a very adverse light on the gambling and drinking set that revolved around his royal person. A visitor to Sandringham in 1890 had found it 'a shocking affair for the Royal Family to play an illegal game every night. They have a real table, and rakes, and everything, like rooms at Monte Carlo'.[38] The Prince, who had once enjoyed dancing but had grown too portly to trip the light fantastic in comfort, relieved the inevitable boredom of the country house circuit, and the same people in different combinations and settings, with a little indoor sport as well as shooting, racing and hunting. He always carried a set of baccarat counters that had been given to him by his friend, Reuben Sassoon. They were in denominations varying from five shillings to ten pounds and were engraved with the Prince of Wales's feathers.[39] They were also illegal currency.

During the St Leger race week in September, the Prince usually stayed with his friend Christopher Sykes, 'the great Xtopher' as he was known, but Sykes was one of those for whom the carousel of extravagant entertaining had brought near bankruptcy, and he was no longer in the position to host a St Leger house party at his home, Brantingham Thorpe, near Doncaster. So in 1890 this was held by the ship owner Arthur Wilson, who Edward did not know well, at his home, Tranby Croft. That first evening, another guest, Lieutenant Colonel Sir William Gordon-Cumming of the Scots Guards, was observed cheating at baccarat by upping or reducing his stakes after he had managed to covertly look at his cards – a sleight-of-hand the French called *la pousette*. Sir William was kept under close surveillance the next night and was seen to cheat on a number of occasions, winning £225 over two evenings, usually from the Prince of Wales, who was the banker. When confronted with his crime, the redress traditional among 'gentlemen' was agreed: those present swore 'to preserve silence' on the matter in exchange for a solemn promise from Sir William that 'I will undertake never to play cards as long as I live'. This was intended to protect the reputation of the Prince of Wales, who kept a copy of the agreement signed by all those present and left Tranby Croft sharpish next morning.

But too many people knew – it was soon common gossip among the smart set (the Countess of Warwick – Daisy Brooke – earned her nickname 'Babbling Brooke' for her part in spreading the news) and Gordon-Cumming announced his intention to sue five of his accusers for the slur on his character. When the case came to court, the country would know that the heir apparent to the throne was a gambler and a participant in illegal games. In the event, the jury found against Sir William, who was dismissed from the Army, blackballed by his clubs and effectively expelled from society. 'The light which it has thrown on [his habits]…alarms and shocks the people,' wrote Victoria of her errant son, but he did not see it quite like that and declined her suggestion that he should send a missive to the Archbishop of Canterbury condemning gambling as a social evil. In his view, gambling was what took place between consenting adults who could well afford it. Finally, he decided to take up bridge in place of baccarat (and one of the many attractions of Mrs Keppel was to be that she played a good hand of bridge, though she once confessed ingenuously that she could 'not tell a King from a Knave' when Edward challenged her at the card table).

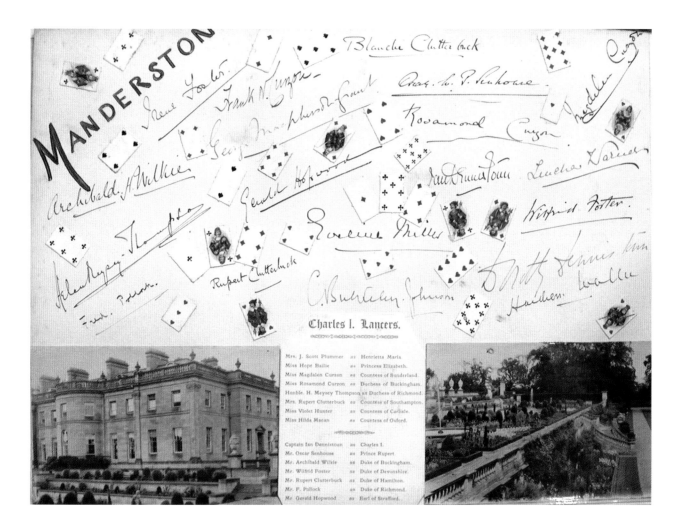

The record of a popular Edwardian evening at cards at Manderston.

After dinner, the Olliff-Coopers would sometimes play games. Particularly if they had company, there was bridge and whist and parlour games; the one they most enjoyed was 'the feather' (which could also be played with tissue paper). 'The players must draw their chairs in a circle as closely together as possible. One of the party begins the game by throwing the feather into the air as high as possible…the object of the game is to keep it from touching anyone, as the player whom it touches must pay a forfeit... it is impossible to imagine the excitement that can be produced by each player preventing the feather from lighting on him [by means of blowing and swotting]. The game must be heartily played to be fully appreciated.'[40] But that night the Olliff-Coopers recalled the Tranby Croft affair as they played baccarat in the chinoiserie-furnished card room by the fire, with the red-lacquered grandfather clock ticking, a chalk line carefully delineating the space so that no repeat of the affair was likely at *their* table. The stakes were high, and again Sir John was lucky as he scooped his winnings into a pile.

Dinner cleared, the servants were in the servants' hall downstairs playing cards too. Sometimes they played dominoes or cribbage, or games such as Old Maid or Loo, but that night their game was poker, a recent import from the United States. The excitement was raucous but the stakes were paltry.

CHAPTER ELEVEN

Imperial Might

A large cloth map of the world, its surface veined with a network of almost imperceptible cracks, hung on the wall of the Edwardian Country House alongside a blackboard, the mounted stuffed head of a startled rabbit, a likeness of the new King, George V, botanical drawings and multiplication tables, while on the desk and windowsills jostled a collection of birds' eggs, a disintegrating nest, some pressed leaves, a fossil, a writing slate and exercise books, reading primers, steel-nibbed pens, lead pencils and wax crayons – all the appurtenances of an early-twentieth-century child's education. It was the domain of Mr Raj Singh, who had been engaged by Sir John to tutor his ten-year-old son, Guy, while the family was living the Edwardian experiment.

Pointing at the map with a ruler, Mr Singh, a teacher in London in the twenty-first century, showed his pupil the island of Fiji where he had been born, and India where his family came from. 'When George V came to the throne, the British Empire had almost reached its apogee,' he explained. 'You can see, all these countries that are coloured pink are British possessions and they spread right round the globe, large parts of Africa, Australia, New Zealand, Canada, India. It was said that the sun never set on the British Empire.'

In January 1911 the newly crowned King and his wife, Queen Mary, set off for India. It was the only visit made to the subcontinent by a reigning King Emperor and it was commemorated 'by a durbar [assembly] of unprecedented scale and extravagance'.[1] The highlight of the Delhi durbar came when the King and Queen, wearing jewel-encrusted crowns of freshly minted imperial gold and ermine-lined robes of purple, sitting on golden thrones in a crimson marquee, received a long procession of Indian princes who came to pay homage to their imperial majesties. They were, wrote the correspondent for *The Times,* 'remote but beneficent, raised far above the multitude [it was estimated that there was a crowd of 100,000 spectators], but visible to all'.[2] After the ceremonials, the King went hunting in Nepal over the New Year, bagging twenty-four tigers and a bear, while eighteen rhinoceroses were also shot by the hunting party.

It was not the first time that George V had visited India: in October 1905, the then Prince and Princess of Wales had left England in the battleship *Renown* for a four-and-a-half-month-long visit of the subcontinent that took them from Bombay to Delhi, to Calcutta, Mysore, Hyderabad and Jaipur. It was an exhausting and exhilarating 9,000-mile tour by train, car and carriage of the 'jewel in the crown' of Britain's Empire. On their arrival in Bombay they were welcomed by Lord Curzon, who had been Viceroy for seven years, but three months earlier had been forced to resign in a bitter row with the British government over the military administration of the subcontinent. George Nathaniel Curzon was the brother of Eveline, who married Sir James Miller, the rebuilder of Manderston, home to the Edwardian Country House experiment. As Manderston owed a profound architectural debt to the Curzon family seat, Kedleston Hall in Derbyshire, so was the Government House in Calcutta modelled on Kedleston.

Though he no longer occupied the top job, in recognition of his meticulous planning of the royal visit, Curzon was grudgingly permitted to welcome the royal couple on their arrival in Bombay, before handing over to his successor, the Earl of Minto, a week later. It was a painful humiliation for the 'very superior person' who was the embodiment of ceremonial pageantry. In

January 1903 Curzon had orchestrated a durbar to proclaim the accession of George's father, Edward VII, to his Indian subjects – a quarter of a billion of them. It was to be 'the biggest show that India will ever have had'. In the early Victorian period the British had been anxious to 'contrast their honest, plain black frock coats with the pretentious glitter of the oriental monarchs they controlled'.[3] But following the Indian mutiny of 1857–9 against the rule of the British Governor General, Lord Dalhousie, its brutal suppression and the assumption by the Crown of responsibility for the governance of India (which had previously rested with the East India Company), British policy in India had changed: its intention now was to present the colonial rulers as the legitimate successors to the deposed Mughal Emperors. Far from being 'reformed', the traditional Brahmanic hierarchies of caste (which had become more extensive and rigid during the period of control by the East India Company) were to be respected as 'capable of integrating into a single hierarchy all [the Empire's] subjects, Indian and British alike' so that social status equated with official position in British India. The model, according to the historian David Cannadine, was that of British metropolitan society in which local government depended on the aristocracy and local gentry 'so their chosen partners in South Asia were the "natural leaders": large landowners, men of "property and rank", of "power and importance", "who exercised great influence" in rural society' – rather like 'the position once occupied by the English Squire'[4]. This in theory meant that the imperial enterprise in India could be administered from Britain in 'collaboration' with 'dependable allies' doing the work of the imperialists much as local government at home implemented the policies of parliament. The third of India not governed directly by the British (first from Calcutta and later Delhi) was divided into some 500 or 600 princely states – 'personal fiefdoms ruled over by rajas and mahrajas, nawabs and nizams', who were no longer to be regarded as strange and reviled but welcomed as a sort of 'feudal social order' that would enable the British to rule that section of India indirectly in a way that they understood.

Queen Mary and King George V at the Delhi durbar in 1911.

Mr Raj Singh, the tutor, and Sir John take a walk.

very icy towards me. I think he resents the fact that I am treated like one of the family, whereas to him, I am just another servant of the family.

'It makes me empathize and sympathize with tutors and governesses throughout history, men and women who were highly intelligent, often well qualified. They were respected to a certain extent, but many doors were closed to them. And in the end they were always employees no matter how well they were treated.

'It is particularly poignant for me because I come from the Fiji Islands and my parents both came from India, though we have lived for four generations in Fiji, and because Fiji was a British colony it is still at least two decades behind Britain. This Edwardian country house reminds me of my childhood. We all had this goal of trying to be terribly English. We lived in an Edwardian way really with strict etiquette and a code of manners and dress, and always taking afternoon tea and things like that, and when I first came to England it was quite a culture shock for me. So coming here to the Edwardian Country House is like coming home because the etiquette and sense of propriety are as they were in my childhood. I think that living in the Edwardian Country House has brought back the colonial experience very vividly to me. We lived in a country controlled by an outside power, the sense of status and hierarchy was very strong, and we lived by somebody else's rules and regulations, and that is exactly how it was for somebody in my position in Edwardian times. But it does amaze me when I see the system in action why Indian people with their thousands of years of culture could somehow have decided to forsake this and try to emulate Edwardian British culture which was so stifling that it smothered freedom and creativity and expressiveness. Why did they want to be like their colonial masters? What was so attractive about something that put them down and debased their culture and made it seem inferior to western ways? I just don't understand.'

Mr Raj Singh was also troubled by the notion that at the time of the Raj an Indian tutor could have been something of a 'trophy' for an English family, an exotic exhibit of 'otherness' in the way that Queen Victoria had had her Munshi (teacher), Abdul Karim from Agra, who had become her trusted and indulged companion/servant, much resented by other members of the royal household. There had not been much encouragement from the British for Indian aspirations: in 1909 only 65 of the 1,244 members of the Indian Civil Service were non-British.[14] There was a small Indian community in Britain by the start of the Edwardian period. Since at least the eighteenth century, the British had imported Indian servants and ayahs (nannies for the children) on their return to the homeland, and a number of lascars (sailors) who were employed on ships that sailed between Britain and India settled in Britain – despite laws that forbade this. Their life could be very hard and little protection or help was offered to them in many cases. In the early years of the twentieth century, the number of Indians coming to Britain to study – mainly law and medicine and for entry to the Indian Civil Service – rose from around 300 in 1900 to roughly 1,750 in 1913.[15] In 1892 the first Indian, Dadabhai Naoroji, was elected to Parliament as a Liberal, and in 1895 Manchererjee Bhownagree was returned as Conservative Member for Bethnal Green.[16]

Duleep Singh, the son of the founder of the Sikh nation, had been forced to renounce his claims as Maharajah of the Punjab (and hand over the famous Koh-i- Noor diamond as a 'gift' to Queen Victoria) when it was annexed by the British in 1849. He subsequently settled in Britain on a stipend. In 1863 Duleep Singh purchased Elveden Hall on the Norfolk/Suffolk borders and soon was part of the Prince of Wales's shooting set, but his extravagant lifestyle, and feeling of betrayal by the British, led him to renounce his Christian faith and set off back to India. He did not get there but died in Paris in 1893. His body was brought back to Elveden Hall (which had been purchased by the Earl of Iveagh) for burial.

Aware that Mr Raj Singh too felt lonely and misunderstood at times, Sir John suggested an occasion that would celebrate aspects of his culture and tell others in the Edwardian Country House more about India both today and under British rule at the start of the twentieth century. He decided to step out of the frame of what would have been likely in an Edwardian Country House in order to hold what he called a Raj supper at Manderston. Mr Singh was enthusiastic about the idea and volunteered to invite some friends of his who would perform traditional Hindu dances for the occasion. Meanwhile the Olliff-Coopers drew up a list of distinguished guests who had close connections with the subcontinent and views both on Empire and issues of race and culture in contemporary Britain.

Mr Edgar serves Mr Raj Singh at dinner.

Evening bag

The narrow silhouette of Edwardian clothes made a little bag an essential fashion accessory for ladies. Called 'Dorothy' bags and often used to carry dancing slippers, these drawstring reticules were very similar to many of today's fashionable evening bags and are simple to make.

The material most often used in the Edwardian era would have been velvet or satin, usually lined in silk and decorated with a tassel, silk embroidery, beadwork or lace as here.

To make a similar bag, you will need a piece of firm fabric such as cotton, velvet, taffeta or satin, and silk, polyester or linen with fine cotton for the lining.

Materials

Two squares of fabric, about 28cm x 28cm (11in x 11in), for the bag and the same amount for the lining
120cm (48in) narrow (0.5cm/¼in diameter) silk cord, cut into two equal lengths for the handles, plus 30cm (12in) for the bottom of the bag
A decorative silk tassel in a matching or toning colour
Decorative trim, of silver, gold or lace, or motifs or small beads (optional)

Method

Lay each square of fabric on its lining, outer faces together. If you are using a decorative trim (as in the illustration), apply this to the right side of the outer fabric before joining it to the lining. (The trim lies between the top and bottom drawstring casings – see below.) Alternatively, beads or a motif can be sewn on to the outside of the finished bag.

Sew the lining and outer fabric together along the top and bottom edges. Turn right side out and press lightly. Now run a line of stitches along the bottom of each square, 1cm (½in) from the edge. This will form the casing for the bottom cord. Then run three parallel lines of stitches along the top of each square, 3cm (1in), 4cm (1½in) and 5cm (2in) from the edge. These will form the casings for the two drawstring handles.

With right sides facing, sew the side seams together, between the bottom and the top rows of stitching.

Thread the 30cm (12in) of silk cord through the bottom casing (using a safety pin); pull tightly and knot firmly. Cut the ends off to 3cm (just over 1in).

Turn the bag right side out. Attach the silk tassel to the centre bottom of the bag.

Insert one of the 60cm (24in) lengths of silk cord in one end of the upper casing at the top of the bag; thread it through to the opposite end, then back through the casing on the other half of the bag. You should now have two ends of cord on one side of the bag. Knot them together firmly about 2cm (just under 1in) from their ends. Repeat this procedure in the lower casing, starting at the other side of the bag. Pull the two sets of knotted cord handles together to close the bag.

The Olliff-Coopers and their guests watch the Empire Day pageant.

fruitful…'[19] A pamphlet issued by the Empire Day League in 1912 had been found in the Edwardian Country House, and it proved the inspiration for pageant to be staged during the Empire Ball, the most glittering event of the Edwardian Country House experience.

The occasion was to be a fancy dress ball on the theme of Empire: there were plenty of precedents. In 1842 Queen Victoria and Prince Albert had thrown a Plantagenet Ball at which Victoria was dressed as Queen Philippa wearing a diamond stomacher (bodice) estimated to be worth £60,000, while Albert masqueraded as Edward III. Encouraged by the success of this venture, the royal couple held a royal *Bal Costume* in 1845 to which guests were required to wear costumes that would have been worn in the decade from 1740 to 1750. In 1874 the artist Sir Frederick Leighton designed a magnificent ball to be held at the home of the future Edward VII, Marlborough House, at which the Princess of Wales, dressed as a grand Venetian lady, led a quadrille with 'Harty Tarty', the Marquis of Hartington. And then, of course, in 1895 there was the Countess of Warwick's ball where the theme was the reigns of Louis XV and XVI, and which led, indirectly, to her conversion to socialism. But perhaps the most famous fancy dress ball of all was the one held by the Duchess of Devonshire to celebrate Queen Victoria's Diamond Jubilee in 1897.

This event was held at Devonshire House, one of the grandest houses in London, which faced on to Piccadilly and looked out over Green Park, to which the guests were instructed to wear any 'allegorical or historical costume before 1815'. This included the servants, who were dressed in Egyptian or Elizabethan outfits hired from theatrical costumiers.[20] The Duchess, a portly woman, was dressed by Worth as Zenobia, Queen of Palmyra, while the Duke paraded as the Holy Roman Emperor, Charles V, as painted by Titian. The then Prince of Wales was togged up as the Grand Master of the Knights Hospitallers of St John of Jerusalem and Chevalier of Malta, which involved an Elizabethan-style costume consisting of a black doublet and hose, a large, feather-plumed hat and silver-spurred boots, while his Princess came positively dripping with pearls as the daughter of Henry II of France and Catherine de Medici, Marguerite de Valois, who married her cousin, Henry of Navarre in 1572. Mrs Keppel, very soon to be *la favorita* of the King, looked customarily beautiful as Madame de Polignac.

Among the rest of the guests could be found almost every historical character of note: some played tribute to their ancestors: the Duke of Somerset reprised his forebear Edward Seymour, 1st Duke and Lord Protector of England in the reign of his nephew Edward VI, while his duchess portrayed the first Duke's sister, Jane Seymour, the third of Henry VIII's six wives. Others rose above themselves: Lady Tweedmouth led a procession as Elizabeth I to her husband's Earl of Leicester; Lady Randolph Churchill elected to be Theodora, wife of the Roman Emperor, Justinian; Countess de Grey dressed as Cleopatra; the Countess of Warwick seemed strangely retrograde as Marie Antoinette (the costume she had worn at her own ball two years earlier); while Viscountess Raincliffe was presumptuous as Catherine the Great, Empress of Russia. Others took classical or metaphysical references: Sibyl, Countess of Westmorland went as Hebe, goddess of youth and culture, as portrayed by Sir Joshua Reynolds (and found the huge stuffed eagle perched on her shoulder something of an inhibition when the dancing started); Lord and Lady Rodney dressed as King Arthur and Queen Guinevere; the Hon. Mrs Reginald Talbot was a Valkyrie; the Countess of Mar and Kellie represented Dante's Beatrice; Lady Doreen Long wore a costume embroidered with the moon and stars as Urania, goddess of astronomy. Others were more modest, representing 'Venetian gentlemen', a 'courtier at the French Court' or 'two Highland gentlemen, 1745', while others were frankly wacky: Margot Asquith came as an oriental snake charmer replete with papier mâché snakes (while her husband, the future Prime Minister H. H. Asquith – who hadn't much wanted to go anyway and didn't stay long – thought it might be held against him if he appeared as Oliver Cromwell, so put on the kit of an ordinary Roundhead soldier); and George Cornwallis-West blacked up as his idea of a slave and donned 'garments like multi-coloured bed quilts'[21] to appear in the retinue of his sister Daisy, Princess of Pless, rather a favourite of Edward VII's, who went as the Queen of Sheba.

The sister-in-law of Lady Miller of Manderston, Mary Curzon (née Leiter, the American heiress to the Marshall Fields Chicago department store fortune), was invited to the Devonshire House ball and went dressed as Valentina Visconti of Milan, though the Curzons were still on their way back from India when the great Manderston ball was held in November 1905. The occasion was the completion of the

Miss Anson enthroned as Britannia, the central figure of the Empire Ball pageant.

Master Guy in the role of Britannia's 'first minister'.

'All those, madam, who have given their lives by noble deeds to found thy mighty Empire, these two thousand years,' replied Guy, as a way of introducing the children who were mainly friends of his from the school he was attending in Berwick. These young actors represented 'ancient Britons', 'King Alfred', 'the sea-dog, Sir Francis Drake', 'the great explorers of the North-West passage', and a roll-call of other British 'heroes' culminating in 'thy warriors who guard thy menaced throne and lead thy men to victory', 'thy mighty sailors, who defend thy shores and keep off all who, through jealousy and world-lust, would ravage thy fair island home'. And finally 'These, madam, are thy aeroplanes, whose wings mount the clouds, making thee supreme in air, as on sea,'[24] as small boys zoomed on to the stage each in a cardboard cockpit with flapping cardboard aircraft wings. The children had been kitted out by Miss Morrison 'with Erika helping out', as Master Guy explained, 'going treadle, treadle, treadle, sew, sew, sew until late into the night for three weeks.'

'Britannia' rose and thanked 'you all, troops and Ministers. Our past, and present and future are secure. Our past granite; our present steel; and our future' – she paused – 'what you make it. With duty, love, and honour as our guide, our Empire still shall hold; and like summer roses perfume the world with freedom's gladsome fragrance. Be bold, be brave, do right! And as long as ye do this, I, Britannia, will proudly be your Queen!' Miss Anson declared with a flourish. As the finale, the stage led a rousing chorus of 'Rule Britannia', which most of the guests joined in singing enthusiastically. But at least one did not.

'I could never sing "Rule Britannia, Britons never, never shall be slaves" because implicit is that other people can be slaves,' explained the broadcaster and writer Darcus Howe. Darcus, who came to Britain from Trinidad in 1961, was intrigued to find out how the essence of Englishness in the first years of the old century was being interpreted in the Edwardian country house. Impressive in the costume of a naval commander in recognition of the Empire's long role in fighting for British causes (or the fact that it was naval power that overthrew British rule in the West Indies), he came to Manderston for the Empire Ball. 'I was interested to see how the young people in the house who came here as servants had adjusted to the mores of a time 100 years ago, and how the middle-aged master of the house and his wife from a typical middle-class English life adjusted to this much more privileged and grander life style,' he explained.

Like Mr Raj Singh, Darcus had been educated in English ways, in his case at his school in Trinidad. 'I enjoyed my education tremendously, but I was in constant revolt against the Edwardian snobbery and prejudices that were still prevalent in the colonial education system. As far as I am concerned, the Empire was a battleground, but when you fight your enemy he becomes part of you, you become like him in many ways because you can't help but admire the way he dresses, his military strategy, his culture even. Those who founded the Empire tried to establish white supremacy, but they never fully succeeded and I think that the impact of the imperial tenancy on Africa, India, the Caribbean, has been exaggerated, it really did not have a lasting cultural impact. At my school, for example, there was no real flag-waving or singing "Rule Britannia" or anything like that, and that was because a lot of the English people who taught there had fought in the Second World War, and they had fought shoulder to shoulder alongside black men, so they couldn't believe in that old idea of imperial superiority any more, and in a way they were subverting it from within. And looking back, I don't think that the Empire was built in order to civilize uncivilized people. In my view it was about the pursuit of wealth. Undoubtedly a number of imperialists *did* transform whole areas of the globe, but now that's over. We are in a post-colonial period, and out of that conflict has come a two-way process. It isn't just that there is a lot of Britain in India, Africa, the Caribbean, but there's also a lot of Africa and India and the Caribbean here in Britain today.

'Sir John is seriously circumscribed by the times he's living in. And he's not an aristocrat any more than the original owner of this house was. So it's not aristocratic licence in his case, it's the assumption of autocracy. It's 1912 and in only two years the most terrible war is going to break out, but already things have changed. We are on the cusp of real change. The rise of working-class consciousness seems to be threatening the old order, and it isn't any longer possible to imagine that the "servant problem" will go away. In fact it will get more acute. And so Sir John may well decide to treat his servants with greater generosity. When those in power are forced by changed circumstances to make concessions, they tend to portray it as generosity. But it isn't. It's that they are losing their power. And they know they are.'

Marie Antoinette and Nelson (a.k.a. Sir John and Lady Olliff-Cooper) dancing at the Empire Ball.

Men of the 1st Nava

CHAPTER TWELVE

Winners
and Losers

Brigade at Manderston

'The servants' hall is a little world of its own,' reckoned Samuel and Sarah Adams in their book of guidance, *The Complete Servant*, 'in which the passions, tempers, vices and virtues are brought into play.'[1] It was in this 'little world of its own' that the final drama of the Edwardian Country House was to be played out.

The servants' hall had proved to be the centre of their daily lives for those who worked below stairs. There were a couple of battered old sofas that had certainly seen better days standing at right angles to the fireplace, and it was into these that the servants would gratefully sink to snatch a moment of relaxation between chores. At such times they might skim a newspaper or magazine, or talk, or just close their eyes for a blessed moment's snooze. In the evening when they had finished work, they would often all gather in the servants' hall to have a game of cards, play dominoes or to read. One of the pleasures of the Edwardian experience, Antonia reckoned, had been the nights when the lower servants had huddled round the fire to read aloud John Bunyan's *Pilgrim's Progress*, taking it in turns to read a chapter a night ('Come with me, Neighbour, there are such things to be had which I spoke of, and many more Glories beside. If you believe me not, read here in this Book…'). 'I couldn't believe it. You'd never find me doing something like that at home. I'd be watching television, but here it was really nice to all gather round together to read a book like that. It almost made me nostalgic for the Edwardian way of life. *Almost*,' she qualified.

There was an upright, almost-in-tune piano in the corner and both Rob and Erika, the third housemaid, were accomplished pianists and would sometimes sit at the keyboard in the evening picking out tunes – Rob even managed Beethoven's 'Moonlight Sonata', which impressed everyone. Most of the servants enjoyed music. Becky had a fine soprano singing voice – her clear, high rendition of 'Pié Jesu' was inclined to bring a tear to most eyes – and Jess loved to dance. One night the servants had had a ceilidh in their hall with Scottish fiddle players. Everyone agreed that it had been a splendid evening with plenty of opportunity for energetic reels, fairly inauthentic 'Scottish' cries, and plenty of noisy clapping in time with the music. It had been refreshing to see the 'upper ten' join in with gusto – Miss Morrison was soon breathless with all the charging across the room, arms folded, and Mrs Davies was puffing a bit too, while the butler, Mr Edgar, smiled benignly as watched what he liked to consider as his 'family' having a good time. All, that is, except M. Dubiard who, disenchanted with the demands of the Edwardian Country House, sat alone in the kitchen plucking a grey partridge and reflecting on the solitary nature of life – and death.

But the servants' hall was not always a warm and friendly place. It could be much as the Adamses had described, a battle ground resulting in misunderstandings, hurt feelings and wounded pride, as thirteen people who had never met before, and really did not have much in common (as Charlie pointed out), lived in very close proximity to each other as they struggled to make sense of the Edwardian experience.

It could also be a confusing place. On the one hand, it had all the elements of a family in the warmth and sympathy that each often expressed for the others. There had been a natural pairing: Becky and Jess worked as a team cleaning the house and almost instantly became very good friends, delighting in how much they shared in their attitudes towards life, and Jess was always interested to hear about Becky's grandmother's experiences in service, and how the first housemaid regarded her time in the Edwardian Country House as a form of homage to her much-loved relation's hard life. Mrs Davies and Miss Morrison soon found that they too had a natural affinity, as upper servants inclined to feel that the younger generation really didn't know the meaning of hard work, though Mrs Davies was always very protective of 'her girls', recognizing how onerous their duties were, and regarded herself as a mother figure and confidante to them. Rob and Charlie were a duo too, sharing a bedroom as well as their footmen's duties, though this could lead to friction at times. And then there were Ellen and Kenny whose burgeoning romance made them a couple, snatching moments alone together whenever they could, but still joining in the general life of the below stairs community.

The situation had all the tensions of family life too, and could erupt into angry accusations, flare-ups, tears and sulks before peace was restored, since, just like a family, they were all in it together for the duration.

But the servants' hall also presented a social microcosm far removed from this family model. It was here that the rigid distinctions of status were enforced with a hierarchy that sharply divided upper and lower servants, with further calibrations woven through the two categories. At first the lower servants had found it hard to comprehend the notion of instant obedience ('discipline, discipline, discipline' was Mr Edgar's mantra), of not speaking until you were spoken to, of the insistence on correct address – 'Sir' for the butler, always *Mrs* Davies, *Miss* Morrison, *Monsieur* Dubiard – and had been bemused and not a little insulted by the strict emphasis on precedence at all times, filing into prayers, sitting in order of rank at all meals, walking the two or three miles to church every Sunday and the same number back whatever the weather, while the upper servants rode in a trap. But gradually the lower servants had come, if not to accept, then to be resigned to the fact that that was how things were, and would be so long as they lived in their Edwardian personas.

M. Dubiard relaxes in the servants' hall by picking out tunes on the battered piano.

Kenny's theory was characteristically to the point. 'It goes right through the ranks in Edwardian society: you've got the rich people upstairs who dump on the footmen, and then the footman dumps on whoever is below him, which happens to be the hall boy in my case. And I know that I should be working hard and showing respect to try to earn promotion to third footman or something, but basically I'd rather be at the bottom of the pile than doing with all these people who are always pulling rank, because they consider themselves to be a notch above the person below them.' As one of the footmen, Rob could see how Kenny had constructed his paradigm, but surveying the dynamics of the hierarchy from *his*

Letters home. Mrs Davies recounts her experiences in the Edwardian Country House.

place on the ladder enabled him to recognize why there was so little solidarity at times among those in the house who might have been thought to have common cause. 'The people at the top don't deal with the people at the bottom. They give their orders to the people half-way down, who then tell the people at the bottom what to do. And that can create animosity between the upper and the lower servants and among the lower servants too.'

On the night of 5 November the entire cosmos of the hierarchy of the Edwardian Country House was created *multum in parvo* right there in the servants' hall. The previous week Sir John had announced at prayers that he had decided that as the Edwardian experiment was coming to an end he would throw a party for the servants. The food would be supplied by caterers, they would be waited on by outside help employed for the occasion, they would eat off the family's china ('the everyday stuff', Mr Edgar interjected hastily), they would be served wine from the family's cellar rather than their usual jugs of beer, and there would be dancing 'exactly the same dances as were danced at the Empire Ball' to the music of a two-piece 'orchestra', and the evening would be rounded off with fireworks and a bonfire. 'I hope that pleases you, thank you and good morning to you all,' the master of the house concluded.

It sounded wonderful. 'I am going to invite some guests,' Mr Edgar announced later at dinner in the servants' hall. 'I am going to invite the family. That's exactly what would have happened,' he added hurriedly, looking around the table at the startled faces of the lower servants staring at him.

Within the limited range of clothes available to them, the servants made an effort for the occasion. 'It's much easier for the boys,' sighed Antonia, who admitted that whatever she did, she did not find that her corset made her feel curvaceous and sexy, but more like 'a frumpy, dowdy, androgynous workhorse that needs a bath'. Nevertheless, like the other maids, she brushed out her hair and found a length of ribbon, and all the servants enjoyed the novelty of sitting at table in their own hall eating food that had been neither cooked nor served by them and talking freely to each other without waiting to be asked. 'To Edwardiana,' Mr Edgar proposed, and they all raised their glasses and repeated enthusiastically: 'To Edwardiana.'

'Sir John and Lady Olliff-Cooper,' announced Mr Edgar a few minutes later, conducting the upstairs family to their own basement to join in the servants' ball. As would have been expected, Sir John led the dancing with the housekeeper, and the butler partnered Lady Olliff-Cooper, while Mr Jonathan asked the first housemaid if she would care to dance and Master Guy made a beeline for the second housemaid, his companion in fire-making. The upper servants seemed delighted to entertain their employers and took them on a tour of the mysteries of the engine rooms of their ship of luxury. For Sir John and Mr Jonathan it was the first time that either had ever ventured below stairs, and Sir John gamely drew a comparison between Kenny's shambolic end of corridor that served as his bedroom, and their own son's 'teenage' room. Lady Olliff-Cooper and Miss Anson had already had a lightning tour of the kitchens when they had been almost forcibly dragged down there by the chef at the height of the servants' discontent, but they tactfully did not refer to that occasion. Master Guy, the only upstairs habitué of downstairs, took a proprietorial pride in showing off his knowledge of the servants' labyrinthine quarters to his parents.

The Titanic

The British liner *Titanic* was built in Belfast for the White Star Line. It was one of the largest liners in existence at the time, and its safety features – including watertight compartments in the hull – were supposed to mean that it was unsinkable. But on 14 April 1912, four days out from Southampton on its maiden voyage to America, the *Titanic* hit an iceberg some 400 miles off the coast of Newfoundland, and sank within two and a half hours. Over 1,500 people perished out of the 2,224 aboard.

The liner was plying the highly competitive Atlantic route and its speed appears to have been excessive for the icy conditions. The ship was also equipped with far too few lifeboats – in all, a shortfall of over a thousand places.

The *Titanic* has become another symbol of Edwardian inequality, since 63 per cent of the 'top deck' first-class passengers were saved, as compared to 38 per cent of the 'below deck' third-class passengers, and 24 per cent of the crew.

position in a household that could oppress and exhaust her. But as she read in the newspaper about the death of Emily Davison – a martyr to the cause of women's right to the vote, who, waving a suffragette banner, had run out in front of the King's horse during the Derby in June 1913 and had been fatally injured by its hooves – Becky knew that this was not a personal struggle: it was a political and economic one for all women. She and Miss Anson studied the report, appalled to see how the popular press trivialized the outrage with no mention of Emily Davison's educational achievements or political beliefs. 'If enough people feel strongly enough to give their life for a cause' (though it was not entirely clear that Miss Davison *had* intended to die), Miss Anson predicted, 'things will change. They just will.'

In the provisions of the first Reform Act in 1832, women had been left out of the process of democratization because their 'natures' were considered to exclude them from public life and keep them in the domestic sphere. By 1914 some eight million men, around 60 per cent of the population, were enfranchised and no women were. The battle was for the vote: but women wanted the vote so that their demands for equal access to education and for legal and economic rights would be forced on to the nation's agenda. The 'women's movement' had a history stretching back into the nineteenth century, and notable reforms for their campaigns included the Married Women's Property Acts in 1870 and 1882; rights in the custody of children in 1873; the right to judicial separation and maintenance in 1878; the raising of the age of consent to sexual intercourse to sixteen in 1885; in 1886 the repeal of the Contagious Diseases Act (legislation introduced in the 1860s in garrison and port towns to combat the spread of venereal disease among enlisted men by identifying and registering 'common prostitutes' who could then be forcibly interned in hospital for up to nine months, while no action was taken to curb the sexual proclivities of men, and often non-prostitutes were degraded); and the gradually widening of access to employment in shops, schools, offices, the civil service and even the medical profession.[4] In 1869 women were granted the right to vote in local government elections; elementary, secondary and university education was extended to women from the 1870s; and propertied women could vote for school boards (1875), county councils (1888) and parish and district councils (1894) – since these were regarded as a legitimate extension of women's concerns for health, education and welfare.

In the Edwardian period 55 per cent of single women and 14 per cent of married women were in paid work; women were active in such organizations as the Mothers' Union (which had 40,000 members), the Girls' Friendly Society (some quarter of a million members and associates), and such bodies as the Women's Council for the Primrose League and the Women's Liberal Unionist Association, which were formed as

auxiliaries to the main political parties; they were prominent canvassers and organizers at election time, sat on school boards, were elected as local councillors, and under their auspices free school meals, subsidized milk for children and outdoor relief for the elderly were introduced. Yet women still laboured under considerable economic and legal inequalities and they did not have the vote in elections to parliament. The largest of the Edwardian suffrage organizations was the National Union of Women's Suffrage Societies (NUWSS), which consolidated sixteen constituent societies under the leadership of Millicent Fawcett in 1897. It was independent of any political party and believed in constitutional means to gain the vote. The WSPU (Women's Social and Political Union) had been founded by Emmeline Pankhurst in 1903: its motto was 'Deeds not words', and during the 1906 election it moved centre stage, challenging the constitutional suffragist movements which the Pankhursts (Emmeline was joined by two of her daughters, Christabel and Sylvia) and their supporters regarded as 'all very polite and very tame'. The WSPU adopted the designation of 'suffragette' scornfully coined for it by the *Daily Mail*, and decided on militant action intended to force the hand of the Liberal government which was, in principle, sympathetic but dilatory.

However, although it was a national demand with activity all over Britain, women's suffrage was not high on the political agenda of the triumphant Liberal Party and when, in 1908, H. H. Asquith, who was an intransigent opponent, succeeded Campbell-Bannerman as Prime Minister, the suffragettes decided that 'argument [was] exhausted'. They escalated their campaign – which had previously consisted of heckling at meetings, refusing to pay fines, and sporadic attempts to storm the House of Commons – into a militant action, the aim of which was to 'to set everyone talking about votes for women, to keep the subject in the press, to leave the government no peace from it'. These tactics, which included throwing stones at politicians' windows, hurling eggs, chaining themselves to railings, scattering marbles under the hooves of police horses and setting fire to pillar boxes, divided the movement. The constitutionalists favoured peaceful lobbying as the way to persuade their political masters that they were sufficiently responsible to have a say in the affairs of the nation, while a more militant wing were convinced that without dramatic and disruptive action, their cause would be disregarded for ever.

For their civil disobedience, many suffragettes were imprisoned. In gaol a number went on hunger strike and, fearful of what it would do to public opinion should one of these women die, the Liberal government ordered forcible feeding and then introduced the infamous 'Cat and Mouse Act' in 1913. Under its terms, women were released from prison on licence when their refusal to eat had weakened them, and were then taken back into custody as soon as they had regained their health.

How would a person in Miss Anson's position have felt about the campaign for votes for women in the Edwardian period? In her role she certainly had the time to organize meetings, get up petitions, write letters and pamphlets, help to sew banners or raise funds if she so chose. Though her brother-in-law had admitted that 'there is no reason on earth why women shouldn't have the vote', he had declared unequivocally 'I will have no suffragettes in this house,' so, without independent economic means, she would have been confined to activities of a gradualist nature. But as an upper-class woman (or certainly living the life of an upper-class woman), resident mainly in the country, she might have been expected to be more conservative in her approach to such matters than her urban, middle-class sisters. They were in the vanguard of modernism and change, benefiting most from new educational and professional opportunities and most eager to link emancipation to social change and be treated as capable citizens with a voice in their governance.

Young patricians were eager to get to the front as soon as possible. 'Our one great fear,' recalled Oswald Mosley, 'was that war would be over before we got there.' Lord Tennyson dressed and packed 'in feverish haste, so anxious was I not to run any chance of missing the war'. The poet Rupert Brooke declared 'the one central purpose of my life, the aim and end of it, the thing God wants of me, is to get good at beating Germans', and he wrote to another friend: 'Come and die. It'll be great fun.'[13] Lord Derby, touring the country to raise volunteers, told a meeting of the Territorial Association that 'If I had twenty sons, I should be ashamed if every one of them did not go to the front when his time came.'[14] But Mary, Countess of Wemyss, who was to see two of her sons killed in the war, was more realistic about the prospect in 'the last days of the Era of Peace'. She described her youngest son, Yvo Charteris, who was killed at Loos when he was just nineteen, reading the Declaration of War posted in the streets in August 1914: 'How many youths must have gazed with innocent, untroubled eyes, and pleasurable thrills of interest and excitement at their own death warrant, as they read the fatal Declaration which was to destroy so many millions of lives, shaking all things to their foundations, wasting the treasures of the past and casting its sinister influence far into the future.'[15]

Country house ladies organized clothing and food parcels for the troops and for prisoners of war, convened knitting parties, ran canteens at railway stations where troops were marching off to war, and some actually crossed over to France. The Duchess of Westminster ran a Red Cross hospital in a former casino at Le Touquet; Mrs Keppel helped in a field hospital in Étaples; Lady Angela Forbes ran a military canteen at Boulogne, while the Duchess of Sutherland organized an ambulance unit in Belgium. Young upper-class women trained as VAD nurses and performed such tasks for strangers as emptying chamber pots, changing soiled sheets, and dressing and washing the wounded – tasks that in pre-war years they would not have dreamed of doing for themselves since servants would have always done it for them – and grieved as their lovers, brothers and friends were killed.

By the end of 1914, six peers, sixteen baronets, ninety-five sons of peers and eighty-two sons of baronets lay among the dead on the Western Front. And so it continued throughout the Great War. Lord Rosebery spoke of 'the fountain of tears [being] nearly dry. One loss follows another until one is dazed.' 'Truly,' wrote Lady Curzon at the end of the war, 'England lost the flower of her young men in those terrible days… there was scarcely one of our friends who did not lose a son, a husband, or a brother.' Although, as David Cannadine points out, the majority of the notables who served did return home, not since the Wars of the Roses had so many 'patricians died so suddenly and so violently'. In *relative* terms, it was on the landed classes that the greatest sacrifice fell.

In the Edwardian Country House, Sir John would have been too old for active service (the upper age limit was extended to fifty-one in April 1918, but he was fifty-six), and if Master Guy could still be thought of as aged ten in 1914, he would still be too young by 1918. But Mr Jonathan was a different matter. Aged eighteen in 1914, he would most likely to have been a member of the legendary 'lost generation' of that terrible war. In the first year of the war 86,000 British fighting men were dead, wounded or missing (compared to 850,000 French and 650,000 Germans in the same period). By the end of the Great War the death toll was not far short of three quarters of a million (722,785) men. One in eight was killed: one in four was injured. The highest losses were in the army among soldiers fighting in the trenches in France and Flanders. Those who served in the army had only a one in two chance of surviving the war without being killed, wounded or taken prisoner.[16]

In absolute terms, because a greater proportion of the population and thus of fighting men was working class, these were the majority of those killed. In the First World War, 450,000 infantrymen died. Only 4 per cent of the infantry who died were commissioned: 96 per cent were from the ranks. But the war mirrored Edwardian social inequalities: many of the working-class men who volunteered were rejected as unfit for active service. Over one million of those examined between 1917 and 1918 were considered to be physically unfit for combat duty and of those from urban industrial areas around seven out of every ten men would be assessed as Grade III or IV, meaning that they were fit only for clerical work. In effect, the humbler a man's social origins were, the less likely he was to see active service, whereas the wealthy who were passed into the services as Grade I – 'men without any disabilities' – were deemed healthy enough to die.

The army hierarchy replicated the social hierarchy: officers were predominantly drawn from the middle and upper classes. In the conditions of trench warfare, junior officers led their men into battle: they were first 'over the top'. Whether they were leading an attack, a night patrol, a *reconnoitre* expedition or crawling out of their trenches to repair a barbed wire fence, they were first in the line of fire. This ideology of glory and sacrifice had been inculcated at home, in church, on the school playing fields, at university, and in books and magazines that recounted Britain's heroic imperial role in the world. Now the tab had to be picked up. There was a direct correlation between age and mortality, and between class and mortality: young officers were the most vulnerable category, the men least likely to survive the war. As J. M. Winter points out, 'Casualty rates among officers were substantially higher than among men in the ranks, and the most dangerous rank in the army – the subaltern – was recruited throughout much of the war from current pupils or old boys of the public schools and ancient universities: the finishing schools of the propertied classes.'[17] Between 1914 and 1918, 37,452 officers were killed and the rolls of honour of the fallen of the universities of Oxford and Cambridge were disproportionately heavy, as were those of the public schools. One in four men under twenty-four in 1914 from these universities would be killed: approximately one in five public school boys would perish.[18]

When he arrived at the Edwardian Country House, Jonathan Olliff-Cooper had just left Winchester school, and that autumn he went up to Magdalen College, Oxford, to read history. Winchester lost 500 boys in the First World War: the fallen from Magdalen College were 200.

Mr Jonathan

When eighteen-year old Jonathan (who is known to his family as Jonty) arrived at the Edwardian Country House, he had taken his A levels and was about to go up to Magdalen College, Oxford, to read Modern History. He was confident that living in the Edwardian period was going to be 'a very interesting historical experience'. But he was apprehensive too: 'I can't just nip down to the pub when I want to, or listen to the sort of music I enjoy, or send e-mails or watch television, and I have to ask my father's permission to do anything since he is the master of the house.' And he wondered how he would find life with servants. 'I ran the Cadet Force at school, so I'm used to telling people what to do, but maybe I will be embarrassed by servants waiting on me, and restrained because I can't be familiar with them. I won't be able to get to know them even though a lot of them are around the same age as I am.'

During the war, numbers of country houses were turned over to nursing the wounded; serried rows of beds filled former ballrooms while exquisitely plastered dining rooms became operating theatres. Others were used as convalescent homes. When the war was over many of the heirs were dead; others, squeezed by higher taxes and falling incomes, were forced to sell. A fifth of the land in Scotland, some 4 million acres, came on the market after the First World War. Death duties were increased to 40 per cent in 1919 and would continue to rise, while changes in the way that land was valued made this levy still more punitive.

And in many ways, the peace was not to bring all that people had fervently hoped for either. Most women munitions workers were laid off at the end of the war and only a limited number of women retained their jobs in aircraft factories and other industries, or moved into jobs that had previously been categorized as 'men's work' in the iron and steel industry, or as labourers in the docks, leather works, sawmills and brewing. Though some were retained as booking clerks and delivery drivers, and many women kept their jobs in shops and offices when peace came, most were dismissed from jobs they had had on the railways or buses. The government was fulfilling its pledge to those men who had left their jobs to go to war under the Restoration of Pre-War Practices Act. which had promised that such work would revert to men when the war was over.[19]

They were reminded that 'their first duty was to the soldier – the man who had done his bit for the past four years – and would now be wanting to return to his normal occupation', and were pressurized to take up traditional 'women's trades': laundry work and domestic service, with assurances that being a servant would be different now since mistresses had learned to 'appreciate' good servants and treat them with consideration. But many women were unconvinced and were determined to resist a return to domestic service even if this had been the work they had done before the war. An interview in the *Daily Chronicle* with a munitions worker who was prepared to take any job 'except domestic service', and employers were obliged to offer higher wages and guarantees of free time and even in some cases a written agreement of working conditions (including an end to the demeaning practice of calling servants by their first name or surname only), and even then 65 per cent of women said they would not go back into service whatever the inducements.[20]

'One day all this will be yours'.
As the elder son, Mr Jonathan contemplates
what might have been his future.

But frequently there was little choice. Unemployment benefit was cut after three months, and if women refused domestic work (whether they had ever done it before or not) their benefit was stopped. The 1920 Unemployment Insurance Act covered all manual workers except agricultural workers and domestic servants, and it was not until 1946 that domestic servants of both sexes were protected by national employment insurance.[21] The slump of the 1920s hit the manufacturing trades hard and reduced women's employment opportunities further. Nevertheless, the number of servants never again reached pre-war levels.

Despite the government's belief that domestic service was the answer to women's unemployment, there was a shift towards non-residential jobs and an overall slow decline until the Second World War, after which the decline was terminal. The number of women in domestic service fell by 46 per cent between 1931 and 1951, and by the latter date there were fewer than three-quarters of a million women domestic servants employed in England and Wales.[22]

It was much the same with men servants: despite government propaganda, the younger ones did not see that the 'home fit for a hero' that they had been promised meant someone else's house, and had no wish to return to life below stairs and replicate their wartime experience of scrubbing, peeling, scouring, polishing and standing to attention when spoken to. Many of the older demobilized men had difficulty finding a job since so many landed families in straitened post-war circumstances were forced to prune their domestic establishments drastically. The 1921 census recorded that of a total of 61,006 male indoor servants, only 48 per cent were working in private houses; the rest were employed as waiters or worked in institutions or commercial organizations.[23]

As the rain poured down on a dank, dark Scottish afternoon, Sir John Olliff-Cooper stood under a dripping umbrella looking out of the Cheviot Hills as the mists rolled around their bracken-covered slopes, and reflected on how difficult he was going to find it to leave the Edwardian Country House. In three months he had grown accustomed to the life and deeply attached to the house where he and his family had lived their Edwardian experiment. Now he was about to leave it for the twenty-first century, and he found that his feelings of proprietorial pride and anxiety conflated with those that he imagined his Edwardian counterpart might have felt in 1914.

Inside the house, sitting in his room with the table lamp throwing a soft pool of light on to the books he was leafing through, Sir John's heir was in a reflective mood too. 'If you had survived the First World War [and he knew how heavily the odds were stacked against that possibility for his age and class], and you had come back to this,' Mr Jonathan mused, 'you would probably view your inheritance with disgust. You would have seen young men who had been your footmen or hall boy or groom fighting shoulder to shoulder with you, going through the same hell in the trenches that you were going through, and being incredibly brave. And then you would come back to a rigid social hierarchy like this and you would think: "This isn't fair and it isn't right. It's not what we were fighting for".'

Julian Grenfell, who was to be mortally wounded at Ypres, acknowledged the debt as a metaphor in a poem he wrote in 1915, two months before he was killed, 'Prayer for Those on the Staff':

Fighting in the mud, we turn to Thee,   But not on us, for we are men
In these dread times of battle, Lord,   Of meaner clay, who fight in clay,
To keep us safe, if so may be,   But on the Staff, the Upper Ten
From shrapnel, snipers, shell and sword.   Depends the issue of the Day.[24]

Footnotes

INTRODUCTION

1   John Betjeman, 'Architecture' in Simon Nowell-Smith (ed.) in *Edwardian England: 1901–1914* (Oxford University Press, 1964), p. 362.

CHAPTER ONE

1   Samuel Hynes, *The Edwardian Turn of Mind* (Princeton University Press, 1968), p. 4.

2   Wilfrid Scawen Blunt, *My Diaries: Being a Personal Narrative of Events, 1888–1914: Part II* (Martin Secker, 1920), p. 1.

3   Jose Harris, *Private Lives, Public Spirit: Britain 1870–1914* (Oxford University Press, 1993), p. 2.

4   Cornelius Rozenraad, 'The International Money Market', quoted in David Kynaston, *The City of London. Volume II: The Golden Years, 1990–1914* (Chatto & Windus, 1995), p. 7.

5   Kynaston, p. 7.

6   Marghanita Laski, 'Domestic Life', in Simon Nowell-Smith (ed.), *Edwardian England, 1901–1914* (Oxford University Press, 1964), p. 141.

7   Harris, p. 97.

8   W. D. Rubenstein, *Men of Property: The Very Wealthy in Britain Since the Industrial Revolution* (Croom Helm, 1981), pp. 30–41.

9   Harris, p. 100.

10 W. H. Mallock, *The Old Order Changes* (London: 1886), p. 28.

11 John Betjeman, 'Architecture' in Nowell-Smith (ed.), p. 353.

12 E. S. Turner, 'Gilded Drainpipes', *London Review of Books*, 10 June 1999, pp. 31–2.

13 Lady Frances Balfour, quoted in J. Mordaunt Crook, *The Rise of the Nouveaux Riches: Style and Status in Victorian and Edwardian Architecture* (John Murray, 1999), p. 65.

14 Quoted in Crook, p. 59.

15 J. B. Priestley, *The Edwardians* (Wm. Heinemann, 1970), p. 61.

16 Martin Daunton, *Trusting Leviathan: The Politics of Taxation in Britain, 1799–1914* (Cambridge University Press, 2001), p. 21.

17 Parliamentary Debates –3rd series 125, 18 April 1853, quoted in Daunton, p. 230.

18 Elizabeth Roberts, 'Women's Work, 1840–1914', in L. A. Clarkson (ed.), *British Trade Union and Labour History: A Compendium* (Macmillan, 1990), p. 231.

19 Pamela Horn, *Life Below Stairs in the 20th Century* (Sutton Publishing, 2001), p. 10.

20 Vita Sackville-West, *The Edwardians* (The Hogarth Press, 1930, reprinted Virago Press, 1983), p. 55.

21 See Peter Mandler, *The Fall and Rise of the Stately Home* (Yale University Press, 1997), in particular Part II: 'Fortresses of Barbarism, 1867–1914', pp. 109–52.

22 [Berwickshire newspaper]

23 Clive Aslet, 'Manderston, Berwickshire', *Country Life*, 15 February 1979, pp. 390–3.

24 Clive Aslet, *The Last Country Houses* (New Haven and London: Yale University Press, 1982), p. 124.

25 From Kinross's obituary in the Council of the Royal Scottish Architects' annual report for 1931, quoted in Aslet (1982), p. 122.

26 *Manderston*: guide book to the house, no named author (Norman Hudson, n.d.), p. 3.

27 Aslet (1979), p. 393.

28 Mordaunt Crook, p. 55.

29 Aslet (1979), p. 126.

30 Aslet (1979), p. 126.

CHAPTER TWO

1   Quoted in Frank Dawes, *Not in Front of the Servants* (1973, the National Trust in conjunction with Random House, 1989), pp. 16–17.

2   Dawes, pp. 16–17.

3   Anon, *The Duties of Servants: The Routine of Domestic Service* (1894: facsimile edition Copper Beech Publishing, n.d.), pp. 73–4.

4   *The Duties of Servants*, p. 73.

5   *A New System of Domestic Cookery* (1860), quoted in Elizabeth Drury, *The Butler's Pantry Book* (A. C. Black, 1981), p. 83.

6   Dorothy Henley, *Rosalind Howard, Countess of Carlisle*, p. 87.

7   *Manderston* guide book, p. 19.

8   Jill Franklin, *The Gentleman's Country House and Its Plan, 1835–1914* (Routledge & Kegan Paul, 1981), pp. 88–9.

9   Margaret Powell, *Below Stairs* (Peter Davies, 1970), p. 156.

10 Margaret Fishenden, *House Heating* (1925), quoted in Franklin, p. 91.

11 J. J. Stevenson, *House Architecture* (2 vols, 1880).

12 K. F. Purdon, *The Laundry at Home* (1902), p. 18.

13 Pamela Sambrook, *The Country House Servant* (Sutton Publishing, in association with the National Trust, 1999), pp. 144–5.

CHAPTER THREE

1   *Beeton's Book of Household Management* edited by Mrs Isabella Beeton (S. O. Beeton, 1861; facsimile edn Jonathan Cape, 1968), p. [?].

2   E. S. Turner, *What the Butler Saw* (Michael Joseph, 1962), p. 158.

3   'Williams', *Footmen and Butler: Their Duties and How to Perform Them* (Dean & Son, n.d.), p. 88.

4   *The Servants' Practical Guide* (London: 1880), quoted in Drury, p. 13

5   Beeton, p. 278.

6   Beeton, p. 963.

7   *The Duties of Servants*, p. 53.

8   *The Duties of Servants*, pp. 52–3.

9   Christina Hardyment, *Behind the Scenes: Domestic Arrangements in Historic Houses* (The National Trust, 1997), p. 45, quoting Viola Bankes of the butler at Kingston Lacy in Dorset.

10 *National Review*, vol. XVIII (1892), pp. 812–20.

11 Sambrook, p. 20.

12 Charles Booth (ed.), *Life and Labour of the People in London*, vol. VIII, 'Population Classified by Trade' (Macmillan, 1896).

13 Drury, p. 33.

14 Beeton, p. 964.

15 Albert Thomas, *Wait and See* (Michael Joseph, 1944), p. 69.

16 Laski, pp. 162–3.

17 Hardyment, p. 35; Sambrook, p. 36.

18 Anne Cobbett, *The English Housekeeper* (1842).

19 Hardyment, p. 35.

20 Samuel and Sarah Adams, *The Complete Servant* (1825: reprint, Southover Press, 1989), p. 144.

21 James Williams, *The Footman's Guide*, quoted in Drury, p. 35.

22 Adams, p. 144.

23 Williams, quoted in Drury, p. 35.

24 Beeton, p. 996.

25 Hardyment, p. 178.

26 *Manderston* guide book, p. 20.

27 Adams, p. 143.

28 Turner, p. 170.

29 Eric Horne, *What the Butler Winked At: Being the Life and Adventures of Eric Horne (Butler) for Fifty-Seven Years in Service with the Nobility and Gentry* (T. W. Laurie, 1923), p. 78.

30 Horne, p. 143.

31 Juju Vail, *Rag rugs: Techniques in Contemporary Craft Projects* (Apple Press, 1997), p. 8.

32 Adams, p. 150.

33 Williams, p. 5.

34 Williams, pp. 5–6.

35 Market Harborough Museum oral history transcripts, quoted in Horn (2001), p. 5.

CHAPTER FOUR

1   Lady Greville, *The Gentlewoman in Society* (Henry & Co. 1892), p. 85.

2   Greville, pp. 88–9.

3   Greville, p. 90.

4   Sackville-West, p. 43.

5   Sackville-West, pp. 43–4.

6   *Punch*, 1843, pp. 40, 59.

7   Mark Girouard, *Life in the English Country House: A Social and Architectural History* (Yale University Press, 1998), p. 301.

8   Mordaunt Crook, pp. 3–4.

9   Dorothy Nevill, *Under Five Reigns* (Methuen, 1910), p. 151.

10 Rubinstein (1981), p. 41.

11 W. D. Rubinstein, 'New Men of Wealth and the Purchase of Land in 19th-Century Britain', in *Past and Present*, no. 92 (1981), p. 135.

12 Mordaunt Crook, p. 17.

13 Girouard, p. 300.

14 David Cannadine, *The Decline of the British Aristocracy* (Yale University Press, 1992), p. 96.

15 Oscar Wilde, *The Importance of Being Earnest* (London: 1895).

16 Cannadine, p. 119.

17 *Estates Gazette*, 15 October 1910, quoted in Cannadine, p. 110.

18 Cannadine, p. 108.

19 Cannadine, pp. 100–101.

20 Mordaunt Crook, p. 239.

21 Richard Wilson and Alan Mackley, *Creating Paradise: The Building of the English Country House, 1660–1880* (Hambledon Press, 2000).

22 Mandler, p. 120.

23 *The Studio Yearbook of Decorative Art*, 1908, pp. xi–xii, quoted in Aslet (1992), pp. 1–2.

24 Quoted in Aslet (1992), p. 19.

25 Thorstein Veblen, *The Theory of the Leisure Class* (Macmillan, 1899).

26 John Cornforth, 'Manderston, Berwickshire: The Seat of Lord Palmer', *Country Life* (26 August 1993), pp. 38–42.

27 Aslet (1979), pp. 466–9.

28 *Country Life* (26 August, 1979), p. 40.

29 Anon, *Etiquette: Rules & Usages of the Best Society* (1886; reprinted Leicester: Bookmart, 1995), p. 110.

30 Mrs Humphry ('Madge' of *Truth*), *Manners for Women* (Ward Lock, 1897), p. 83.

31 Mrs Humphry, pp. 83–4.

32 Mrs Humphry, p. 111.

33 *Etiquette*, p. 113.

34 *Etiquette*, p. 116.

35 Beeton, p. 12.

36 Beeton, pp. 18–19.

37 Sir Bernard Burke, *The Book of Precedence. The Peers, and Knights and the Companions of Several Orders of Knighthood Placed According to their Relative Rank* (London, 1881).
38 Leonore Davidoff, *The Best Circles: Society: Etiquette and the Season* (Croom Helm, 1973), p. 47.
39 Gwen Raverat, *Period Piece: A Cambridge Childhood* (Faber & Faber, 1952), p. 78.
40 Beeton, p. 13.
41 Beeton, p. 13.
42 Greville, p. 91.
43 Quoted in Drury, p. 134.
44 Sarah and Samuel Adams, p. 141.
45 Sabine Baring-Gould, *Royal Court* (1886), p. 47.

CHAPTER FIVE
1   Sarah and Samuel Adams, p. 83.
2   Sackville-West, p. 36.
3   Elizabeth Ewing, *History of Twentieth Century Fashion* (B. T. Batsford, 1974), pp. 8–10.
4   Cecil Beaton, *The Glass of Fashion* (Weidenfeld & Nicolson, 1954), p. 7.
5   Valerie Steele, *The History of the Corset*.
6   Sackville-West, pp. 39–40.
7   Frances Hodgson Burnett, *The Making of a Marchioness* (1901: reprint Persephone Books, 2001), p. 95.
8   *The Duties of a Lady's Maid* (London: 1825).
9   *The Duties of a Lady's Maid*, quoted in Drury, p. 103.
10 Greville, p. 135.
11 Sackville-West, p. 39.
12 Jane Ashelford, *The Art of Dress: Clothes and Society 1500–1914* (The National Trust, 1996), p. 250.
13 Ashelford, p. 250.
14 Alison Adburgham, *Shops and Shopping, 1800–1914* (George, Allen & Unwin, 2nd edn, 1981), p. 249.
15 Quoted in Ashelford, p. 262.
16 William Morris, *Hopes and Fears for Art* (London: 1880), p. 170.
17 Arthur J. Taylor, 'The Economy', in Simon Nowell-Smith (ed.), p. 107.
18 C .E. Montague, *Disenchantment*, (Chatto & Windus, 1922), quoted in Taylor, p. 106.
19 Greater London, Inner London Population and Density History: http://www.demographia.com/dm-lon
20 Ewing, p. 5.
21 Quoted in Ewing, p. 7.
22 Mrs Humphry, p. 64.
23 Laurel Brake, *Subjugated Knowledge: Journalism, Gender and Literature in the Nineteenth Century* (Macmillan, 1994), p. 132.
24 Janice Winship, *Inside Women's Magazines* (London: Pandora Press, 1987), p. 27.
25 Ros Ballaster, Margaret Beetham, Elizabeth Frazer and Sandra Hebron, *Women's Worlds: Ideology, Femininity and the Woman's Magazine* (Macmillan,1991), pp. 98–107.
26 Adburgham, p. 101.
27 Adburgham, p. 249.
28 Adburgham, p. 257.
29 Adburgham, p. 125.
30 Ashelford, p. 259.
31 Ewing, p. 6.
32 *Etiquette*, p. 116.
33 *Etiquette*, p. 118.
34 Mrs Humphry, p. 91.
35 Mrs Humphry, p. 90.
36 Beeton, p. 954.
37 *Etiquette*, p. 119.
38 Sackville-West, p. 44.

39 *The Footman and Butler*, p. 43.
40 *Etiquette*, pp. 120–8.
41 *Etiquette*, p. 119.
42 Mrs Humphry, pp. 91–2.
43 Mrs Humphry, p. 92.

CHAPTER SIX
1   Franklin, p. 1.
2   Jessica Gerrard, *Country House Life: Family and Servants, 1815–1914* (Blackwell, 1994), p. 45
3   *A Few Rules for the Manners of Servants in Good Families* (Ladies' Sanitary Association, 1901).
4   Gerrard, p. 143.
5   John Burnett (ed.) *Useful Toil: Autobiographies of Working People from the 1820s to the 1920s* (Penguin, 1977), p. 154.
6   Robert Kerr, *The Gentleman's House, or how to plan English residences from the Parsonage to the Palace* (1864), p. 223.
7   Roberts, pp. 218–19.
8   Gerrard, p. 168.
9   Mary Russell Mitford, *Our Village* (Harrap & Co., 1947; Oxford University Press paperback edn, 1982), p. 29.
10 Laski, p. 143.
11 Roberts, p. 231.
12 Quoted in Horn (2001), p. 3.
13 Nina Slingsby Smith, *George: Memoirs of a Gentleman's Gentleman* (Jonathan Cape, 1984) p. 35.
14 Dawes, pp. 103–5.
15 *Warne's Model Cookery* (London: *circa* 1899), p. 75.
16 Sambrook, p. 89.
17 Alexis Soyer, *The Gastronomic Regenerator* (1846) quoted in Drury, p. 155.
18 Gerrard, p. 11.
19 Beeton (1901 edn), p. 1456.

CHAPTER SEVEN
1   *Berwickshire Advertiser*, 1 September 1911.
2   Susan Tweedsmuir, *The Edwardian Lady* (Duckworth, 1966), pp. 84–6.
3   Quoted in Mandler, p. 206.
4   Leonore Davidoff, *The Best Circles: Society, Etiquette and the Season* (Croom Helm, 1973), pp. 56–7.
5   Jessica Gerrard, 'Lady Bountiful: Women of the Landed Classes and Rural Philanthropy', in *Victorian Studies*, Vol. 30, No. 2 (Winter 1987), p. 206.
6   Greville, pp. 155–6.
7   Anne Summers, 'A Home from Home – Women's Philanthropic Work in the Nineteenth Century', in Sandra Burman (ed.), *Work Fit for Women* (Edward Arnold, 1979), p. 39.
8   Frank Prochaska, 'Female Philanthropy and Domestic Service in Victorian England', *Bulletin of the Institute of Historical Research*, 54, 1981, pp. 79–80.
9   *The Lady's Companion*, 28 January 1911, p. 266.
10 Elaine Kilmurray and Richard Ormond (ed.), *John Singer Sargent* (Tate Gallery Publishing, 1998), p. 144.
11 Sophia Murphy, *The Duchess of Devonshire's Ball* (Sidgwick & Jackson, 1984), pp. 161–2.
12 Census, Registrar General's Annual Reports, 1971. Age, Marital Conditions and General Tables: Table 6 (HMSO, 1974), p. 13.
13 Jane Lewis, *Women in England, 1870–1950* (Wheatsheaf Books, 1984), pp. 3–4.
14 Sue Bruley, *Women in Britain since 1900* (Macmillan, 1999), p. 16.

15 Mary Stocks, *My Commonplace Book* (Peter Davies, 1970), p. 6.
16 Mrs Humphry, p. 56.
17 *The Freewoman*, 23 November 1911, quoted in Juliet Gardiner (ed.), *Women's Voices, 1880–1918: The New Woman* (Collins & Brown, 1993), pp. 200–203.
18 Davidoff, p. 50.
19 Denis Pye, *Fellowship is Life: The National Clarion Cycling Club, 1895–1995* (Clarion Publishing, 1995), p. 6.
20 Pye, p. 3.
21 Quoted in Ashelford, p. 236.
22 *Punch*, 2 June 1883.
23 Richard Ellman, *Oscar Wilde* (Hamish Hamilton, 1987), pp. 244, 268.
24 Pye, pp. 9–10.
25 Frances, Countess of Warwick, *Life's Ebb and Flow* (Hutchinson & Co., 1929), pp. 89–92.
26 Henry Pelling, *Origins of the Labour Party, 1880–1900* (Oxford University Press, 2nd edn, 1965), p. 173.
27 Eric Horne, *More Winks: Being Further Notes from the Life and Adventures of Eric Horne (Butler), for Fifty-Seven Years in Service with the Nobility and Gentry* (T. W. Laurie, 1932), pp. 215–16.
28 Roberts, p. 230.
29 Roberts, pp. 256–7.
30 Roberts, p. 257.
31 Roberts, p. 229.
32 Dawes, p. 164.

CHAPTER EIGHT
1   A. P. Herbert, *Tantivy Towers* (London: Ernest Benn, 1930).
2   Phyllida Barstow, *The English Country House Party* (1989; Sutton Publishing, 1998), p. 85.
3   Barstow, p. 86.
4   Jonathan Garnier Ruffer, *The Big Shots: Edwardian Shooting Parties* (Debrett-Viking Press, 1977), p. 21.
5   Ruffer, p. 134.
6   Christopher Hibbert, *Edward VII: A Portrait* (1976; Penguin, 1982), pp. 94–5.
7   *Country Life*, 21 January 1911.
8   Pamela Horn, *High Society: The English Social Elite,1880–1914* (Alan Sutton Publishing, 1992), p. 138.
9   Horn (1992), pp. 138–9.
10 John Vincent (ed.), *The Crawford Papers: The journals of David Lindsay, twenty-seventh Earl of Crawford and tenth Earl of Balcarres, 1871–40* (London, 1984), entry for 6–10 August 1913, p. 316.
11 Ashelford, p. 240.
12 A. Escoffier, *A Guide to Modern Cookery* (Wm. Heinemann, 1907), pp. 549–50.
13 H. Cholmondeley-Pennell, *Fishing* (Longman, Green & Co., 1912), p. 197.
14 Quoted in Horn (1992), p. 138.
15 MORI poll conducted for the *Mail on Sunday*, 14–15 July 1999. p. 1.
16 Pamela Horn, *Victorian Countrywomen* (Alan Sutton, 1991), p. 54.
17 Countess of Warwick, pp. 95–7.
18 Countess of Warwick, pp. 96–7.
19 The Side Saddle Association, *Member's Handbook, 2001*, p. 58.
20 *Manderston* guide book, p. 23.
21 Quoted in David Cannadine, *Aspects of Aristocracy* (Yale University Press, 1994), p. 56.
22 H. J. Perkin, *The Age of the Railway* (Panther, 1970), pp. 171–2.
23 Cannadine (1994), p. 62.
24 Cannadine (1994), p. 63.

CHAPTER NINE

1   *Manderston* guide book, p. 22.
2   Booth, vol. VII, p. 224.
3   'A Butler's View of Menservice' in *Nineteenth Century* (1892), XXXI, p. 925.
4   William Taylor, *Diary 1837* (ed. Dorothy Wise, 1962), quoted in Franklin, p.106.
5   Franklin, p.106.
6   Davidoff, p. 41.
7   *The Lady, a Magazine for Gentlewomen*, 9 February 1893.
8   Lady Colin Campbell, *Etiquette of Good Society* (1911), p. 63.
9   Powell, pp. 146–7.
10 C. E. Vuillamy (ed.), *The Polderoy Papers* (London: 1943), quoted in Gerrard, p. 251.
11 John R. Gillis, 'Servants, Sexual Revelations and the Risks of Illegitimacy' in Judith L. Newton, Mary P. Ryan and Judith R. Walkowitz, *Sex and Class in Women's History* (Routledge & Kegan Paul, 1983) pp. 145-6.
12 Derek Hudson (ed.), *Man of Two Worlds: The Life and Diaries of Arthur J. Munby, 1828–1910* (1972).
13 *Ann Morgan's Love: A Pedestrian Poem* (A. J. Munby, 1896), quoted in Leonore Davidoff, 'Class and Gender in Victorian England: The Diaries of Arthur J. Munby and Hannah Cullwick', *Feminist Studies*, 5, No. 1, Spring 1979, p. 87.
14 *Cassell's Book of Sports and Pastimes* (Cassell & Co., 1904), p. 334.
15 Chris Cook and John Stevenson, *The Longman Handbook of Modern British History* (Longman, 1983), p. 68.
16 Mandler, p. 174.
17 Mandler, p. 80.
18 Paul Johnson (ed.), *Twentieth-Century Britain: Economic, Cultural and Social Change* (Longman, 1994), p. 1.
19 Horn (2001), p. 17.
20 *Daily Mail*, 20 November 1911.
21 Horn (2001), pp. 17–18.
22 B. K. Murray, *The People's Budget of 1909–10: Lloyd George and Liberal Politics* (Oxford University Press, 1980), p. 256.
23 *The Times*, 31 July 1909, p. 9.
24 Hynes, p. 5.
25 Johnson, p. 80.
26 Johnson, pp. 66–7.
27 Johnson, p. 68.

CHAPTER TEN

1   Lucy Cohen, *Lady de Rothschild and her Daughters* (John Murray, 1935), pp. 269–70.
2   George Dangerfield, *The Strange Death of Liberal England* (1935, MacGibbon & Kee, 1966), pp. 40–41.
3   Roger Fulford, 'The King' in Nowell-Smith, p. 5.
4   Hibbert, p. 294.
5   Dangerfield, pp. 41–2.
6   Blunt, p. 320.
7   Quoted in James Fox, *The Langhorne Sisters* (Granta Books, 1998), p. 116.
8   Frances, Countess of Warwick, *Afterthoughts* (Cassell, 1931), p. 39.

9   Aronson, p. 41.
10 Antony Allfrey, *Edward VII and his Jewish Court* (Weidenfeld & Nicolson, 1991), p. 8.
11 Countess of Warwick, p. 77.
12 Hibbert, p. 155.
13 Aronson. pp. 125–6.
14 Elinor Glyn, *Romantic Adventure* (Ivor Nicholson & Watson, 1936), pp. 74–5.
15 Quoted in Aronson, p. 177.
16 Fox, p. 115.
17 Fox, p. 217.
18 Keith Middlemas, *The Life and Times of Edward VII* (Weidenfeld & Nicolson, 1972), p. 68.
19 T. H. S. Escott, *Society in the New Reign* (1904).
20 Rubinstein, *Men of Property*, p. 156.
21 Quoted in Mordaunt Crook, pp.156–7.
22 Countess of Warwick, quoted in Allfrey, p. 23.
23 Beatrice Webb, *Our Partnership* (ed. Barbara Drake and Margaret Cole) (Longman, 1948), pp. 412–13, 27 July 1908.
24 Allfrey, p. 12.
25 Allfrey, p. 15.
26 Blunt, p. 318.
27 Quoted in Cowles, p. 361.
28 Cornwallis-West, p. 159.
29 Cornwallis-West, p. 150.
30 The Duke of Portland, *Men, Women and Things* (London: Faber, 1937).
31 Philip Magnus, *King Edward VII* (London: John Murray, 1964), p. 254.
32 Magnus, p. 210.
33 Ross McKibbin, *Classes and Cultures: England 1918–1951* (Oxford University Press, 1998), p. 353.
34 Quoted in Ross McKibbin, *The Ideologies of Class* (Oxford University Press, 1990), p. 104.
35 McKibbin, (1990), p. 132.
36 McKibbin, p. 120.
37 J. L. Paton, 'Gambling' in *Encyclopaedia of Religion and Ethics*, 12 vols (Edinburgh, 1913), vol. VI, p. 164.
38 Miss Winifred Sturt to her fiancé, Charles Hardinge, quoted in Magnus, p. 222.
39 Magnus, p. 223.
40 *Cassell's Book of Sports and Pastimes* (London: Cassell & Company, n.d.), p. 764.

CHAPTER ELEVEN

1   Lawrence James, *Raj: The Making and Unmaking of British India* (Little, Brown and Co., 1997), p. 320.
2   Quoted in James, p. 321.
3   Bernard S. Cohen, 'Representing Authority in Victorian England', in Eric Hobsbawm and Terence Ranger (eds.), *Inventing Tradition* (Routledge & Kegan Paul, 1981), pp. 165–210.
4   David Cannadine, *Ornamentalism: How the British Saw their Empire* (Allen Lane, The Penguin Press, 2001), pp. 43–4.
5   Cannadine (2001), p. 45.
6   *The Times*, 30 December 1902.
7   Quoted in David Cannadine, 'Lord Curzon as Imperial Impresario', in *Aspects of Aristocracy: Grandeur and Decline in Modern Britain* (Yale University Press, 1994), p. 85.
8   Cannadine (1994), p. 90.

9   Quoted in Cannadine (1994), p. 90.
10 Lawrence James, *The Rise and Fall of the British Empire* (Little, Brown and Company, 1994), p. 204.
11 James (1994), p. 207.
12 Quoted in James (1994), p. 207.
13 *The Empire Book of Patriotism* (1912), p. 12.
14 James (1994), p. 347.
15 Shompa Lahiri, *Indians in Britain: Anglo-Indian Encounters, Race and Identity. 1880–1930* (Frank Cass, 2000), p. 5.
16 Rozina Visram, *Ayars, Lascars and Princes: Indians in Britain, 1700–1947* (Pluto Press, 1986), pp. 78–96.
17 Beeton (1901 edn), p. 1263.
18 James (1994), pp. 210-11.
19 *The Empire Day Book of Patriotism* (1912), p. 3.
20 Sophia Murphy, *The Duchess of Devonshire's Ball* (Sidgwick & Jackson, 1984), p. 47.
21 Murphy, p. 138.
22 *The Berwickshire News*, 14 November 1905.
23 *The Berwickshire News*, 14 November 1905.
24 *Empire Day Book of Pageants* (London: 1916), p. 10.

CHAPTER TWELVE

1   Samuel and Sarah Adams, p. 23.
2   Raverat, pp. 75–6.
3   Raverat, p. 49.
4   Martin Pugh, *Women and the Women's Movement in Britain* (Macmillan. 2nd edn, 2000), pp. 1–2.
5   Jill Liddington and Jill Norris, *One Hand Tied Behind Us: The Rise of the Women's Suffrage Union* (Virago, 1978).
6   Lisa Tickner, *Imagery of the Suffrage Campaign, 1907–14* (Chatto & Windus, 1987), p. 179.
7   Quoted in Horn (2001), p. 20.
8   Horn (2001), p. 20.
9   Rosina Harrison, *Rose: My Life in Service* (Cassell, 1975), p. 22.
10 Horn (2001), p. 24.
11 J. M. Winter, *The Great War and the British People* (Harvard University Press, 1986), p. 27.
12 *Country Life*, January 1915, quoted in Horn (2001).
13 Christopher Hassal, *Rupert Brooke: A Biography* (Faber & Faber, 1964), pp. 471, 480.
14 Quoted in David Cannadine, (1990), p. 72.
15 Quoted in Angela Lambert, *Unquiet Souls: The Indian Summer of the British Aristocracy, 1880–1918* (Macmillan, 1984), p. 166.
16 Winter, p. 72.
17 Winter, p. 66.
18 Winter, pp. 98–9.
19 Gail Braybon and Penny Summerfield, *Out of the Cage: Women's Experiences in Two World Wars* (Pandora Press, 1987), p. 120.
20 Braybon and Summerfield, p. 123.
21 Horn (2000), p. 27.
22 Horn (2000), p. 191.
23 Horn (2000), p. 30.
24 Quoted in E. L. Black (ed.), *1914–18 in Poetry* (Hodder and Stoughton, 1970), p. 102.

Further reading

A selection of the books available on the Edwardian era. Further books and articles referred to in the text can be found in the endnotes.

RECENT HISTORIES
These include the 1905–14 era and/or discuss the context of the Edwardian Country House.

Aslet, Clive, *The Last Country Houses* (Yale University Press, 1982)

Barstow, Phyllida, *The English Country House Party* (Thorsons, 1989; Sutton Publishing, 1998)

Cannadine, David, *The Decline and Fall of the British Aristocracy* (Yale University Press, 1990, Macmillan Papermac, 1996)

Cannadine, David, *Aspects of Aristocracy: Grandeur and Decline in Modern Britain* (Yale University Press, 1994; Penguin, 1995)

Cannadine, David, *Class in Britain* (Yale University Press, 1998; Penguin, 2000)

Cannadine, David, *Ornamentalism: How the British Saw their Empire* (Allen Lane: Penguin, 2001)

Clarke, Peter, *Hope and Glory: Britain 1900–1990* (Allen Lane, 1996; Penguin, 1997)

Cowles, Virginia, *Edward VII and His Circle* (Hamish Hamilton, 1956)

Dangerfield, George, *The Strange Death of Liberal England* (1935; MacGibbon & Kee, 1966)

Daunton, Martin, *Trusting Leviathan: The Politics of Taxation in Britain, 1799–1914* (Cambridge University Press, 2001)

Davidoff, Leonore, *The Best Circles: Society, Etiquette and the Season* (Croom Helm, 1973)

Dawes, Frank, *Not in Front of the Servants* (Wayland, 1973; the National Trust in conjunction with Century, 1989)

Drury, Elizabeth, *The Butler's Pantry Book* (A. C. Black, 1981)

Franklin, Jill, *The Gentleman's Country House and Its Plan, 1835–1914* (Routledge & Kegan Paul, 1981)

Gerrard, Jessica, *Country House Life: Family and Servants, 1815–1914* (Blackwell, 1994)

Girouard, Mark, *Life in the English Country House: A Social and Architectural History* (Yale University Press, 1998)

Hardyment, Christina, *Behind the Scenes: Domestic Arrangements in Historic Houses* (The National Trust, 1997)

Harris, Jose, *Private Lives, Public Spirit: Britain 1870–1914* (Oxford University Press, 1993; Penguin, 1994)

Hartcup, Adeline, *Below Stairs in the Great Country Houses* (Sidgwick & Jackson, 1980)

Hibbert, Christopher, *Edward VII: A Portrait* (Allen Lane, 1976; Penguin, 1982)

Holden, Edith, *The Country Diary of an Edwardian Lady* (Michael Joseph, 1977)

Horn, Pamela, *Ladies of the Manor: Wives and Daughters in Country-House Society, 1830–1918* (Sutton Publishing, 1991)

Horn, Pamela, *High Society: The English Social Elite,1880–1914* (Sutton Publishing, 1992)

Horn, Pamela, *Life Below Stairs in the 20th Century* (Sutton Publishing, 2001)

Hugget, Frank E., *Life Below Stairs: Domestic Servants in England from Victorian Times* (Book Club Associates, 1977)

Hynes, Samuel, *The Edwardian Turn of Mind* (Princeton University Press, 1968)

James, Lawrence, *The Rise and Fall of the British Empire* (Little, Brown, 1994)

James, Lawrence, *Raj: The Making and Unmaking of British India* (Little, Brown, 1997)

Kynaston, David, *The City of London*, vol. II, *The Golden Years, 1890–1914* (Chatto & Windus, 1995)

Lambert, Angela, *Unquiet Souls: The Indian Summer of the British Aristocracy, 1880–1918* (Macmillan, 1984)

Magnus, Philip, *King Edward VII* (John Murray, 1964)

Mandler, Peter, *The Fall and Rise of the Stately Home* (Yale University Press, 1997)

McKibbin, Ross, *The Ideologies of Class: Social Relations in Britain, 1880–1950* (Oxford University Press, 1990)

Mordaunt Crook, J., *The Rise of the Nouveaux Riches: Style and Status in Victorian and Edwardian Architecture* (John Murray, 1999)

Nowell-Smith, Simon (ed.), *Edwardian England, 1901–1914* (Oxford University Press, 1964)

Plumptre, George, *The Fast Set: The World of Edwardian Racing* (André Deutsch, 1985)

Priestley, J. B., *The Edwardians* (Heinemann, 1970)

Pugh, Martin, *Women and the Women's Movement in Britain* (Macmillan, 2nd edn, 2000)

Rose, Kenneth, *George V* (Weidenfeld & Nicolson, 1983)

Rubinstein, W. D., *Men of Property: The Very Wealthy in Britain Since the Industrial Revolution* (Croom Helm, 1981)

Ruffer, Jonathan Garnier, *The Big Shots: Edwardian Shooting Parties* (Debrett-Viking Press, 1977)

Sambrook, Pamela, *The Country House Servant* (Sutton Publishing, in association with the National Trust, 1999)

Thompson, F. M. L., *Gentrification and Enterprise Culture: Britain, 1870–1980* (Oxford University Press, 2001)

Turner, E. S., *What the Butler Saw* (Michael Joseph, 1962)

MEMOIRS AND MANUALS
The memoirs cover the Edwardian period, or have relevance to it, and the advice manuals are among those used in the Edwardian Country House.

Adams, Samuel and Sarah, *The Complete Servant* (1825; reprint, Southover Press, 1989)

Beeton, Isabella, *The Book of Household Management* (S. O. Beeton, 1861; also 1901 edn; facsimile edn Jonathan Cape, 1968)

Blunt, Wilfrid Scawen, *My Diaries: Being a Personal Narrative of Events, 1880–1914* (Martin Secker, 1920)

Campbell, Lady Colin, *Etiquette of Good Society* (1911)

Cassell's Book of Sports and Pastimes (1904)

Cassell's Household Guide, 4 vols (c1900), vol. 5, 1911

Cornwallis-West, G., *Edwardian Hey-Days, Or a Little About a Lot of Things* (Putnam, 1930)

Duties of a Lady's Maid, The (1825)

Duties of Servants, The: The Routine of Domestic Service (1894: facsimile edn Copper Beech Publishing, n.d.)

Escoffier, A., *A Guide to Modern Cookery* (Heinemann, 1907)

Etiquette: Rules & Usages of the Best Society (1886; reprinted Bookmart, 1995)

Everywoman's Encyclopaedia, 8 vols (1910)

Glyn, Elinor, *Romantic Adventure* (Ivor Nicholson and Watson, 1936)

Greville, Lady, *The Gentlewoman in Society* (Henry & Co., 1892)

Horne, Eric, *What the Butler Winked At: Being the Life and Adventures of Eric Horne (Butler) for Fifty-Seven Years in Service with the Nobility and Gentry* (T. W. Laurie, 1923)

Humphry, Mrs ('Madge' of *Truth*), *Manners for Men* (1897: facsimile edn Pryor Publications, 1993)

Humphry, Mrs, *Manners for Women* (1897: facsimile edn Pryor Publications, 1993)

James, Mrs Eliot, *Our Servants: Their Duties to Us and Ours to Them* (1883)

Keppel, Sonia, *Edwardian Daughter* (Hamish Hamilton, 1958)

Ladies' Sanitary Association, *A Few Rules for the Manners of Servants in Good Families* (1901)

Raverat, Gwen, *Period Piece: A Cambridge Childhood* (Faber & Faber, 1952)

Servant's Practical Guide, The (1880)

Warne's Model Cookery (c.1899)

Warwick, Frances, Countess of, *Life's Ebb and Flow* (Hutchinson & Co., 1929)

'Williams', *The Footmen and Butler, Their Duties and How to Perform Them* (Dean & Son, 8th edn, n.d.)

EDWARDIAN NOVELS (RELEVANT TO THE THEME OF THE BOOK) IN REPRINT EDITIONS

Burnett, Frances Hodgson, *The Making of a Marchioness* (1901; reprinted Persephone Books, 2001)

Leverson, Ada, *The Little Otleys* (1908–16; reprinted Virago Press, 1962)

Sackville-West, Vita, *The Edwardians* (1930; reprinted Virago Press, 1983)

Wells, H. G., *Tono-Bungay* (1909; J M Dent, Everyman's Library, 1994)

Timeline

1899
Outbreak of the Second Boer War.

1900
Labour Representation Committee formed.
Conservative–Liberal Unionist coalition under Lord Salisbury returned to power in 'khaki election'.

1901
22 January: Death of Queen Victoria, aged eighty-one, after a reign of sixty-three years. Edward VII succeeds to the throne.
September: Taff Vale judgement, a landmark in the development of the Labour Party. Workers on the Taff Vale Railway took unofficial action to gain the right to join a trade union. The dispute was then made official by the Amalgamated Society of Railway Servants but, after the strike was settled, the railway company sought damages from the union for losses incurred during the strike. This was rejected on appeal, but in July 1901 the House of Lords reversed the appeal and granted £42,000 plus costs against the union. The judgement severely limited the right to strike and convinced many working people of the need for an independent political party to support the interests of labour. The Labour Representation Committee made immunity from prosecution for trade unions a condition of joining the 'LibLab' pact made before the 1906 election.
October: Britain's first submarine launched.
December: First Nobel Prizes awarded.

1902
January: Smallpox outbreak in London.
March: Cecil Rhodes, 'the architect of Empire', dies.
May: Boer War ends.
July: Arthur Balfour succeeds Salisbury as Conservative Prime Minister.
9 August: Coronation of Edward VII, delayed from July because of the King's appendicitis.
Charles Booth's survey of poverty, *Life and Labour of the People of London*, published.
Windsor Castle opened to the public.
Beatrix Potter's *Peter Rabbit* published.
Rudyard Kipling's *Just So Stories* published.

1903
1 January: Edward VII proclaimed Emperor of India.
October: Formation of the suffragette Women's Social and Political Union (WSPU), by Emmeline and Christabel Pankhurst.
December: Marie Curie the first woman to win the Nobel Prize.
Orville and Wright make the first successful flight in a petrol-powered aeroplane.

1904
February: War breaks out between Russia and Japan when the Russian fleet attacks at Port Arthur.
April: Entente Cordiale signed with France.
Licence plates for cars compulsory.
May: Rolls-Royce car manufacturing company formed.
November: Figures released reveal that poverty is rising dramatically – 122,000 people in London and 800,000 in England and Wales are in receipt of poor relief, with a quarter of a million in workhouses.
December: J. M. Barrie's *Peter Pan, or The Boy Who Wouldn't Grow Up* opens in London.

1905
January: 'Bloody Sunday' in St Petersburg, when Tsar Nicholas II's troops fire on demonstrators led by Father George Gabon, killing 500 people.
By popular demand, Arthur Conan Doyle brings his famous detective back from the 'dead' in a new book, *The Return of Sherlock Holmes*.
April: More than 10,000 people perish in an earthquake in Lahore, India.
May: Women's Suffrage Bill 'talked out' in Commons.
June: Mutiny of Russian sailors on battleship *Potemkin*.
Automobile Association founded.

July: Einstein's Theory of Relativity proposed.
August: Lord Curzon resigns as Viceroy of India.
October: Christabel Pankhurst and Annie Kenney arrested: start of the militant phase of the Suffragette movement.
Aspirin on sale in Britain.
December: Balfour resigns; Henry Campbell-Bannerman invited to form a government.
First motorized ambulances for traffic accident victims introduced by London County Council (previously ambulances were used only for people suffering from infectious diseases).
John Galsworthy's *A Man of Property* (the novel that becomes the first part of *The Forsyte Saga*) published.

1906
February: Liberal landslide at General Election; Labour wins thirty seats.
HMS *Dreadnought* launched.
Formation of the Labour Party.
Trade Disputes Act overturns Taff Vale Judgement.
Free school meals introduced for children in need.
April: Mount Vesuvius erupts, killing hundreds.
San Francisco earthquake: 800 die.
SOS becomes the international distress signal.

1907
Women can stand for election in county and borough election and can take the office of mayor.

April: War Office objects to plan to construct a Channel tunnel: Bill withdrawn.

Baden-Powell founds the Boy Scout movement.

Entente Cordiale becomes Triple Alliance when Russia joins.

New Zealand achieves dominion status.

1908

April: Ill-health forces Campbell-Bannerman's resignation; Herbert Asquith succeeds him as Prime Minister.

Old Age Pensions (with a means test) introduced for a minority of old people.

Coal Mines Regulation Act legislates for a maximum working day of eight hours underground.

Territorial Army (volunteer home defence force that could be mobilized in the event of war) founded. By 1914 it had over a quarter of a million members.

England plays the first ever international football match, against Austria – and wins 6–1.

June: Edward VII visits Russia.

Olympic Games staged in London.

National Farmers' Union founded.

December: Professor Ernest Rutherford awarded the Nobel Prize for Chemistry for his work on radiation and the nature of the atom.

E. M. Forster's *Room with a View* published.

1909

Labour Exchanges established.

Trade Boards Act establishes minimum wage in some of the lowest-paid trades.

July: Blériot makes the first cross-Channel flight, taking forty-three minutes.

November: The House of Lords throws out Lloyd George's 'people's budget' – the 'most radical budget in the nation's history'.

1910

Liberals under Asquith win general election in February and December.

Union of South Africa formed.

21 May: Death of Edward VII; succeeded by George V.

July: Dr Crippen arrested at sea for the murder of his wife, the first criminal suspect to be caught by radio. He was travelling with his mistress Ethel Le Neve, disguised as a boy.

20 August: Florence Nightingale dies.

Osborne Judgement bans trade unions from funding political activities.

Girl Guide movement founded by Baden-Powell and his sister, Agnes.

1911

February: Ramsay MacDonald succeeds Keir Hardie as chairman of the parliamentary Labour party.

March: Shops Act legislates for sixty-hour week and all employees entitled to a half-day holiday each week.

Parliament Act restricts power of the House of Lords.

Payment of MPs introduced.

23 June: George V crowned in Westminster Abbey.

July: Agadir crisis when Germany sent a gunboat to Moroccan port allegedly to protect German trading interests against the French. Britain was concerned at this possible threat to Gibraltar. Although Germany and France negotiated a settlement, the incident fuelled Britain's concern about Germany's expansionist aims.

November: Balfour resigns as leader of the Conservative Party; succeeded by Andrew Bonar Law.

Period of industrial unrest from 1911 to 1914.

1912

January: Captain Scott's expedition reaches the South Pole – Amundsen has beaten them. All perish on the return journey.

April: The 'unsinkable' *Titanic* sinks after hitting an iceberg, with the loss of more than 1,500 lives.

May: Irish Home Rule Bill introduced.

September: Edward Carson organizes the Ulster Volunteers to resist Home Rule for Ireland.

British Board of Film Censors established.

Royal Flying Corps (precursor of the Royal Air Force) established.

1913

March: Cat and Mouse Act introduced in an attempt to deal with the problem of suffragettes' hunger strikes in prison.

May: Stravinsky's *Rites of Spring* performed to shocked audiences in Paris.

June: The suffragette Emily Davison throws herself under the King's horse at the Derby and dies from her injuries.

The zip fastener patented by a Swedish engineer.

Trade Union Act reverses Osborne Judgement.

September: Ulster Volunteer Force established.

D. H. Lawrence's *Sons and Lovers* published.

1914

Immigration, already restricted since 1905 Act, further restricted

March: Velazquez's *Rokeby Venus* slashed in the National Gallery by a suffragette with a meat cleaver.

Wyndham Lewis's Vorticist magazine, *Blast*, signals arrival of modernism in Britain.

April: George Bernard Shaw's *Pygmalion* opens in London, starring Mrs Patrick Campbell.

James Joyce's *Dubliners* published.

Edgar Rice Burroughs' *Tarzan of the Apes* published.

28 June: Archduke Franz Ferdinand of Austria assassinated by a Serbian nationalist in Sarajevo.

1 August: Germany declares war on Russia and, on the 3rd, France.

4 August: Britain declares war on Germany when it violates Belgian neutrality. Fighting continues on the Western Front until 11 a.m. on 11 November 1918. By this time, 772,000 British have been killed, and 1,676,037 wounded.

Author's acknowledgements

Writing any book incurs debts: in a book such as this they are manifold and direct. My first thanks must go to those who peopled the Edwardian Country House: the 'upstairs' family of John and Anna Olliff-Cooper, Jonathan and Guy, and Avril Anson; the 'tutor', Rejit Singh; and the 'servants' downstairs: Tristan Aldrich, Carly (Ellen) Beard, Charlie Clay, Rob Daly, Jean Davies, Denis Dubiard, Hugh Edgar, Eva Morrison, Erika Ravitz, Jessica Rawlinson, Kenneth Skelton and Rebecca Smith. Without their willingness to share their experiences and to supply a mass of information and advice, this book could not have been written. Nor could it of course without the Wall to Wall team to whom I am most grateful: I am particularly indebted to Caroline Ross Pirie, the series producer and director, to Melanie Lindsell and to Fiona Blair with whom I seem to have been in almost daily contact. My thanks too to Nick Murphy, co-director, and to Emma Willis, executive producer, to Mark Ball, Rachel Bliss, Joyce Cope, Andrea Kohn, Amy Leader and Donna Luke.

At Channel 4 Books Charlie Carman and her team have, once again, been exemplary publishers and my thanks are due to Emma Tait, Annie Schafheitle, Verity Willcocks, and particularly to Sarah MacDonald for efficient and encouraging editorial support; to Christine King for meticulous and tactful copy editing; and to Isobel Gillan for inspired design solutions, and thanks to my agent Deborah Rogers.

Dr Peter Mandler and Daru Rooke have both read the manuscript and I have hugely benefited from their comments and suggestions, though any errors and omissions of course remain solely my responsibility. Rosalind Ebbutt has been a mine of information on costume and effects, and I am also most grateful for the help of Polly Bell-Hughes, Simon Berry, Robin Darwell-Smith, Dr John Davies, Guy Dymond, Mike Everett, Neil Freeman, Professor Henry Horwitz, Arthur Inch, Patrick MacLure, Jim Matthews, John Ormiston, Jane Pryor, Caroline and Patricia Rose, and Professor Richard Sheppard.

No book like this can be written without drawing on the work of those who traversed the terrain before: my debt to them is acknowledged in the endnotes and the suggestions for further reading.

Producer's acknowledgements

This project would not have been possible without the kindness and enthusiasm of the people who live and work in and around Duns. For their help throughout filming, Wall to Wall would like to thank Lord and Lady Palmer, Reverend Donald Gaddis, Rona and Andy Lang, Geoffrey and Valerie Dymond, Sarah Gash, Tommy and Helen Noon, Mr and Mrs Grant, Agnes and Robert Crawford, Mark Dawson, Bill Hardie, Marion Smith, John and Joan Bimson, Brenda Leddy, Johnny Rutherford, Diane Youngman, Mary and Bill Bryson, Maggie and Brian Gray, David and Marlene Young, the Knoll Hospital, the Gardeners' Royal Benevolent Society, the Berwickshire Hounds, Ronald Drummond, Christina Cowan, Sarah Hogg, Jenny Leggett, the Whip and Saddle, Christine Taylor, Gordon Morrison, Neil Mountain, Kay Melville, Roxburgh Lacemakers, Langton Rural, Dorien Irving, Professor Jimi Langley, Madame Christine Quick, Sheila Massie, Joan Russell, Robert Allott, Nan Eddy, R. Welsh and Son, Fred Baxendale at Howe and Blackhall, Richard Landale at Kelso Races, the staff and pupils at Longridge Towers, the Brownies, Guides and Cubs of Duns and the Greggs Bakery Band.

The Edwardian Country House was graced with a number of visitors. The producer would like to thank Merlin Evans, Sandy Broadhurst and Graham Pearce from the Clarion Cycling Club, Dr Morrice McCrae, Arthur Inch, John Myatt, Lady McEwen, Colonel Simon Furness, Simon Berry, Mrs Elizabeth Whinney, David Liddell Grainger and Lady de la Rue, Mr and Mrs Richard Baillie, Judith Linton and her ceilidh band, Shearings, Prince Mohsin Ali Khan of Hyderabad, Yasmin Alibhai-Brown, Krishnan Guru-Murthy, Priya Pawar, Sushma Mehta and the dancers and musicians she brought with her, Jeffrey Bates of Bates and Hindmarch antiquarian books, Darcus Howe, David Mellor, Lord Deedes, Lord and Lady Steel, Alan Beith MP, Baroness Maddock, Lady Chelsea, Robert Swan OBE, Andrew Motion, the Edinburgh University Savoy Opera Group, the two 'chauffeurs' Don Moore and George McCartney, John Adderley and everyone else who came to the fête, dinner party or Empire Ball.

For restoring the house to its Edwardian splendour, thanks are extended to our art director, Maggie Gray, who was ably assisted by Fiona Gavin with Craig Dewar, Bill Purvis, Ronnie Thompson, the two Neil Jordans and Jim Louden all helping to get the house ready on time. Special thanks to costume designers Ros Ebbutt and Amanda Keable, Pat Farmer and Lesley Docksey who made some of the clothes. Thanks also to Fran Needham and Heather Squires.

Wall to Wall researched this project with the help of our historical consultants Daru Rooke, Peter Mandler and Paul Atterbury. Further help came from Pamela Horn, David Moore, John Davis, Neil Freeman, Bill Leader, Martin Pugh, Derek Scott, Judith Lask, the Museum of Labour History, Northern Herald Books, Dr Harvey Osborne, Sara Paston-Williams, Dennis Pye, Adrian Greenwood, Jim Spencer and John Macmillan at Historic Newspapers, Dinosaur Disks, the Victorian Society, Whitechapel Art Gallery, the Working Class Movement Library, the National Library of Scotland, the Yorkshire Car Collection, the British Library, Eyemouth Museum, John Hayes at the Museum of Childhood in Edinburgh and the Victoria Research web. Thanks also to all who applied to take part, particularly those who took the time to write to the production team with country house stories of their own.

Finally, thanks to Camilla Deakin and Janice Hadlow at Channel 4 Television.

Suppliers

Stationery: Smythson of Bond Street; pens: Parker; chinaware: Josiah Wedgwood & Son; glassware: Stuart Crystal; toiletries: Rose & Co Apothecary, D. R. Harris & Co Ltd, Trumpers (for razors); Edwardian hospitality: Gore Hotel, London, Caledonian Hotel, Edinburgh; silverware: Robbe & Berking; diamonds and pearls: Hamilton & Inches; packaging: Robert Opie, Unilever; magazines and newspapers: Vinmag Archive, Historic Newspapers; wines: Berry Bros & Rudd; art materials: Windsor & Newton, Fired Earth; spectacles: Specsavers; guns: Holland and Holland; flowers for special occasions: Banks Florist, Edinburgh; ball gowns: Angels & Berman Costumier, Cosprop. LOCAL PRODUCE: Vegetables: Betty Snow (herbs), Thisselcockrig Farm, Reiver Country Farm Foods, Wild Tastes, Dicksons; eggs and dairy: Stichill Jerseys, Oxenrig Farm; fish: Waddells of Eyemouth, D. R. Collins of Eyemouth, Lindesfarne Oysters; meat: Prentice Butchers, Duns; game and poultry: Burnside Farm Foods; other products: Heatherslaw Corn Mill, Campbell & Neill (ice), Chainbridge Honey Farm, Crema (tea and coffee), Beers of Scotland, Theakstons, Pam's Flower Box.